MANAGING POLARITIES IN CONGREGATIONS

MANAGING POLARITIES IN CONGREGATIONS

Eight Keys for Thriving Faith Communities

Roy M. Oswald and Barry Johnson

Herndon, Virginia
www.alban.org

The Alban Institute
2121 Cooperative Way, Suite 100
Herndon, VA 20171

Cover design by Spark Design.

Library of Congress Cataloging-in-Publication Data

Oswald, Roy M.
Managing polarities in congregations : eight keys for thriving faith communities / Roy M. Oswald and Barry Johnson.
p. cm.
Includes bibliographical references.
ISBN 978-1-56699-390-6
1. Church. I. Johnson, Barry Allan, 1942- II. Title.
BV600.3.O74 2009
253--dc22
2009026750

09 10 11 12 13 VG 5 4 3 2 1

DEDICATIONS

By Roy M. Oswald:

To Loren Mead, who was always there encouraging me to continue my research within congregations.

To Speed Leas, who was also taken by Barry's material when he first presented it to us.

By Barry Johnson:

I dedicate this book to some of the Protestant, Roman Catholic, and Jewish clergy and a Native American spiritual teacher who have been important in my life. I have had the privilege to work with, learn from, and be inspired by each of them. They are listed in the order I came to know them.

Rev. Bill White
Rev. Bill Webber
Rev. William Sloane Coffin
Rev. Richard Fernandez
Rabbi Abraham Heschel
Rabbi Balfour Brickner
Fr. Richard Neuhaus
Fr. Robert Drinan
Rev. John C. Bennett
Fr. Art Melville
Rev. Martin Luther King Jr.
Rev. Ray Kretzschmer
Rev. Terry Hager
Rev. Jerry Toshalis
Rev. Speed Leas
Rev. Roy M. Oswald
Rev. John Scherer
Rabbi Shoshana Boyd Gelfand
Herb "One White Horse Standing" Stephenson

CONTENTS

ACKNOWLEDGMENTS

The first polarity map was created in 1975. (See chapter 1, page 11.) Since then, the map and the polarity principles have become richer through application and experiences in a variety of settings. A number of people have contributed to the evolution of the map. Thank you to John Scherer for creating the rectangle at the top of the map and for coming up with the name for it, "Greater Purpose Statement" (GPS, a little play on "global positioning system"); Bob de Wit and Ron Meyer for the Synergy Arrows; Todd Johnson for the measurable Early Warnings; and Sallie Snyder for the idea of converting the original polarity circle into an infinity loop.

When Barry Johnson introduced the concept of Polarity Management to the consultants at the Alban Institute, both Roy Oswald and Speed Leas took an immediate interest. Roy, Speed, and Barry attempted to write a book on polarities within the church, but that book was not to be. We acknowledge Speed's contributions to our work.

Roy acknowledges the contributions to our eight polarities made by participants in Alban Institute training events. Whenever Roy has used polarity principles in a workshop, he has kept the participants' work, written on newsprint during the event, and has used their ideas to develop more fully the discussion of the eight polarities.

We acknowledge the long hours editor Beth Gaede has put into this book. She consistently challenged anything that was not clear or that did not make sense. She went far beyond normal editing in the production of this book. We owe Beth our hearty thanks.

We also acknowledge Luke Mossman-Johnson for the graphics that appear in these pages.

CHAPTER 1

Why Managing Polarities Is Important to Congregational Health

Are we going to have a highly nurturing and caring congregation whose members manifest God's unconditional love, *or* are we going to have a congregation whose members feel challenged to change their lives—to grow up spiritually and to accept accountability for living lives of commitment and service? This question is driven by a double message about God we get in congregational education and from our clergy. On the one hand, we are told that God is a nurturing God who loves us unconditionally just as we are. On the other hand, we are told that God consistently challenges us to grow spiritually and to lead lives that promote justice, mercy, and compassion. This God demands transformation in our lives and holds us accountable for our actions. Which is it? Is God essentially loving or essentially demanding? The answer is yes. This question captures a polarity. A polarity is a pair of truths that are interdependent. Neither truth stands alone. They complement each other. We call this the *Nurture AND Transformation* polarity. It is one of the eight polarities we will examine in this book.

What Are Polarities?

Congregations often find themselves in power struggles over the two poles of a polarity. Both sides believe strongly that they are right. People on each side assume that if they are right, their opponents must be wrong. We call this assumption "either/or" thinking. *Either* we are right *or* they are right—and we know we are right! When people argue about the two truths, both sides will be right, and they will need each other to experience the whole truth.

For example, when you look at this picture, what do you see?

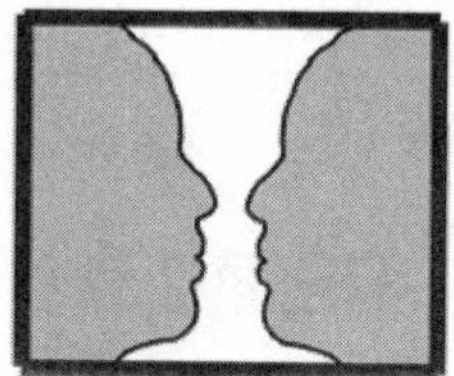

Figure 1.1

Do you see a goblet? Let's say that you and some members of your congregation see a goblet. You all think this reality is obvious and look askance at those who would suggest that it is *not* a picture of a goblet. You are right, and those who disagree with you are wrong—period. Let's say that others in your congregation see two heads. They are equally convinced that they are right. If you try to tell them that they are wrong—that it is not a picture of two heads; it is a picture of a goblet—you will have a fight on your hands. You are contradicting their perception of the truth, and you are not likely to convince them otherwise—nor they you!

This picture shows how either/or thinking can draw us into unnecessary conflicts. This picture is like a polarity in that both views are accurate and depend on each other. If you take away the goblet, you also lose the two heads. If you take away the two heads, you also lose the goblet. What is required in this situation and with all polarities is both/and thinking. This is a drawing of *both* a goblet *and* two heads.

Notice how foolish it is to fight from either position—as if the picture were *either* a goblet *or* two heads. It is equally foolish and painfully destructive to treat congregational polarities from an either/or perspective. To deal with polarities, we need to recognize that each side is accurate but that neither side by itself is complete. We need to see the whole picture.

When Barry Johnson first introduced Polarity Management to Roy Oswald in 1989, Roy immediately said, "I am consulting with congregations every week that are fighting over polarities with an either/or mindset. The pain and suffering that result are tragic."

IN WHAT FOLLOWS, ROY'S VOICE IS HEARD: Over the years, I have continued to work with congregations, pastors, and lay leaders and have deepened my conviction of the potential value of Polarity Management for congregations and their leaders. I have noticed that thriving congregations are thriving in large part because they manage some key polarities well. Many of them have leaders who through their own experience, intuition, and wisdom have developed the ability to manage polarities without knowing formally about Polarity Management. I have been learning with these congregations about polarities that seem to show up again and again, and how thriving congregations have been managing them effectively. I have also been teaching Polarity Management, and congregations have found it useful, especially in addressing chronic and loaded issues.

In what follows Barry speaks: Meanwhile, I have written a book on Polarity Management[1] and have been learning how to apply it with a great variety of organizations on four continents. I have increased my appreciation for the phenomenon of polarities as a wonderful gift from God. It is a gift found in nature, like gravity, ice, or a forest. Polarities are everywhere in our daily lives for us to tap to enhance the quality of our lives and to help our congregations thrive.

The importance of this phenomenon has been recognized and written about for centuries in philosophy and religion. It is at the heart of Taoism, in which we find the familiar polarity of yin and yang energy. It is only in the past fifty years that business and industry have come to appreciate the phenomenon, often called dilemma or paradox. No matter what it is called, the research is clear: leaders and organizations that manage polarities well outperform those that don't. Books supporting this statement are listed in appendix D.

The Elements of Polarities

What is exciting for the two of us is that this phenomenon, explored first within religious traditions and later found useful by business and industry, is being reclaimed by faith communities with a new appreciation. Polarity Management brings three elements to this ancient wisdom:

1. An *infinity loop* follows the normal flow of energy around the two poles of a polarity. This infinity loop both holds the poles together as an interdependent pair and keeps them apart as distinct entities.

2. A robust and user-friendly *map* enables us to see key dimensions of any polarity.
3. A *set of principles* describes how all polarities work.

We are not suggesting that your congregation is not managing polarities and needs to start. You are already managing polarities, because they are an integral part of life, including the life of your congregation. This book will help you manage them more intentionally, effectively, and sustainably. We hope that this book will help you and your members either *become* a thriving congregation or *sustain* yourselves as a thriving congregation in the service of your mission.

Eight Key Polarities for Thriving Congregations

In his work with congregations, Roy has identified eight polarities that thriving congregations manage well. Each polarity can be expressed as a question that highlights the positive aspects of each pole. Here are the eight polarities Roy has identified.

- *Tradition AND Innovation:* How do we stay rooted in our historic faith and heritage *AND* foster creativity in our life together?
- *Spiritual Health AND Institutional Health:* How do we nurture our mission and spiritual health *AND* maintain a healthy institution that sustains our corporate life?
- *Management AND Leadership:* How do we create or sustain a well-organized, stable congregation *AND* create or sustain a congregation that inspires members to embrace change?
- *Strong Clergy Leadership AND Strong Lay Leadership:* How do we support strong leadership by our clergy *AND* ensure broad, active participation by our laity?
- *Inreach AND Outreach:* How do we respond to members' needs *AND* take care of those outside our membership?
- *Nurture AND Transformation:* How do we manifest God's unconditional love for us *AND* challenge people to grow spiritually and to serve others with commitment?

- *Making Disciples—Easy Process AND Challenging Process:* How do we make it easy for people to become members *AND* ensure that membership has meaning and depth?
- *Call AND Duty:* How do we help members recognize their particular call from God to serve others *AND* ensure that the mundane tasks needed to sustain congregational life are accomplished?

Thriving congregations thrive in part because they manage these polarities well. They have learned to carry out both components of each polarity, rather than chronically fighting about the two points of view. They have found ways to use the inherent tension between the two in a synergy that helps the congregation thrive. Unlike declining congregations, they have learned to manage the polarities skillfully.

Declining congregations have seen one or more of these polarities as an either/or choice; they have believed that they must support one pole and abandon the other. This approach leads to win/lose power struggles that become vicious circles, sapping the energy of the congregation and contributing to its decline.

Arguments over polarities take place in all families, organizations, and nations. Often in congregations, the arguments take on additional significance because the stakes are high. When one's congregation and faith are the bedrock of life, anything that appears to threaten the congregation or the faith can quickly generate fear and anger. It is precisely because the stakes are high that it is important to understand whether the difficulty confronting the congregation is essentially a *polarity to manage* with both/and thinking or a *problem to solve*, a situation in which either/or thinking is most useful. As you read this book, you will learn how thriving congregations manage these eight polarities. You will also learn how all polarities work so that you can more effectively manage these polarities and any others you might identify.

How Do Polarities Work?

Before examining the eight congregational polarities, let's take a look at two obvious examples of polarities: (1) *Inhaling AND Exhaling* and (2) *Activity AND Rest*. We will use these two polarities to show the underlying energy system in all polarities, which has the shape of an infinity loop. We will then show how this energy moves within a polarity map. Finally, we will describe some of the basic principles of how polarities work.

Two Poles and an Infinity Loop

First, let's look at the basic energy system for all polarities. A polarity has two poles, or centers of gravity. There is a natural oscillation of energy around the two poles that takes the shape of an infinity loop. Breathing is our first example.

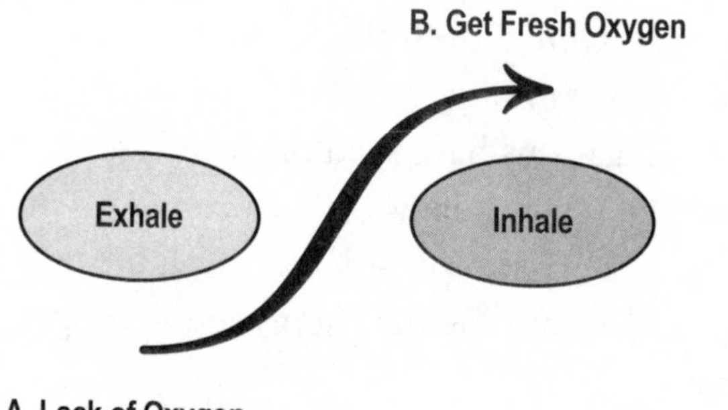

Figure 1.2

Focus on your own breathing for a moment. Exhale deeply and hold that position. As you hold it, you will start to experience the limits of exhaling alone—(a) a lack of oxygen (see fig. 1.2). Now inhale deeply and hold your breath. Notice how natural and good it feels to move from the downside of exhaling (a) to the upside of inhaling (b) as you take in fresh oxygen.

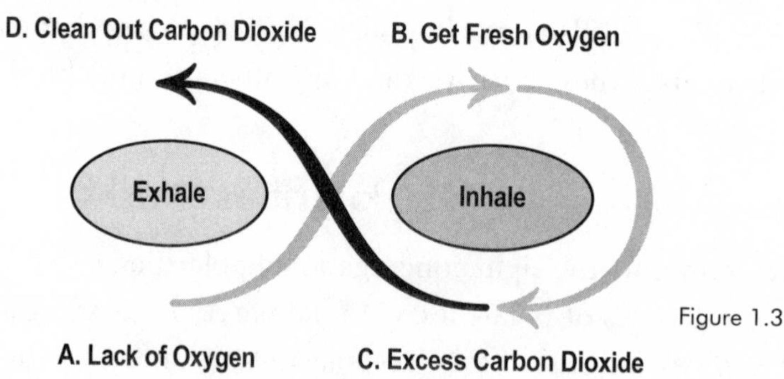

Figure 1.3

However, as we see in figure 1.3, this move to the upside of inhaling is not a sustainable "solution."

After getting the benefits of inhaling, you start to experience the limits of inhaling alone: (c) excess carbon dioxide. Again you experience discomfort. Go ahead and exhale. Notice how good it feels to move from the downside of inhaling (c) to the upside of exhaling (d) as you breathe out the carbon dioxide. Cleaning out carbon dioxide is the benefit of exhaling. It is essential, but it also is not a "solution" to the "breathing issue." After enjoying the benefit of exhaling, you again start to experience the limit of exhaling, a lack of oxygen (a). The energy continues to follow this infinity loop as long as you live.

Figure 1.4 illustrates the self-correcting oscillation within the breathing polarity.

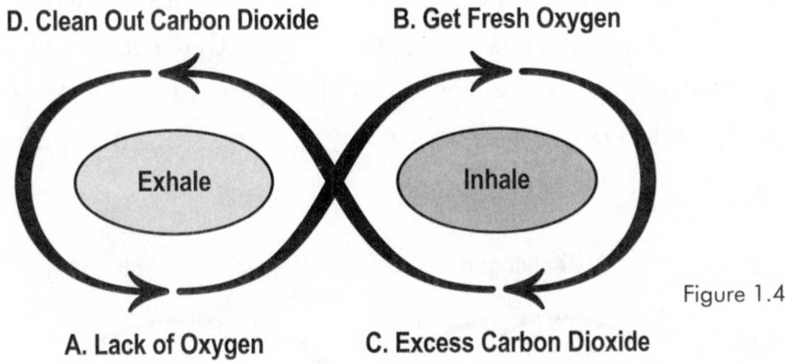

Figure 1.4

This example is simple, but it demonstrates the natural oscillation between two poles that is characteristic of all polarities. Because the time needed to complete the infinity loop is so short, it would obviously be foolish to suggest that you choose either inhaling or exhaling as the wave of the future for your congregation. Because the time needed for a congregation to cycle through the infinity loop is often much longer, we often think of the upside of one pole as the "solution" rather than as a segment of an ongoing process.

Let's look at one more example of a polarity that we manage every day: *Activity AND Rest* (see fig. 1.5 on page 8.)

When you have had too much activity to the neglect of rest, you get burned out (a). This condition can easily be identified as a "problem"—and

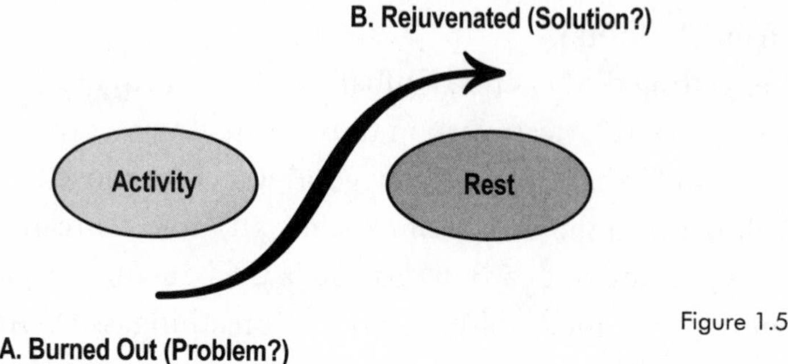

Figure 1.5

at one level it is. When we suffer burnout, the natural thing to do is to get some rest so as to be rejuvenated (b). Rejuvenation can easily be identified as the "solution." Even though resting is the best thing to do when one is exhausted, the upside of rest is not an ultimate "solution." It is more accurate to see it as a necessary segment (a to b) of an ongoing, self-correcting infinity loop. A polarity is self-correcting in that the downside of one pole naturally moves us to the upside of the opposite pole. As in breathing, we constantly make course corrections by moving from one pole to its opposite.

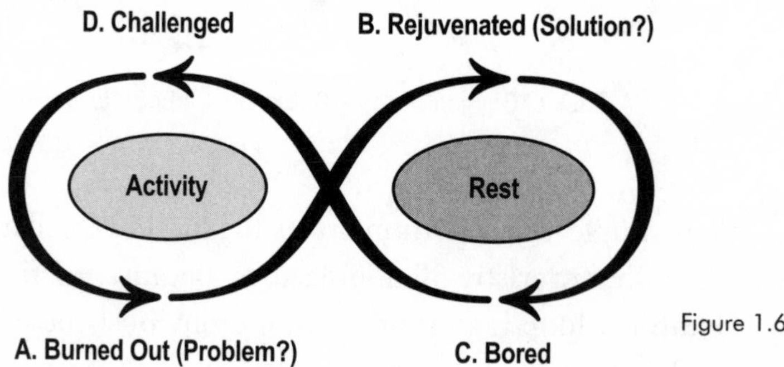

Figure 1.6

There is a point at which we maximize the benefits of rest; those benefits start to diminish as we move toward boredom (c). What drives the continued movement through the infinity loop is our anticipating or experiencing the downside of a pole, combined with our attraction to the upside of the other pole (fig. 1.6). In this case, we need to get up off the couch and do something! This is just the self-correction necessary when we experience the downside of rest. It takes us to the upside of activity, where we feel challenged and invigorated (d). The upside of activity is not a sustainable "solution" either, and will inevitably reach its limits, so then we start to move toward the downside of activity, becoming burned out (a). We manage this process in one way or another every day.

We have used these two basic polarities to show how all polarities function. Here are a few key principles of all polarities to draw from these examples:

1. All polarities contain two poles and an energy system that flows around them in an infinity loop.

2. Polarities are ongoing. As long as we are alive, we will be managing *Inhale AND Exhale* and *Activity AND Rest.* Likewise, as long as a congregation exists, it will be managing the eight polarities we have identified. Thriving congregations manage them well. Declining congregations don't.

3. If we have a polarity to manage, there will be an upside and a downside to each pole.

4. When we experience the downside of one pole—for example (as in figure 1.5), Burned Out—we see it as the "problem." At the same time, the upside of the opposite pole—for example, Rejuvenated—becomes increasingly attractive as the "solution."

This view of the solution is reasonable, and it is half right. When we experience the downside of one pole, the upside of the opposite pole is the necessary correction; however, it is not the ultimate "solution." It is a temporary self-correction in an ongoing process. If we were to stick with Rest as a "solution," we would soon find ourselves in the downside of Rest—(c) Boredom—and look at Rest as if it were a mistake! It was not a mistake to Rest. But neither was it a sustainable "solution."

5. If we overfocus on one pole to the neglect of the other member of this interdependent pair, we always get to the downside of the pole on which we overfocus.

6. In an argument over a polarity, both sides are right. It might be more appropriate to say both sides are accurate but incomplete.

When we argue about a polarity, we are like the blind people feeling an elephant. One feels a leg and says that the elephant is like a tree. Another feels the tail and says the elephant is like a snake. Both descriptions are accurate, but neither is complete. Feeling the leg is like focusing on a segment of the infinity loop (a to b) and thinking we know the whole process. Another group might be focusing on another segment of the infinity loop (c to d), and its members may think they know the whole process. Many congregational fights arise from this misperception by good people dedicated to helping their congregation.

7. With all polarities, both sides are dependent on each other over time. To be sustainable, Activity needs Rest, and Rest needs Activity.

8. Polarities are unavoidable, unsolvable (in that neither pole alone is a sustainable solution), and indestructible. They must be managed over time.

The Polarity Map

The polarity map is a helpful structure for organizing information that goes beyond the basic structure of the two poles and the infinity loop. Map 1.1 is a polarity map with an expanded version of the *Activity AND Rest* polarity.

Upside of Activity

1. Mind remains sharp.
2. Body stays toned.
3. Person is stimulated and challenged.

Upside of Rest

1. Thoughts are integrated.
2. Body is rejuvenated.
3. Person is relaxed and refreshed.

Downside of Activity

1. Mind is overloaded.
2. Body is exhausted.
3. Person becomes overwhelmed, burned out.

Downside of Rest

1. Mind is dulled.
2. Body is out of shape.
3. Person is bored, unstimulated.

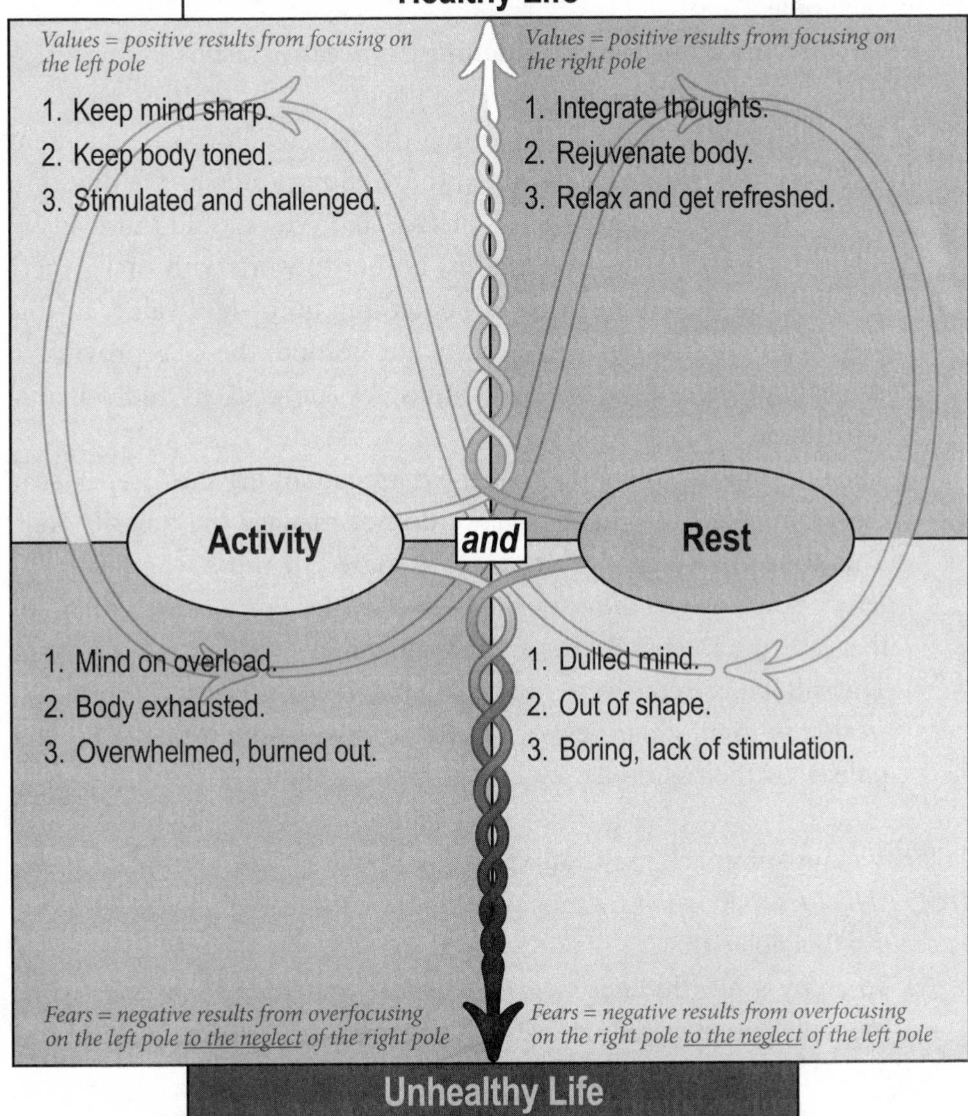
Polarity Management® Map
Greater Purpose Statement (GPS)—why balance this polarity?
Healthy Life
Values = positive results from focusing on the left pole
1. Keep mind sharp.
2. Keep body toned.
3. Stimulated and challenged.
Values = positive results from focusing on the right pole
1. Integrate thoughts.
2. Rejuvenate body.
3. Relax and get refreshed.
Activity
and
Rest
1. Mind on overload.
2. Body exhausted.
3. Overwhelmed, burned out.
1. Dulled mind.
2. Out of shape.
3. Boring, lack of stimulation.
Fears = negative results from overfocusing on the left pole to the neglect of the right pole
Fears = negative results from overfocusing on the right pole to the neglect of the left pole
Unhealthy Life
Deeper Fear from lack of balance

Map 1.1

The polarity map contains the following elements:

1. The two poles of the polarity.
2. The infinity loop showing the normal flow of energy around the two poles.
3. Two upside quadrants containing the positive results that come with each pole.
4. Two downside quadrants containing the negative results from overfocusing on one pole to the neglect of the other.
5. The rectangle at the top containing the Greater Purpose Statement (GPS) serves two purposes. First, the GPS responds to the question "Why bother to manage this polarity well?" Why should those favoring activity and those favoring rest bother to work with each other? The answer, the GPS, has to be something both sides value. In this case, the answer could be a healthy life. Second, the GPS provides a constant reference point when things get complicated and possibly disorienting.
6. The rectangle at the bottom of the map containing the Deeper Fear represents what will happen if we do not manage the polarity well. This concern, which also needs to be shared by those who favor different poles, will be the opposite of the Greater Purpose Statement. In this case, the Deeper Fear is an unhealthy life.
7. The small box in the center of the map that contains "*AND*" reminds us that with all polarities, to be effective over time we need the left pole *AND* the right pole.

Polarity maps summarize several aspects of a polarity. For example, the *Activity AND Rest* map (map 1.2 on pages 14–15) confirms what we all experience with this polarity.

1. To enjoy a healthy life (Greater Purpose Statement), we have to be mentally and physically active *AND* we need to take some time for rest and rejuvenation.
2. We end up with an unhealthy life (Deeper Fear) if we don't manage this polarity well. We can become unhealthy by overfocusing on either activity or rest.

3. If we are experiencing burnout (lower-left quadrant), the natural thing to do is to get some rest (go to upper-right quadrant) so that we can relax and be refreshed. The upside of rest is the natural response to the downside of activity.
4. However beneficial the upside of rest may be, it is not an ultimate solution. Over time, too much rest will lead to a dulled mind and an out-of-shape body.

The congregational polarity maps will also confirm our experience with the polarities we discuss and will apply directly to all polarities in a congregation.

Virtuous and Vicious Circles

Two additional features of polarity maps are (1) a pair of arrows coming from the two poles and spiraling up toward the GPS and (2) a pair of arrows spiraling down toward the Deeper Fear. The arrows are called Synergy Arrows. Together, they represent the possibility that the separate energies directed toward each pole can be combined in a positively reinforcing way or a negatively reinforcing way.

1. *Virtuous Circles*. When the energy from two poles is combined in a positively reinforcing way, the result is a "virtuous circle." If you do a good job of getting to the upside of one pole, you will more easily get to the upside of the other pole. In this case, staying active mentally and physically will improve your ability to rest. And getting adequate rest will improve your ability to be active. Staying active and getting adequate rest form a virtuous circle that moves a person toward a healthy life.

Preparing to run a marathon is an example of intentionally tapping the energy of a polarity. In our day-to-day life we may get up, go to work, come home, and go to sleep. At one level we are managing the *Activity AND Rest* polarity without much thought or intention. However, if we want to run a marathon, we must become mindful of tapping this energy system and creating a virtuous circle between the two poles.

Each day we may run a little farther as we build up the activity pole. The increased activity requires that we deliberately get a good night's sleep—sleep that increases our ability to run even farther the next day. The in-

Action Steps

How will we gain or maintain the positive results from focusing on this left pole? What? Who? By when? Measures?

1. Read books and newspapers to keep current.
2. Work out six days a week.
3. Consult and train in new settings.
4. Kayak regularly.

Early Warnings

Measurable indicators (things you can count) that will let you know that you are getting into the downside of this left pole.

1. Eyes need Visine in the morning.
2. Increased tiredness.
3. Increase in forgotten items.
4. Dana says I look tired.

Polarity Management®

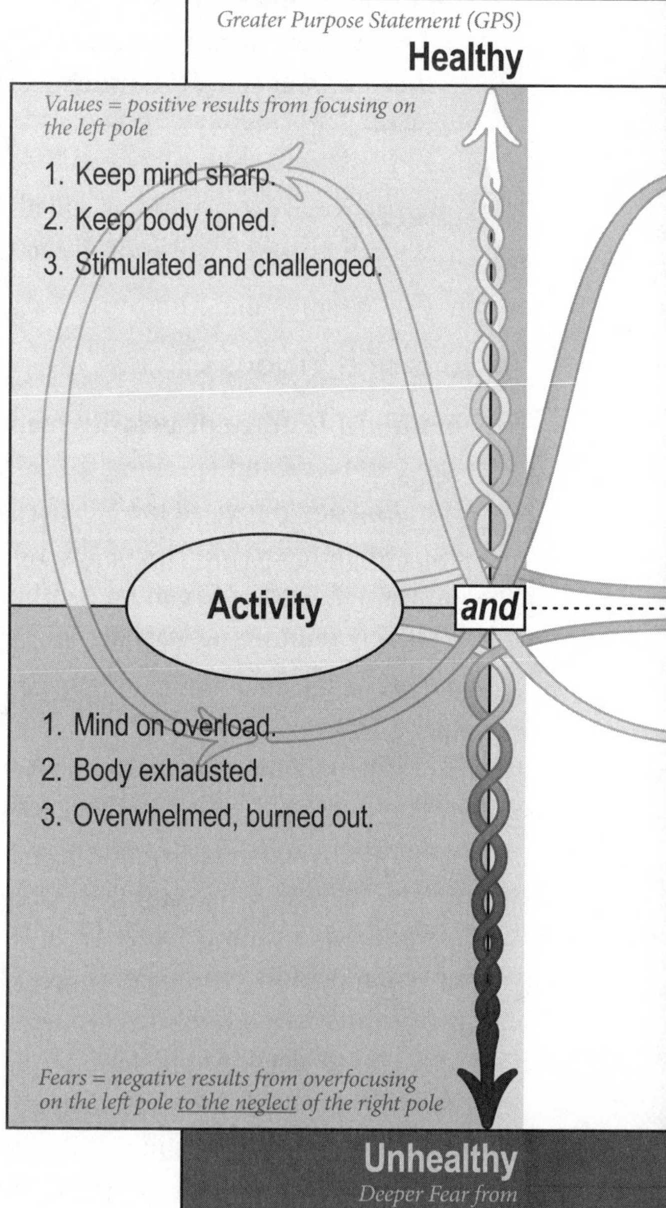

Map

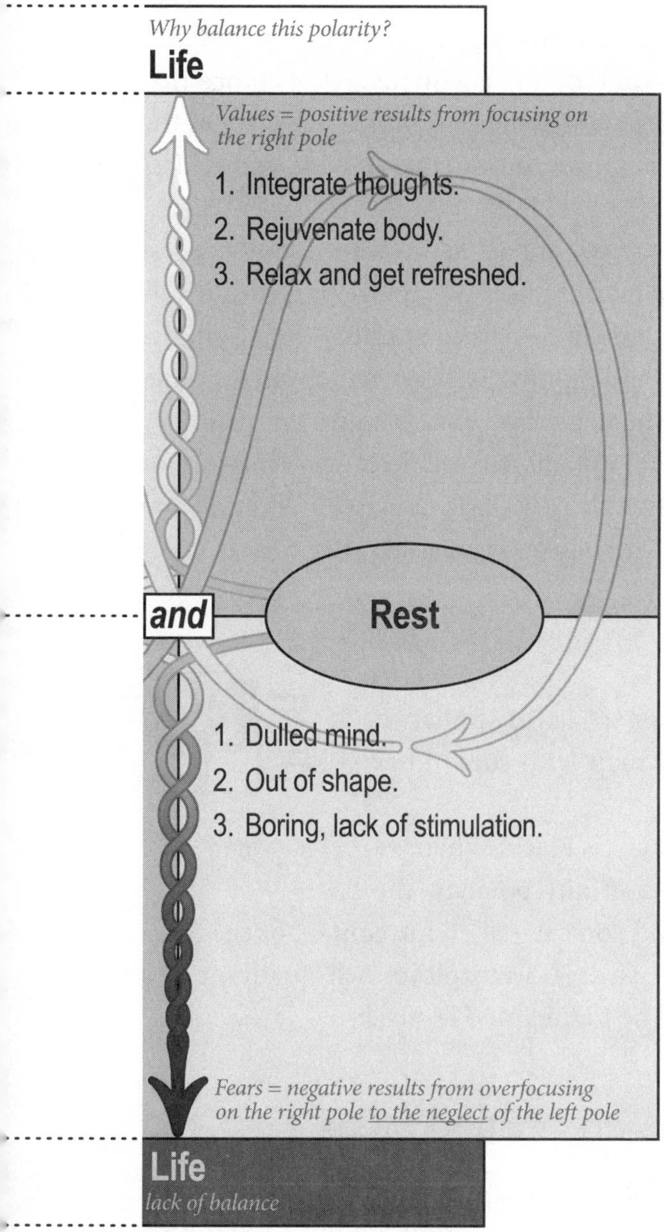

Why balance this polarity?

Life

Values = positive results from focusing on the right pole

1. Integrate thoughts.
2. Rejuvenate body.
3. Relax and get refreshed.

and

Rest

1. Dulled mind.
2. Out of shape.
3. Boring, lack of stimulation.

Fears = negative results from overfocusing on the right pole to the neglect of the left pole

Life

lack of balance

Action Steps

How will we gain or maintain the positive results from focusing on this right pole? What? Who? By when? Measures?

1. Get eight hours sleep.
2. Take one day a week off from working out.
3. "Free" time each week and eight weeks off each year.
4. Kayak regularly.

Early Warnings

Measurable indicators (things you can count) that will let you know that you are getting into the downside of this right pole.

1. Increased TV watching.
2. Two or three days without working out.
3. Gaining weight—pants tightening.
4. Reduced work on calendar.

Map 1.2

creased activity and the improved rest reinforce each other. We have created a virtuous circle that enables us to run a marathon—a venture that was beyond our capacity before we tapped this energy system.

2. *Vicious Circles.* When the energy from two poles is combined in a negatively reinforcing way, the result is a "vicious circle." It is created when we are so preoccupied with activity that we don't get adequate rest, a choice that undermines our subsequent activity and leads to an unhealthy life. On the other hand, if you don't engage in vigorous, productive activity, you undermine your capacity for rest.

To continue the marathon analogy, overfocusing on either activity or rest will undermine our ability to run a marathon. If we run too far, with insufficient rest between runs, our muscles will be damaged rather than built up. *Activity AND Rest* are needed for building muscle. The vicious circle comes into play when we overexercise to the neglect of rest, risking a sports injury that could put us to bed. When that happens, we are no longer training for a marathon—in fact, we can barely walk. The lack of activity while we are recovering moves us further from the ability to run a marathon.

Icons

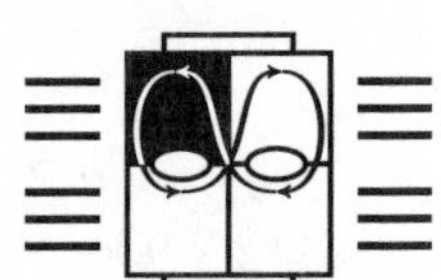

Upside Left

Throughout the book, you will also see icons similar to this one—an outline of a polarity map with some lines on either side.

Notice that the upper-left quadrant is black. When we talk about the upper-left quadrant of any polarity, the section will begin with this icon; and you can see, in the context of the overall map, where our attention is focused. As we explore each quadrant of a polarity in turn, that quadrant will be highlighted in black.

Early Warnings and Action Steps

To manage a polarity well, we need to maximize the upside of each pole and minimize the downside. We do this by creating Action Steps for the upside and Early Warnings for the downside. We take Action Steps to make sure we get to the upside. Early Warnings are measurable indicators that let us know we are moving into a downside.

Early Warnings for the Activity Pole

Early Warnings Left

When we attempt to manage a polarity well by pursuing two sets of Action Steps, the intent is to stay in both upside quadrants and out of the downside quadrants. Early Warnings let us know we are on the downside of a pole. They must be measurable indications that are either increasing or decreasing. They must be different for each downside so that we know which downside we need to address with corrective action.

The Early Warnings that let Barry know he is getting into the downside of activity include irritated eyes in the morning from lack of sleep; extreme fatigue, especially after lunch; pronounced forgetfulness; and comments from his wife, Dana, that he looks tired.

When Early Warnings crop up, it's time to revisit the Action Steps for the opposite pole. For example, when Barry feels extremely tired, he will ask himself if he is taking the Action Step of getting eight hours of sleep a night. (If not, he might find it useful to *take* that Action Step, rather than just writing it down.) If we check the Action Steps and find that we are doing all the steps, we probably need to modify them in some way. For example, Barry might start taking a short nap during the day or doing yoga or meditation.

Early Warnings for the Rest Pole

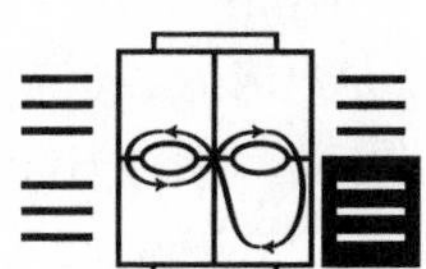
Early Warnings Right

Barry enjoys activity so much that he is more vulnerable to the downside of Activity than to the downside of Rest. This is true of all polarities: we are more likely to get into the downside of our preferred pole than that of our less preferred pole. When Barry gets into the downside of Rest, the Early Warnings include excessive TV watching, often accompanied by the observation at the end of a program that it was not worth the time; the passage of two or three days when he doesn't work out; pants that seem to be "shrinking"; and work that also starts shrinking, because Barry is not developing new clients.

The constructive response to these Early Warnings is for him to look to the Action Steps for the Activity pole and see if he is taking those steps. If not, he probably needs to start. If he is taking the Action Steps and still ending up in the downside of the Rest pole, he probably needs to alter the Action Steps in some way. For example, he could limit his TV watching to a few favorite programs, rather than clicking through the channels to find something of mild interest that encourages his couch-potato inclinations.

Action Steps for the Activity Pole

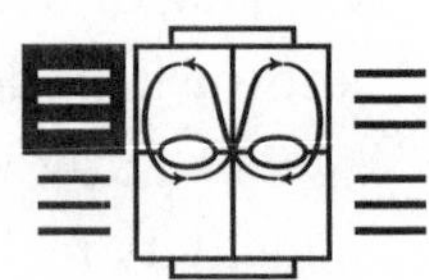

Action Steps Left

We will use the *Activity AND Rest* polarity to demonstrate how the Action Steps and Early Warnings work. An icon like this one indicates that the Action Steps needed to reach the upside of Activity, the left pole, are discussed in the material that follows.

In this case, the question is, "What is Barry doing to get to the upside of Activity—to keep his mind sharp and body toned and to feel stimulated and challenged?" His Action Steps include reading, working out, consulting in new settings, and kayaking regularly. These Action Steps are intended to maximize the upside of Activity and to minimize the downside of Rest.

Action Steps for the Rest Pole

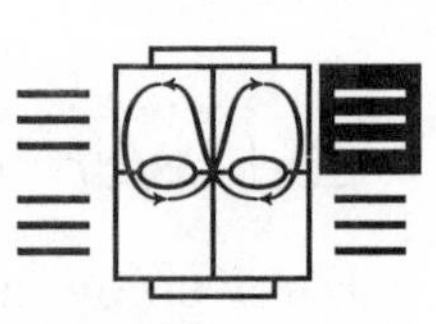

Action Steps Right

If Barry does Action Steps only for Activity and neglects Actions Steps for Rest, he will find himself in the downside of Activity. This is why it is important, as with all polarities, to empower both poles, making sure we have solid Action Steps for gaining or maintaining the benefits of each upside.

To get to the upside of Rest, Barry needs to get eight hours of sleep a night, take a day off each week from his regular workouts, reserve some free time in the week when he is not working or thinking about work, build in eight weeks a year for vacation, and kayak regularly. Notice that kayaking shows up in both sets of Action Steps. This is what we call a "High-leverage" Action Step, because it simultaneously supports both upsides. Kayaking provides activity for Barry's body and rest for his mind.

How Polarities Function

The list of polarity principles below summarizes seven key ideas about how polarities function. In chapters 2 through 9 we examine additional key polarity principles and offer a summary map with Action Steps and Early Warnings for each polarity. A central message of this first chapter is that thriving congregations thrive in part because they manage polarities better than declining congregations do. This assertion is consistent with research in business and industry showing that leaders and organizations that do a good job of managing polarities (sometimes called *paradoxes* or *dilemmas*) outperform those that don't.

The authors are convinced that it is difficult, if not impossible, for a congregation to thrive without managing well the eight polarities we discuss in this book. A congregation can manage some of these polarities well, yet failing to manage all eight will damage congregational health. A congregation can manage these polarities more or less well, but when it manages them all well, its efforts will have a noticeable positive effect. Congregations may experience declines in membership, finances, energy, or other dimensions partly because of external circumstances that impinge on congregational life. Because a congregation has much less power to deal with external circumstances than internal ones, addressing internal issues will have a greater impact on the congregation's well-being. Managing the eight polarities well is a good place to start.

POLARITY PRINCIPLES

1. Polarities are interdependent pairs of truths that are a natural and integral part of our daily lives. Like all other natural phenomena, they are a gift from God.
2. We are constantly managing polarities, because they are embedded in congregational life. The polarity map and principles are

intended to build on the intuitive and tacit wisdom about polarities that we have acquired by dealing with them more or less well our whole life. The map and principles provide a common model, language, and understanding of this phenomenon. This understanding will allow us to be more collaborative and intentional about tapping this phenomenon to create or maintain a thriving congregation.

3. Either/or thinking, though essential in some situations, does not enable us to manage polarities effectively. To manage polarities well, we must supplement our either/or thinking with both/and thinking.
4. If we treat a polarity to manage as if it were a problem to solve, we will find that we are dealing with unnecessary, often painful and draining power struggles in which the congregation loses twice. It loses the first time because energy is wasted and relationships are damaged during the struggle. It loses again when one side "wins," and the congregation has to deal with the downside of the winners' preferred pole.
5. The normal flow of energy in all polarities is an infinity loop, which reflects the ongoing self-correction of the polarity from the downside of one pole to the upside of the other. Over time, the upside of one pole will reach its limits, especially if it is focused upon to the neglect of the other pole, and we will begin to experience the downside of the pole. As we anticipate or experience the downside of a pole, we are naturally driven in a self-regulating way to the upside of the opposite pole.
6. A polarity map contains two pole names with an *"AND"* box between them; an upside and downside for each pole; a Greater Purpose Statement (GPS) and a Deeper Fear; positively reinforcing Synergy Arrows leading in a virtuous circle toward the GPS; and negatively reinforcing Synergy Arrows leading in a vicious circle toward the Deeper Fear.
7. A polarity can be managed well. First, it must be recognized as a polarity to be managed rather than a problem to be solved. To manage it well, we have to create Action Steps to get to the upside of each pole and identify Early Warnings to let us know when we are moving to a downside.

CHAPTER 2

Tradition AND Innovation

Chapter 1 provided an overview of the polarity map and a few key principles. We are ready to look at the first of the eight polarities that, when managed well, can help a congregation thrive. We will use "Thriving Congregation" as the Greater Purpose Statement (GPS) for all eight polarities. The Deeper Fear will be "Declining Congregation."

The content of the various boxes within a polarity map depends on the language and values of those filling out the map. If, as you read this book, some of the content in one of the maps does not work for you or others in your congregation, by all means revise the content. We are not dictating any particular map or map content as the best way to describe the polarities in your congregation. We are suggesting that polarities do exist within your congregation and that recognizing and managing them will be helpful. Feel free to modify the content in a way that reflects the language and values of your congregation.

For example, the pole names we have given to our first congregational polarity are *Tradition AND Innovation*. Another possible pair of words for this dimension of congregational life is *Stability AND Change*. The names of the poles and the content of the map should reflect the values and language most useful for your congregation.

The map is a tool that helps us organize knowledge as well as clarify language and values. We trust you and others in your congregation to fill in the content, including a Greater Purpose and a Deeper Fear, and statements summarizing the upside and downside of each pole.

Once you have agreed on the map content, the principles that apply to all polarities will also hold in predictable ways for the elements you identify. This consistency will allow you to manage the polarity over time. For example, you can be certain that if you overfocus on one pole to the neglect of the other, you will find yourself on the downside of the pole on which you have overfocused—as we saw with the *Activity AND Rest* polarity in chapter 1.

So let's look at the polarity of *Tradition AND Innovation* and explore how it might function in a congregation.

Honoring the Past AND Staying Relevant

Pastors Jill Buhler and Jack Smothers moved to new program-size congregations—that is, churches with 150–350 average worship attendance—at about the same time. Both congregations had been slowly declining over the previous ten years. Jill planned to apply a recommendation she had heard from an Alban Institute consultant: that for the first nine to twelve months, her job as pastor was to be a historian and a lover—to get to know people, to find something to love in everybody, and to learn about the congregation's history as a way of trying to understand its personality. Certain leaders of the congregation became impatient with her. The congregation was losing members, and people wanted to know what she was going to do to help them grow again. She held her ground and insisted that she would soon get to that task, but first she wanted to explore the congregation as an organism and to get to know its people. These leaders cut her some slack and stayed off her case for the first year.

Trouble began brewing, however, when after eighteen months Jill still had not begun to explore ways the congregation might become stronger and more vibrant. During this time she had gotten to know many of the long-time members and learned that they valued their rich tradition and the stability the congregation had enjoyed over the years. Every time she thought of ways the congregation might grow, she felt a lump in her throat, because she knew that the strategy would upset some of the people she had come to know and love. At the end of twenty-four months, when Jill had still not initiated any changes, the governing board began to ponder whether it had made a mistake in calling her as pastor in the first place. Board members went to their regional executive to see about having her removed.

Jack Smothers, on the other hand, had heard somewhere that if a pastor is going to make any changes, he should do so within the first six months. A new pastor who waits longer than that may not succeed in making changes. For years, the congregation had had only one worship service, with Sunday school at 9:00 AM and a traditional service at 10:15, followed by a coffee time. Within three months of arriving, Jack had persuaded the board that if the congregation wanted to grow, it would have to change its Sunday morning schedule to include a traditional service at 8:30 AM, Sunday school classes at 9:45, and a contemporary service at 11:00. The congregation went along with these changes for a while. Some longtime members who loved the traditional service began to complain about having to get up so early, and attendance began to slump. The contemporary service had not really gotten off the ground because its leaders did not take time to plan it well. They did not identify a target audience for the service or plan how they would let that target audience know about the new worship service. The players in the worship band, mostly congregation members, did not mesh well, and often the music was not wisely chosen or well executed. Longtime members who attended the service complained that the music was too loud and clearly inferior to what should be heard in a church like theirs. Within two years, the grumbling and complaining had become so fierce and constant that the governing board went to the denomination's regional executive to have Jack removed as pastor.

In each of these cases, the new pastor was attending to something important. Jill was paying attention to Tradition, including the need for stability. Jack was paying attention to Innovation, including the need for change. Each got into trouble by not seeing the underlying polarity and by overfocusing on one pole without giving adequate attention to the other pole. In other words, both led their congregations into the downside of their preferred pole.

The Polarity to Be Managed

At first glance this polarity seems obvious. If you have been involved in congregational life for long, you have probably participated in several conflicts involving these two poles. Still, you may not recognize how important it is for a congregation to manage this polarity well. It is a polarity we share with the corporate world. The book *Built to Last,* by business consultant

Jim Collins and organizational development professor Jerry Porras, is devoted to this polarity.[1] Three chapters discuss ways to "preserve your core ideology" (Tradition), which includes having such an ideology, developing "a cultlike culture" without becoming a cult, and developing homegrown management. Three other chapters discuss ways to "stimulate progress" (Innovation), which includes setting "big hairy audacious goals," trying many initiatives and keeping the ones that work, and remembering that "good enough" never *is* good enough. The book details how "gold" (i.e., financially successful) companies have hung onto the Tradition (stability) pole while at the same time supporting the Innovation (change) pole.

Many religious systems are good at preserving their core ideology. In the corporate world, the average life of a company is about forty years, and a one-hundred-year-old company is impressive for its staying power. In the church, many faith communities are hundreds of years old; their longevity would indicate that they have managed this polarity well. None of these congregations would be around today if they hadn't. We believe, however, that it is more challenging to manage this polarity well in the twenty-first century than it was in earlier years. The rate of change in the world is rising rapidly, requiring church boards to give more attention to the Innovation pole while holding on to the Tradition pole. Moreover, in our post-Christendom era, belonging to or attending a church has become less important than it once was to people in North America.[2] Many congregations did not manage this polarity well and consequently went out of existence, or declined to the point that they are no longer viable. We see hundreds of old church buildings around the country that are no longer home to active congregations. Some of these buildings have been converted into restaurants, libraries, office spaces, community theaters, or museums.

If every congregational governing board managed this polarity well, it would help ensure the congregation's continued growth and vitality by maintaining the traditions and practices that put the church on the map in the first place, while continually scanning the horizon for new ways to reach out to people with the good news of the gospel. Such congregations would hold fast to the best of their tradition while continually testing new ways of engaging and making disciples of people who are outside any religious tradition. This polarity is summarized on map 2.1.

Polarity Management® Map

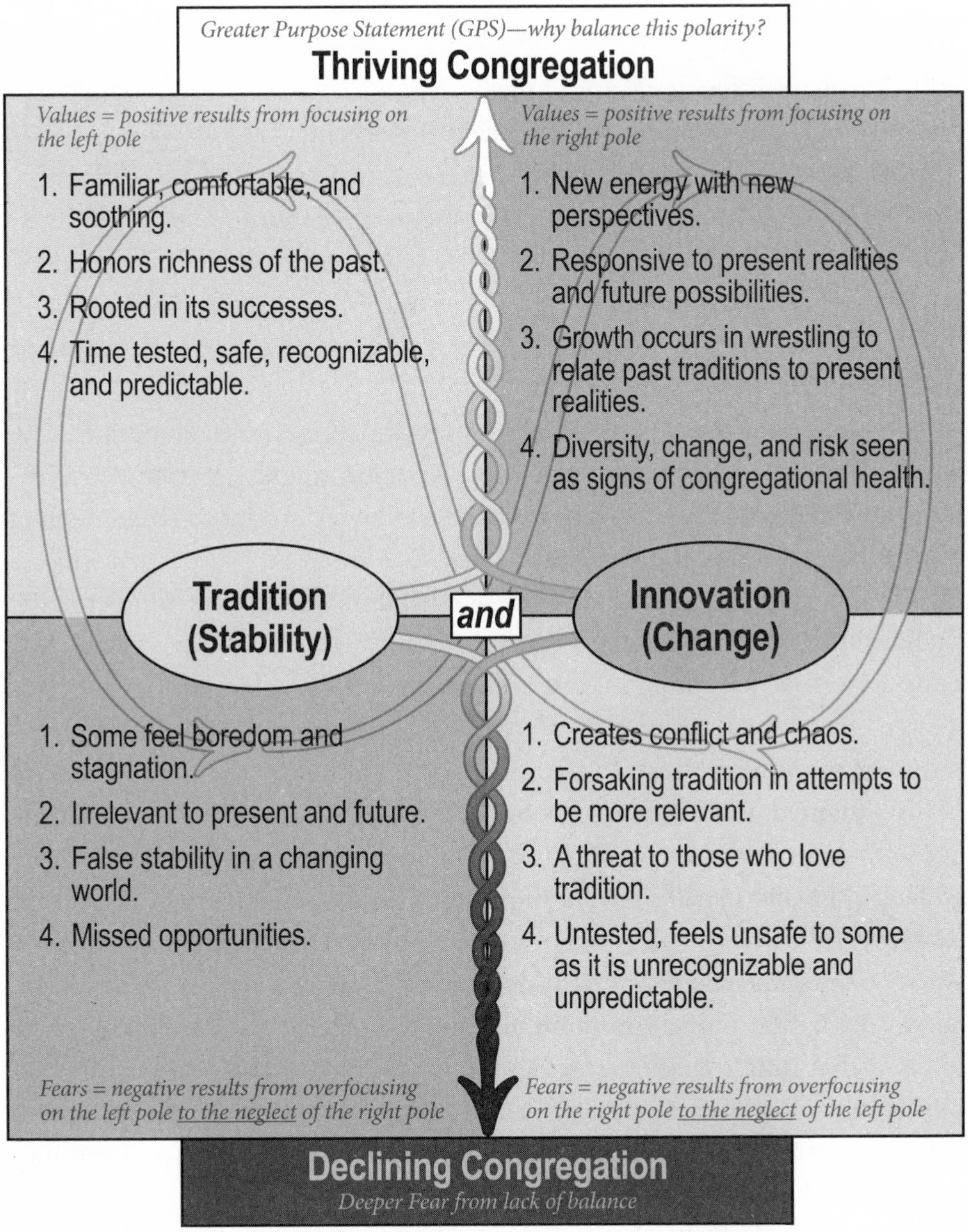

Greater Purpose Statement (GPS)—why balance this polarity?

Thriving Congregation

Values = positive results from focusing on the left pole

1. Familiar, comfortable, and soothing.
2. Honors richness of the past.
3. Rooted in its successes.
4. Time tested, safe, recognizable, and predictable.

Values = positive results from focusing on the right pole

1. New energy with new perspectives.
2. Responsive to present realities and future possibilities.
3. Growth occurs in wrestling to relate past traditions to present realities.
4. Diversity, change, and risk seen as signs of congregational health.

Tradition (Stability) *and* **Innovation (Change)**

1. Some feel boredom and stagnation.
2. Irrelevant to present and future.
3. False stability in a changing world.
4. Missed opportunities.

Fears = negative results from overfocusing on the left pole to the neglect of the right pole

1. Creates conflict and chaos.
2. Forsaking tradition in attempts to be more relevant.
3. A threat to those who love tradition.
4. Untested, feels unsafe to some as it is unrecognizable and unpredictable.

Fears = negative results from overfocusing on the right pole to the neglect of the left pole

Declining Congregation

Deeper Fear from lack of balance

Map 2.1

In the context of the map, let's look at each of the quadrants in more detail.

The Upside of Tradition (Stability)

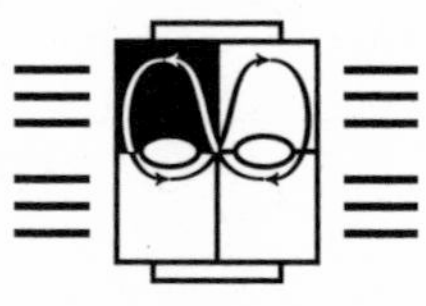
Upside Left

1. *A congregation that enjoys the upside of Tradition feels familiar, comfortable, and soothing.* Preserving the core theology is central to every congregation, as are some of its time-honored rituals and practices. Without tradition and stability, congregational life would be chaotic and would eventually drive people away. All of us need continuity and stability in our lives, or we will die early from excessive stress. The familiar and predictable help us anchor our lives.

A widely used stress scale, the Holmes and Rahe Life Changes Rating Scale,[3] lists a variety of possible changes a person might experience and assigns a numerical value to each. Some life changes are more stressful than others. For example, the death of a spouse is rated at 100 points, while a speeding ticket is rated at 11. Survey participants add up the points for the changes they have experienced in the previous twelve months. When Roy leads a seminar for clergy on stress and burnout, he often administers this survey. Occasionally, some clergy have had total scores of less than 100, indicating only minimal stress. In a younger group of clergy, many of whom are newly ordained, it is not uncommon to see scores in excess of 700, indicating significant stress. Depending upon their psychological hardiness, those scoring over 500 usually have a high score on a second survey, the Strain Response Inventory,[4] which measures such physical symptoms as headaches, sweaty palms, and the inability to sleep. High scores on the Strain Response Survey are a clear indication that the changes in clergy lives are taking their toll and that unless these pastors dramatically reduce their stress, they are candidates for serious illness such as a heart attack or cancer, or for an accident. Together these two surveys demonstrate that tradition and stability are central to longevity and a healthy life.

One theory suggests that some members vigorously resist any departure from congregational traditions because the high rate of change in their daily lives leads them to want at least one significant part of their life to be unchanging. Clergy and lay leaders must continually deal with this polarity; some members want things to stay the same for very good reasons, yet the congregation must be brought into the twenty-first century.

2. *A congregation that enjoys the upside of Tradition honors the richness of the past.* Studies have shown that many members of generation X and the millennial generation want to join congregations rooted in solid tradition. To the surprise of many, there has been a resurgence of younger families attending Greek Orthodox congregations, because the Orthodox have stuck with the ancient symbols of worship. These younger families, the children of baby boomers, experienced little that was familiar and predictable in early life and are particularly drawn to denominations that have had a long history in Christendom. People are attracted to Orthodox Judaism for similar reasons. The boomers have been labeled, fairly or not, as a "me" generation of people who were not about to sacrifice their lives for the sake of their children, as many of their own parents did. Hence, their children were, in many cases, the "latchkey kids" who came home to an empty house and whose parents were often harried and distracted. No wonder familiarity and predictability became important to these children.

3. *A congregation that enjoys the upside of Tradition is rooted in its successes.* Some of every North American denomination's traditions have proved successful through the generations. These ancient traditions contain eternal truths and are part of the identity of these denominations. Congregational decision makers who forsake these rich traditions to become thoroughly contemporary are selling their birthright for the sake of attracting a few new members. Some congregations may experience a decline in attendance by staying with too many of these old traditions, but it is possible that, over time, these traditions may once again attract new members. There is rich material in the upside of the Tradition pole of this polarity.

4. *A congregation that enjoys the upside of Tradition is time tested, safe, recognizable, and predictable.* When people attend worship in their own congregations, they usually want things to be familiar and predictable. Of course, familiarity with the pastor contributes to worshipers' sense of well-being. There also ought to be at least one or two hymns members know well and can sing with gusto. Worshipers' familiarity with the liturgy or the flow of the service also contributes to predictability. Every congrega-

tion has a liturgy—that is, worship follows a certain order every Sunday. But in what are known as liturgical churches—such as Roman Catholic, Orthodox, Episcopal, and Lutheran—many elements remain the same from Sunday to Sunday, or at least for a season of the church year. Worshipers in every tradition want the liturgy to be relatively predictable, but when churchgoers are accustomed to saying exactly the same words and singing the same liturgical responses in worship and then these liturgies change dramatically, some people become upset and stop attending. The Roman Catholic Church, for example, lost many members after Vatican II as a result of the decree that the mass be celebrated in the vernacular rather than in Latin. Some Episcopalians left their church after that denomination replaced the 1928 *Book of Common Prayer* with a revised prayer book in 1979. And some Lutherans became disenchanted when predecessor church bodies of the Evangelical Lutheran Church in America replaced *The Service Book and Hymnal* (published in 1952) with the *Lutheran Book of Worship* (published in 1978). The people who left these denominations did not have the patience to stay around long enough to allow these new liturgies to become familiar. They quickly concluded that worship "just doesn't feel like church anymore."

The Upside of Innovation (Change)

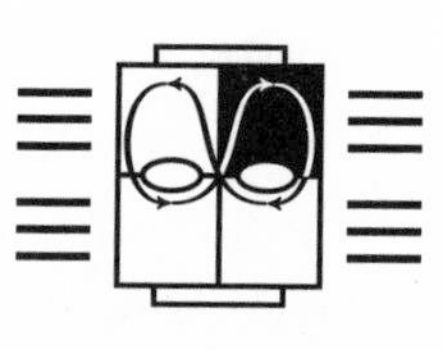
Upside Right

1. *A congregation that enjoys the upside of Innovation brings new energy with new perspectives.* New energy enters congregational life with innovative, fresh ideas. Along the way, those advocating change need to persuade the congregation that it might be exciting to venture into new ways of engaging younger people, younger families, and children.

2. *A congregation that enjoys the upside of Innovation responds to present realities and future possibilities.* The present reality of a congregation may be that it is losing its younger individuals and families. One possibility for such a congregation is to focus more of its financial resources on families with young children, hiring a part- or full-time church professional with a good track record of reaching this group. If the church does not have the

financial resources to add staff, it might move other leadership and volunteer resources to this area of ministry.

The most challenging change to be made in moving to the upside of change and innovation is the development of alternative worship opportunities. It is here that past and present are integrated most profoundly. Any alternative worship service will include elements similar to the traditional service. Scripture, music, sermon, and prayers will still be present. How they are presented may differ, sometime radically. The music will more than likely reflect a style other than traditional hymnody, which we have come to view as proper "church music."

A congregation should not plan an alternative worship service simply for its own members. It ought to focus the new service to attract a group of people who are not already part of the congregation, yet who live in or are moving into the congregation's ministry area. It would be unfair, however, to assume that "praise music" is the only alternative. For many mainline denominations, "praise songs" do not jibe with their theology and would therefore not be an option for worship. Rather, we should think of at least a half-dozen types of alternative worship services that can begin to draw in new members. If the most popular radio station in the county plays country-western music, then that is probably the kind of music a congregation needs to use to attract new members. This approach would most certainly bring a different crowd into the congregation.

3. *A congregation that enjoys the upside of Innovation struggles to relate past traditions to present realities.* The upside of the *Innovation AND Change* pole, however, involves much more than just offering a new worship opportunity. The order of services on Sunday morning could change. The way people are greeted and invited to stay for coffee and doughnuts could change. (In fact, snacks that contain less saturated fat than doughnuts might be offered.) In some cases, a second Sunday school might be formed. Or, more substantively, the whole organizational structure of the congregation could be the focus for change.

4. *A congregation that enjoys the upside of Innovation sees diversity, change, and risk as signs of congregational health.* St. Mark's Episcopal Church, on Capitol Hill in Washington, D.C., often shows up in Alban Institute

literature as a congregation that has for years been in the forefront of innovation. Several years ago, the congregation took all the pews out of its sanctuary and brought in movable chairs. The most radical move was abandoning the high altar at one end of the sanctuary and building a platform along one wall in the middle of the worship space. On the platform is a smaller altar with a lectern and pulpit on either side. At the congregation's 9:00 AM service, the sermon is preached at the end of the service. Worshipers then take a short break, get some coffee, and come back to their seats for a sermon seminar. Members ask questions and make comments about the sermon. Floor microphones are available. On some occasions the sermon comes under heavy attack, and a heated discussion ensues. By the norms of the congregation, such a discussion is acceptable. The rector has come to expect that his sermons will be seriously questioned, and the sanctuary seating was designed to make this kind of dialogue possible. The 11:00 AM service at St. Mark's is more traditional, although the high altar at the end of the sanctuary is not used (it is used on certain rare occasions). After the service, a pub-style lunch is on offer at a moderate cost, and beer and wine are available. Members stay to enjoy fellowship over lunch.

The sanctuary is used for other types of social gatherings as well. It has become an all-purpose hall. For a dance, event planners clear out the chairs and bring in the food and music. They also present plays in this space. St. Mark's continues to be one of the most vital congregations on Capitol Hill. An extremely heterogeneous congregation, it welcomes many visitors. Even though the congregation retains the tradition of celebrating communion every Sunday, what is done with that liturgy is novel and unexpected. The continued innovation is seen by some people as one of the congregation's key strengths.

THE IMPORTANCE OF ADMITTING DOWNSIDES

Unless congregational leaders admit that a pole has a downside, those resisting that pole will begin to identify all the reasons not to move to the upside of the pole they oppose. Their fears about that pole will increase, because those advocating its upside seem unwilling or unable to recognize its downside. If a congregation works through the polarity together, advocates will readily acknowledge serious downsides to any pole. When they are willing to recognize the downside, they affirm the wisdom of those who are fearful of that downside. In this discussion, if someone comes up with another reason for not taking an action that would support a pole, the group facilitator can simply pick up a felt-tip marker and add the comment to the list on the downside of this pole. Rather than arguing against the idea, the group acknowledges it and adds it to the polarity map. In this way, opposition becomes a resource. Those resisting an action are seen as resources to help the congregation manage this polarity well, because they contribute to a more complete understanding of the situation by providing information for one of the lower quadrants. Having an appreciation for a lower quadrant, along with the rest of the map, can help the congregation address both poles more effectively.

The Downside of Tradition (Stability)

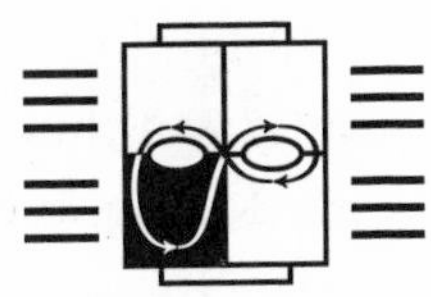

Downside Left

In every polarity, each pole has a downside. Any congregation that places too much emphasis on maintaining its traditional way of worshiping or conducting other activities to the neglect of innovation will increasingly experience more of the downside of that pole.

The downside of Tradition is one that gives many clergy and key lay leaders heartburn. These leaders are only too aware that many members, perhaps a majority, would like their church to stay as it is. Yet these leaders also know that the longer they delay changes that make the congregation more relevant to newcomers or to those outside the church, the more likely it is that they will lose out down the line. This phenomenon raises a question: How can we as a congregation remain an anchor of stability and continuity for our members while bringing congregational life into the present age? How can we move from the downside of the Tradition pole to the upside of the Innovation pole? Let's look at some possible elements in the downside of the Tradition pole.

1. *The downside of Tradition causes some to feel bored and stagnant.* As rich and meaningful as a liturgical service can be, it can also become downright boring—going over the same old thing one more time. The same can be true of a nonliturgical worship service. The routine is only too familiar. The same old hymns can lose their luster.

Looking around the congregation on a Sunday morning, we see the same crowd looking older and more tired. The new problem is that the crowd is shrinking. Some of the people who used to bring energy and excitement to the place are no longer coming. Stagnation has set in.

2. *The downside of Tradition is being out of touch with the present and future.* The challenge of preparing a sermon is to bring the message of Scripture in a way that relates it to listeners' daily lives. This aim requires that the preacher have some idea of what people are experiencing and bring hope, comfort, and challenge to them. As H. Grady Davis, Roy's homiletics professor, used to say, "You can start in Jerusalem and end up in New York City, or you can start in New York City and end up in Jerusalem, but one way or the other, you need to connect the two." If any sermon is to be relevant, the preacher is likely to have to take some risks. The preacher needs to go out on a limb to reach people where they are and to indicate what Scripture has to say about their situation. Sometimes the preacher connects, and sometimes she doesn't. But without taking risks, the preacher is likely to be irrelevant to either the present or the future.

When neither the sermon nor the adult education classes nor any church activity connects with people, the church has become irrelevant to its members. The church no longer has a message worth hearing in today's culture. Members stop showing up for worship or other church events. If things don't change, the slow, steady decline of the church continues.

3. *The downside of Tradition gives rise to false security in a changing world.* In an early Alban publication, *The Life Cycle of a Congregation,*[5] author Martin F. Saarinen takes us through the birth side of the cycle and then over the top to the downside of the cycle. The upside includes birth, childhood, and adolescence. Riding with a congregation as it goes through these stages of development can be exhilarating. The top of the curve has two stages: prime on the upside and maturity on the downside. Further along the downside lie bureaucracy, autocracy, blaming, and death.

The two highest points on this cycle are relevant here. When a congregation hits its prime, everything is going well. Trained leaders are keeping programs relevant and exciting. The congregation has a solid organizational system that keep things running smoothly. Members stay in touch and encourage one another to keep commitment high. The place runs like a well-tuned engine.

The seeds of decline can easily be sown in the prime of life. Everything is going so well that there appears to be no need to consider new and possibly controversial ideas to keep the place growing. The situation is almost like that of Jesus and the disciples on the Mount of Transfiguration. Peter says to Jesus, "Let's stay here and build three tabernacles—one for Moses, one for Elijah, and one for you" (Matt. 17:4, paraphrase). Jesus would have no part in Peter's wishful thinking. Down the mountain we must go, as we still have lots of work to do. When a congregation begins to put most of its energy in keeping things the way they are (in effect, building booths on the mount), it moves to the stage we will call "maturity."

In maturity everything still seems to be running well, but there is resistance to new ideas that might rock the boat. The governing board no longer wrestles with the issues that would keep the congregation on its "growing edge," as it did in the past. Instead the board sees itself as a management group, keeping all the wheels greased and the motor running smoothly. The next stage, bureaucracy, is already on its way. The board begins to run the church in bureaucratic fashion: everyone is asked to abide by the old rules and regulations.

Saarinen's theory is relevant in that it points up the temptation of going for stability when that can be the kiss of death for a congregation that had momentum in its growth phase. Stability without change slows everything down, and the energy and excitement people had for their congregation begin to dissipate. It is almost as though everyone had unconsciously concluded that we are big enough, and it would be nice to plateau for a while. As churches make this choice, their stability offers a false sense of security in a changing world. The congregation begins to be run by a group of managers, who fight hard to preserve what has made the congregation great up to this point. The leaders of the congregation who continue to push for change are not given much support. We will deal with this topic in greater depth when we move to the *Manager AND Leader* polarity.

4. *The downside of Tradition leads to missed opportunities.* The congregation that stays with tradition or stability may miss out on a promising idea for outreach. When, for example, the traditional vacation Bible school fails to reach out to children in the neighborhood, a well-considered change could draw in more neighborhood kids. Holding sessions in the evening and

involving parents might engage far more people in the school, addressing all ages. An overfocus on what has worked in the past may mean that people do not have their heads up and are not scanning the environment for opportunities to reach new people in the area.

The Downside of Innovation (Change)

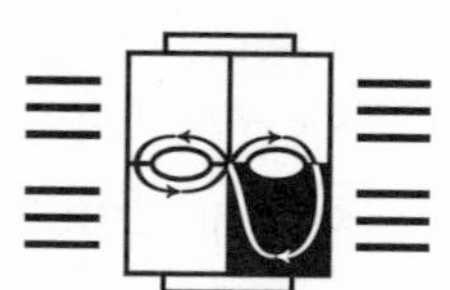

Downside Right

The fear of the downside of Tradition, combined with a strong valuing of Innovation, can lead to the downside of Innovation.

1. *The downside of Innovation can create conflict and chaos.* Innovation will clearly shift the identity of the congregation, for better or worse. It has the potential for creating conflict within the congregation, and causing some people to leave—possibly some big givers. These people may feel as though the church isn't theirs anymore, that the congregation's former identity has been replaced by one that is hard to recognize.

This scenario applies to Jack Smothers in one of our opening stories. Jack brought about changes so quickly when he came to his new congregation that he created enormous conflict, so much so that the governing board voted to have him fired. This story was lived out not many years ago in a large congregation in the Washington, D.C., area, whose new pastor was removed in less than a year.

In many congregations the most controversial elements of church life have to do with the introduction of alternative worship services. Many people object to bringing what they think of as "junk music" into their sanctuary. They think leaders are "dumbing down" their tradition just to attract a few new members. Some do not object at the time these innovative worship celebrations are begun. It is when attendance at an alternative worship experience outstrips attendance at the traditional service that conflict begins. Tradition-minded worshipers begin to feel as though the change in attendance is a judgment upon their preferred service. A large part of the conflict has to do with the kinds of people who attend the alternative worship services and how they dress. For contemporary services people are often encouraged to dress casually, and some come to church in T-shirts, jeans, cutoffs, shorts, and sandals.

2. *The downside of Innovation forsakes tradition in attempts to be more relevant.* Innovation and change can be risky and expensive, as any innovation requires volunteer energies and money. A good example is Marble Collegiate Church in New York, which spent over a million dollars in an effort to build what the members called "Spirit Cafe." This bar and restaurant would use religious themes in its entertainment and music. Marble Collegiate was forsaking its tradition of offering spiritual nourishment within worship and courses on religious themes in the church, and attempting instead to provide spiritual nourishment within the context of a cafe. The experiment failed badly. To this day some generous givers to the congregation remain upset about this failed project. (We should add that unless a church is failing occasionally, it likely is not taking enough risks.)

3. *The downside of Innovation threatens those who love tradition.* When a congregation continues to experiment with new ideas, members may feel as though they are living in chaos and that they are being deprived of the continuity and stability that are important to their health and sanity. For some members innovation will seem to devalue past successes and the rich tradition on which the congregation based part of its identity. Should some innovations draw in a new cadre of people, longtime members and newcomers may have trouble relating to one another.

An example of the way change threatens those who love tradition is a denomination that decided to experiment with the way it formed new congregations. National outreach leaders wanted to test whether a megachurch could be formed without going through all the growth stages that congregations normally experience. The denomination bought a large piece of property and hired a team of clergy to begin functioning as if the congregation would soon become a two-thousand-member church. The pastoral leaders began "seeker services," which used entertainment evangelism—Sunday worship with hard-rock music, liturgical dance, movie clips, and easy-to-learn songs that would get people through the door. Spiritual transformation would take place, they predicted, once people were drawn by the congregation's faith and wanted to delve deeper into what it means to be a Christian. Megachurches that use this form of evangelism expect conversion to occur when those attending Sunday worship become engaged in a small group in which participants seriously discuss matters of Christian faith.

The project was a costly failure. The surrounding congregations of this denomination took exception to the experiment. They got together and mounted serious opposition to the new church. They argued that "entertainment evangelism" ran counter to the theology and liturgy that had been the hallmark of the denomination since the Reformation. These nearby congregations were able to persuade the denomination's national board of mission to shut down the experiment, sell the property, and go elsewhere for any similar effort. The experiment became a threat to nearby congregations whose leaders believed the new church compromised the rich tradition of their denomination.

4. *The downside of Innovation feels unsafe to some, as it is unrecognizable and unpredictable.* In 1969, in his role as assistant to the bishop for youth ministry in the Central Pennsylvania Synod, Lutheran Church in America, Roy took a five-piece band made up of teenagers across the synod, using it to provide the music for fairly traditional Lutheran worship services. The instruments in the band were keyboard, electric guitar, drums, saxophone, and trumpet. He received rather severe criticism from certain clergy and lay leaders, who thought he was deliberately trying to shock people. They accused him of degrading Lutheran hymnody and of trying to be sensational. Forty years later, in 2009, that band would be considered tame in many Lutheran churches. How times have changed! Back in 1969, however, the attempt was seen as dangerous. Because the innovation was unrecognizable, it was seen as unfit for Lutheran worship. In the minds of some, such music could only lead to the disintegration and demise of the church.

Dynamics at Work in a Polarity

We have suggested content for the four quadrants of the *Tradition AND Innovation* polarity map. Before moving on to Action Steps and Early Warnings, let's review some of the dynamics that take place between those advocating one pole or the other. On page 37 is a small, simplified map of the *Tradition AND Innovation* polarity containing only item 1 from each of the four quadrants of the larger map.

The more we value the upside of one pole, the more we will fear the downside of the opposite pole. The potency of the value and the fear is the

Polarity Management® Map

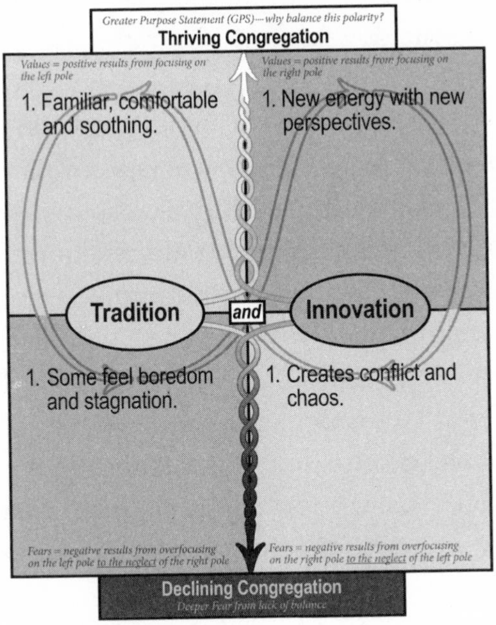

Greater Purpose Statement (GPS)—why balance this polarity?
Thriving Congregation
Values = positive results from focusing on the left pole
1. Familiar, comfortable and soothing.
Values = positive results from focusing on the right pole
1. New energy with new perspectives.
Tradition
and
Innovation
1. Some feel boredom and stagnation.
1. Creates conflict and chaos.
Fears = negative results from overfocusing on the left pole to the neglect of the right pole
Fears = negative results from overfocusing on the right pole to the neglect of the left pole
Declining Congregation
Deeper Fear from lack of balance

Map 2.2

same. If we value the upside of one pole at nine on a ten-point scale, we will fear its loss at nine on a ten-point scale. The more people value the upside of one pole, the more they will denigrate the opposite pole by pointing out why it is a bad idea and adding more items to the downside of that pole. So, for example, the more a congregation values the upside of Tradition (feels familiar, comfortable, and soothing), the more it will fear the downside of Innovation (can create conflict and chaos).

If we mistakenly think that only one pole can be adopted (either/or thinking) *and* hold strong values and fears, as above, we will find it difficult to embrace the other point of view, fearing that we must let go of something we value dearly.

When the rich upside of Tradition is valued highly and the downside of Innovation is greatly feared, a congregation is likely to be insensitive to the downside of Tradition as it begins to appear. A congregation is also likely to overtolerate the downside, even when members become aware of it. A comment reflecting this overtolerance might be heard: "We have our problems, sure. But at least we aren't creating chaos in our church like *they* are."

"They," of course, are congregations that highly value the upside of Innovation and fear the downside of Tradition. As a result, the first congregation is overtolerating the downside of Innovation, which increases others' fear of "them."

Congregations and denominations that highly value the upside of Innovation (it brings new energy with new perspectives) will, if caught in an either/or mindset, be equally fearful of those congregations that appear to be doing well while staying within their traditional format.

Both sides have values essential to a thriving congregation. Both sides have legitimate fears of the downside. What is needed is a polarity perspective to support *both* Tradition *AND* Innovation. When the issue is addressed as a polarity to be managed, however, with a downside to each pole, the nature of the discussion will change. We no longer believe we will lose what we value dearly. Rather, we become willing to support the other pole, because we are confident that our favorite pole will always be valued.

With this overview of the content of this polarity, let's shift to the ways we manage polarities.

Managing the Polarity Poorly

Your congregation may prefer one pole of the polarities we are exploring. More likely, your congregation is split, with some members preferring one pole and some the other. Having a preference is not a problem. Focusing on one pole *to the neglect of the other* is a problem. When this happens, the dynamic balance between the poles is upset, and the natural oscillation over time doesn't happen as easily as it should. In those situations, the polarity is not managed well, and the congregation ends up in the downside of the pole preferred by those with more power.

If your congregation sees this polarity as a problem to solve by adopting competing solutions, it will get into a power struggle between those supporting Tradition and those supporting Innovation, and your congregation will lose twice.

1. You lose first by spending a significant amount of time and energy trying to "win" the argument and to persuade people to support one

side. Relationships will be undermined, and the important work of the congregation will be neglected.

2. You lose a second time when one side does indeed "win." Whenever that happens, first you experience the downside of the "winner's" preferred pole. Then you experience the downside of both poles.

The result of treating a polarity to manage as if it were a problem to solve is that this response contributes to the decline of the congregation.

Below are two icons representing poorly managed polarities. In the first, the overemphasis is on Tradition. In the second, the overemphasis is on Innovation.

Early Warnings

How will we know that we are getting into the downside of one pole or the other? Here the Early Warnings are helpful. They let us know early on what is happening, so we can make corrections as needed. Because polarities will always be with us, we'll have repeated opportunities to identify Early Warnings and learn to recognize them as time goes on. Below are some examples of Early Warnings that help congregations minimize the amount of time they spend in the downside of either pole of this polarity. Feel free to modify them or add to them in whatever way makes sense for your congregation. The important thing is to recognize that managing a polarity over time means that we will periodically experience the downside of one or both poles and need to make a course correction.

Early Warnings for the Downside of Tradition (Stability)

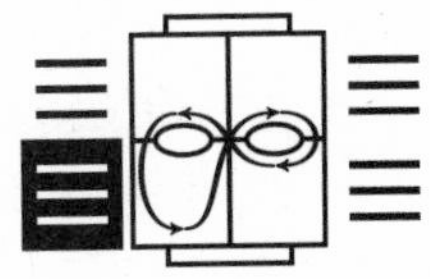

Early Warnings Left

1. Attendance at the traditional service begins to drop, and comments suggesting that "We just don't have the life in our worship that we once had" are increasingly heard.
2. Couples with children leave because they are having trouble keeping the kids interested.

3. The average age of members rises as few younger families join the church.
4. The governing board vetoes ideas that do not support its conception of what the congregation ought to be doing.
5. Members boycott committee meetings as any new idea they suggest gets shot down by more tradition-oriented people.
6. New members complain that the congregation's decision-making bodies seem to be closed to them.
7. The average age of people serving on congregational committees continues to rise.

Early Warnings for the Downside of Innovation (Change)

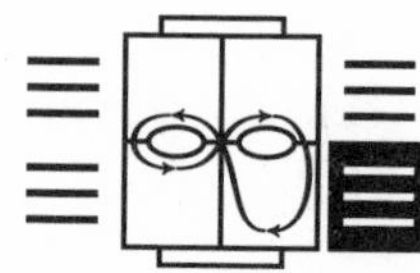

Early Warnings Right

1. Longtime members grumble that this church no longer feels like "our church."
2. Members object that the pastor and staff are spending too much time with new programs and that their needs are being ignored.
3. Some members stop attending church functions, saying they believe that the changes taking place in the church are not faithful to the tradition and theology of the denomination.
4. Members of the congregation's decision-making bodies stop asking whether the changes they contemplate will sacrifice the core identity of the congregation.
5. Only those outside speakers who advocate innovation and change are invited to make presentations to mebers; guest speakers who would emphasize the value of the denomination's tradition are never heard from.
6. Anyone resisting a change effort is labeled as an "old fogy" or a "stick-in-the-mud" and is made to feel less valued within the congregation.
7. Staff members become so focused on instituting creative new ideas that they trample the feelings of those resisting change; as a result, some members feel disenfranchised.

New ideas may also cost money, so innovative ideas can be a financial drain on the congregation. People new to the faith are not used to giving large sums of money to a congregation. It will take time and transformation before these new members begin carrying their share of the financial load. Congregations first need to pay for establishing programs that have the potential to attract new members; then they need to deal with the cost of caring for the new people. Some longtime members will believe that the clergy are paying more attention to newer members than to long-term members, and the congregation may need to hire additional staff to care for either newcomers or longtime members.

Declining congregations are marked by chronic power struggles between members who value Tradition and members who value Innovation. The inherent tension between the two poles generates a vicious circle in which each pole points toward the downside of the other pole. The advocates of Tradition accuse the advocates of Innovation of disrespecting the bedrock on which the church is built and of leading the congregation into conflict and chaos. The Innovation advocates accuse the Tradition advocates of being out of touch and incapable of relating to today's world. Both are half right. Each group's accusation generates defensiveness and counteraccusations by the other, a continuing routine that hastens congregational decline.

Some congregations see one pole as "the answer." No matter which pole the congregation prefers, to the degree that members focus on that pole to the neglect of its counterpart, the congregation will end up in the downside of its preferred pole. This approach will over time undermine its ability to thrive.

Managing the Polarity Well

When you experience these Early Warnings or the ones you have identified for your congregation, the way to correct your course is to revisit the Action Steps you have identified. For example, if you are experiencing Early Warnings that your congregation is moving into the downside of the Tradition pole, revisit your Action Steps for getting to the upside of Innovation. These Action Steps are intended to keep you out of the downside of Tradition. If you are getting into the downside of Tradition, the first questions to ask is, "Are we taking the Action Steps we decided on to avoid the downside of Tradition and to get to the upside of Innovation?" If the answer is no, then you need to start doing those Action Steps or find others you are willing to do. If the answer is, "Yes, we are doing the Action Steps we planned," then you may need to explore additional Action Steps to support steps you have already taken.

Action Steps for the Upside of Tradition (Stability)

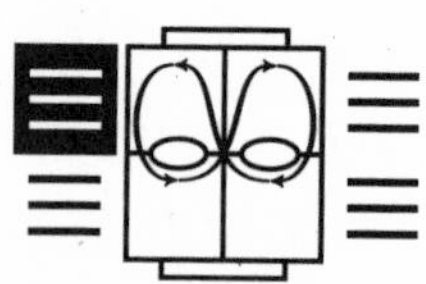

Action Steps Left

These steps are offered only as suggestions. The Action Steps you create should come from the congregation's key stakeholders.

1. *Ask the music and worship committee of the church to begin wrestling with ways to bring a spark of excitement and freshness to the congregation's traditional service.* For example, bring in a string or woodwind quartet to accompany traditional hymns, or invite a harpist or violinist to play the prelude and other service voluntaries, in addition to accompanying the hymns. Some classical hymns work well with other classical instruments. A violinist playing a favorite traditional hymn can enhance the sense of reverence in a service. This idea would offset some members' impression that the energy of the staff or governing body and the congregation's money are all being expended on innovative worship.

This may be a High-leverage Action Step, because it supports the tradition of the church while bringing some innovation into the traditional service. (Remember that we call something a High-leverage Action Step when it supports the upside of both poles.)

2. *In multiple-staff congregations, ensure that both traditionalists and innovators are hired as staff members.*

3. *Sponsor a variety of Bible study groups for the congregation, with some presenting a more traditional view of Scripture and others offering a more innovative perspective.* A good text for an innovative Bible study would be Marcus Borg's book *Meeting Jesus Again for the First Time* or his *Reading the Bible Again for the First Time.*[6] When outside speakers are considered

for special occasions, make sure to invite a balance of traditional and innovation-minded specialists. This may be another High-leverage Action Step as it supports both a traditional approach to Bible study and an innovative perspective.

4. *In the congregation's confirmation class, ask students to write a paper based on an interview with an older adult in the congregation about that person's spiritual journey, and ask students to read their papers to the rest of the class or to a small group in the class.*

A byproduct of this exercise is providing an opportunity for a young person and an older member of the congregation to get acquainted. The younger person will come to appreciate what the older member has had to endure as well as the blessings she has received. Young people may also learn that it's possible to feel blessed and grateful even in the face of tough experiences, and as a result come to respect traditional values and practices. Such conversation would also give the older member some idea of what it is like to be a teenager today.

5. *Celebrate the historical markers in a congregation's life—for example, the congregation's fiftieth anniversary.* At these celebrations, members might recall the history of the congregation and its heroes and villains.

Action Steps for the Upside of Innovation (Change)

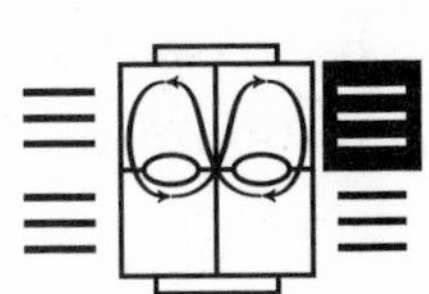

Action Steps Right

1. *Create a task force to visit other congregations periodically to observe some of the innovations they are trying. When task force members discover a new idea that would fit the congregation, they can take it to the appropriate committee.*

2. *Ask the Christian education committee to plan a monthly activity that brings excitement and surprise to Sunday school children, making the Sunday school hour an outreach opportunity and encouraging children who attend to invite a friend to join them.* The committee can plan an activity that lasts for only ten to fifteen minutes before children go to their regular classes—bringing in a clown, singing an action song, or serving fresh fruit. When

children become excited about these monthly activities, they may be more likely to invite a friend to come with them to Sunday school.

3. *Hire a young staff member who will emphasize children's and family ministries within the congregation.* This Action Step might be useful to congregations whose senior pastor is older and relates more easily to the older crowd than to younger members.

4. *Encourage the nominating committee to invite younger or newer members to participate in decision-making groups.*

5. *Develop a policy that all clergy and program staff may take a three-month sabbatical every four years, encouraging staff members to use part of their sabbatical to visit congregations that appear to be doing an outstanding job in the staff member's own ministry area.* Sometimes when congregational decision makers become advocates of change, they need to assure longtime members that they are not going to abandon all of the music, liturgy, and tradition that have great meaning for longtime members. Congregational leaders should be open and upfront with this action. They should have a series of meetings with more traditional members, setting out the game plan. They should ask whether more tradition-oriented members would be willing to allow the congregation to experiment with some new forms of worship and activities if they were assured that everything they hold dear will not be taken from them. For the most part, leaders will find those who prefer traditional aspects of congregational life to be reasonable in their responses to this suggestion. Most longtime members have an investment in their congregation's survival in a vigorous state for the next hundred years. They want their congregation to have the transforming impact on future generations that it had on them. In this way, past and present are integrated.

Another Action Step that a congregation could take to ensure that the Innovation pole gets as much energy as the Tradition pole is to review its decision-making process. Church consultant Bill Easum estimates that most church committees spend 80 percent of their time saying no to the creative ideas brought forward by other members. He favors a permission-giving church in which any group is free to start a new ministry, as long as it is in keeping with the mission statement of the church. The group is free to raise the money without going through a committee and the governing board. Clergy and governing boards may feel threatened by this wide-open way

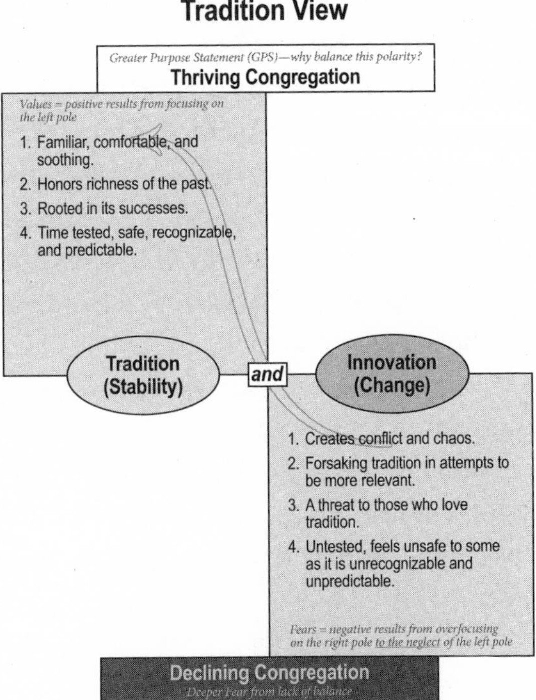

Map 2.3

of doing things, fearing that they have lost control over what happens in the church. There are times we should ask ourselves, "Whose church is this anyway? And why do the minister and the governing board need to give their approval for anything for which members have energy, if it conforms to the mission statement of the congregation?" Some members no longer have patience with a cumbersome committee-and-board decision-making process. When they get excited about a new idea, they might simply drop it if they don't have the energy to work through the usual decision-making process before trying it out. If they are given the option of trying an idea without having to gain approval all the way up the line, they may pursue it. If it fails, they are the ones who take responsibility. If it succeeds, the congregation gets a new spurt of energy.

A Picture of Managing Well

A polarity is managed well when a congregation is maximizing both upsides through Action Steps and minimizing both downsides through Early Warnings. Map 2.3 is a picture showing what the infinity energy loop might look like when a polarity is managed well.

This map contains abbreviated Action Steps and Early Warnings so that you can get an overview of the whole picture. Again, we remind you that the content of the map and the Action Steps and Early Warnings are suggestions. If the words do not speak to your congregation, modify them so that they work for you. Remember, if you are dealing with a polarity, you will experience an upside and a downside to each pole, and your congregation will need to empower both upsides to thrive.

Thriving congregations manage to support both *Tradition AND Innovation*. If they pursue Action Steps and heed Early Warnings, the inherent tension between the two poles becomes a virtuous circle in which Tradition becomes a platform for Innovation, and Innovation helps sustain Tradition. Doing this well helps congregations thrive, even if they have never heard of Polarity Management.

Points of View in Polarities

In chapter 1 we explored seven polarity principles. Principle 8 below is about another helpful concept, the two "points of view" revealed by a polarity map.

POLARITY PRINCIPLE 8

All polarity maps contain two "points of view." The point of view is composed of the upside of one pole, which is valued, and the downside of the opposite pole, which is feared.

This principle summarizes the ideas discussed in "Dynamics at Work in a Polarity" on page 36. Let's briefly look at how some people become entrenched as one-pole advocates. In the *Tradition AND Innovation* polarity, the point of view of those who value Tradition looks like the partial map on page 45 (using item 2 from the larger map content).

The diagonal quadrants including the upside of Tradition and the downside of Innovation represent a point of view. Seeing only this part of the map

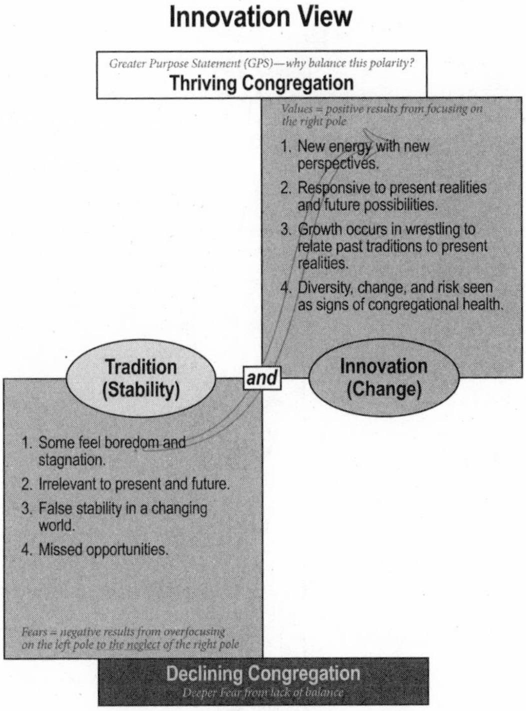

Innovation View

Greater Purpose Statement (GPS)—why balance this polarity?
Thriving Congregation

Values = positive results from focusing on the right pole

1. New energy with new perspectives.
2. Responsive to present realities and future possibilities.
3. Growth occurs in wrestling to relate past traditions to present realities.
4. Diversity, change, and risk seen as signs of congregational health.

Tradition (Stability) *and* **Innovation (Change)**

1. Some feel boredom and stagnation.
2. Irrelevant to present and future.
3. False stability in a changing world.
4. Missed opportunities.

Fears = negative results from overfocusing on the left pole to the neglect of the right pole

Declining Congregation
Deeper Fear from lack of balance

Map 2.4

is like seeing only the goblet, but not the two heads, in the picture in chapter 1. If people strongly value the importance of the tradition and historical roots on which the church was founded, they will strongly fear forsaking those roots and losing the basic platform that has been a source of life for the congregation.

From this perspective, it appears ridiculous to choose Innovation over Tradition. The fear of Innovation's downside makes it difficult to see its upside. This fear can also make people insensitive to and overtolerant of Tradition's downside. This point of view helps explain why some congregations have difficulty tapping the upside of Innovation, and to the degree that they fail to tap this potential, they will undermine their ability to thrive. This point of view is incomplete, however. What is absent is the equally valid and essential opposite point of view, shown in map 2.4 above.

Those with this point of view are equally certain that they are right. They are like those who see only the two heads, but not the goblet, in the picture in chapter 1. And the stronger their value and fear, the more they will overtolerate the downside of Innovation and the more difficult it will be for them to tap the upside of Tradition. Like those who hold only the first point of view, they will undermine the congregation's capacity to thrive.

Polarity Management®

Action Steps

How will we gain or maintain the positive results from focusing on this left pole? What? Who? By when? Measures?

1. Working to add excitement and freshness to the traditional service.
2. In multiple-staff congregations, ensure that both traditionalist staff and those emphasizing innovation are hired.
3. Offer variety of Bible study groups with some emphasizing a traditional view of Scripture and other a more innovative perspective.
4. Have confirmation students interview and write up the spiritual journey of an older member.
5. Celebrate the historical markers of congregational life.

Early Warnings

Measurable indicators (things you can count) that will let you know that you are getting into the downside of this left pole.

1. Attendance at the traditional service begins to drop.
2. Couples with children leave to join other churches.
3. The average age of membership rises.
4. Members boycott committee meetings as any new idea they suggest gets shot down by more tradition-oriented members.
5. New members complain that the congregation's decision-making bodies seem to be closed to them.

Greater Purpose Statement (GPS)

Thriving

Values = positive results from focusing on the left pole

1. Familiar, comfortable, and soothing.
2. Honors richness of the past.
3. Rooted in its successes.
4. Time tested, safe, recognizable, and predictable.

Tradition (Stability)

and

1. Some feel boredom and stagnation.
2. Irrelevant to present and future.
3. False stability in a changing world.
4. Missed opportunities.

Fears = negative results from overfocusing on the left pole to the neglect of the right pole

Declining

Deeper Fear from

Map

Why balance this polarity?

Congregation

Values = positive results from focusing on the right pole

1. New energy with new perspectives.
2. Responsive to present realities and future possibilities.
3. Growth occurs in wrestling to relate past traditions to present realities.
4. Diversity, change, and risk seen as signs of congregational health.

and

Innovation (Change)

1. Creates conflict and chaos.
2. Forsaking tradition in attempts to be more relevant.
3. A threat to those who love tradition.
4. Untested, feels unsafe to some as it is unrecognizable and unpredictable.

Fears = negative results from overfocusing on the right pole to the neglect of the left pole

Congregation

lack of balance

Action Steps

How will we gain or maintain the positive results from focusing on this right pole? What? Who? By when? Measures?

1. Create a task force to visit other congregations to observe some innovative ideas that have been tried and succeeded.
2. Have the Sunday school plan a brief celebratory event monthly before classes and challenge the children to bring their friends to these events.
3. Hire a young staff that will emphasize children and family ministries.
4. Encourage the nominating committee to invite younger and newer members to participate in decision-making groups.
5. Provide clergy/staff sabbaticals and encourage staff to spend part of that time visiting other congregations that specialize in specific aspects of ministry.

Early Warnings

Measurable indicators (things you can count) that will let you know that you are getting into the downside of this right pole.

1. Longtime members grumble that this church no longer feels like "our church."
2. Members object that the pastor and staff are spending too much time with new programs.
3. Some members complain that the congregation is no longer faithful to the tradition and theology of the denomination.
4. Only those outside speakers that advocate innovation and change are invited to speak to the congregation.
5. Some members feel disenfranchised as the members pushing for change trample over them without really hearing them.

Map 2.5

CHAPTER 3

Spiritual Health AND Institutional Health

What is the primary task of a congregation? Should it be transforming lives or maintaining healthy congregational structures? Transforming lives has to do with affirming and helping people understand their personal experience of God. It further entails encouraging them to grow in their faith, committing their lives to it. Maintaining congregational health involves helping people understand the importance of church membership and their need to support the church with their finances and volunteer energies so that the congregation, in turn, is better able to support them in their faith journey. Will there be tension between these two desires in a thriving congregation? No question about it! Congregations can lose their way by focusing on one to the exclusion of the other. We rarely see congregations that keep these two in healthy balance.

Spiritual Vitality AND Administrative Competence

The voices of the governing board at First Church grew louder and louder. Generally, board members did not argue, but this issue had a few members steaming. There was a clear consensus among board members that the congregation was understaffed. Current staff members, including the full-time pastor and four part-timers—a musician, a director of children's ministries, a secretary, and a custodian—were obviously stretched to the limit. The part-time people were working many more hours than their salaries and job descriptions allowed, and they were beginning to resent it. The board members were arguing over whether to hire a parish administrator or a director of evangelism and outreach.

Bill Clark was the chief proponent of the view that the congregation's first priority ought to be a parish administrator. "This place is a permanent disaster area," he insisted. "There is no one to supervise our custodian, to keep the building looking halfway decent. Rooms are double-booked, so one group ends up angry and meeting in the kitchen. We are supposed to have a volunteer receptionist working from 9:00 AM to 12:00 noon Monday through Friday, but on some days, two people show up, and on other days no one does. Newcomers visiting our church will certainly be put off by the chaos."

Frieda Schwelander had a different perspective and made her case with equal conviction. "As a community of faith, our first priority shouldn't be having a spiffy church. It ought to be reaching out to people who have never heard of a loving God, one who sacrificed his Son so we could be reconciled to him. There is a spiritual hunger in our neighborhood, and our first priority should be reaching out and helping people experience the joy and peace that can come from knowing Christ. We need someone to help us become a congregation that is constantly reaching out to the unchurched."

Bill shot back, "A capable lay volunteer can motivate us to be that kind of church, but not until we deal with the organizational mess we're always in."

Frieda retorted, "We can also have a capable lay volunteer as our parish administrator."

A neighboring congregation had been dealing with a variation on this tension. Between fourteen hundred and fifteen hundred people attended Sunday worship, and the congregation continued to grow numerically, mainly because it had a clear focus on the spiritual formation of its members. The congregation's beloved senior pastor insisted that he was not good at administration, but he provided strong leadership for the spiritual growth of the members. The congregation's leaders set a goal that within four years, at least one hundred small groups would be meeting biweekly in homes for study of Scripture, theology, and prayer. To compensate for the senior pastor's lack of administrative skill, the large congregation had hired an administrative pastor.

Yet an incident a year ago had revealed the congregation's lack of organizational competence. During a major building and renovation program, the staff had to move into temporary quarters, and administrative disaster ensued. Staff members argued over who should use which spaces. Church programs faltered, owing to a lack of attention from the staff members in charge of them. The organizational dysfunction of the staff and congregation became all too obvious to board members, many of whom had key roles in managing major corporations. Finally, the board called in a consultant to help the congregation.

The board's decision was unusual. Most congregations seek a consultant when the congregation is well managed and adequately staffed but not growing spiritually, numerically, in social-justice outreach, or in members' caring for one another. This congregation, however, was dealing with the opposite problem—a spiritually vital community that was falling apart administratively.

POLARITY PRINCIPLE 9

If you are building a map with a group of people that includes two subgroups, each of which feels strongly about one pole, it is best to deal with both upsides first. A wise facilitator will start with the upside supported by the group most anxious about being heard. Once that group's upside has been affirmed, its members are more likely to be able to hear that there is a second upside as well.

Notice that in this chapter we are starting with the upside of the left pole and then following the normal flow of the infinity loop through the four quadrants. This approach will help you understand the normal flow of energy through the quadrants as you read about them.

The Polarity to Be Managed

The tensions described in the scenarios at the beginning of this chapter are not examples of a problem to be solved but rather of a polarity to be managed. Map 3.1 on page 54 illustrates how this dilemma looks on a polarity map.

Polarity Management® Map

Greater Purpose Statement (GPS)—why balance this polarity?

Thriving Congregation

Values = positive results from focusing on the left pole

1. People's experiences of God are affirmed and explained. People are supported in experiencing God more deeply and committing their lives to God.
2. Engaging in programs that deepen and strengthen faith is encouraged.
3. Staff is focused on the spiritual nurture of members and the unchurched.
4. Members are keen on sharing their faith story with others and being with others at times of spiritual crisis.
5. Members are aware of their needs for spiritual transformation in their lives, other members, and those outside the church.

Values = positive results from focusing on the right pole

1. People need an institution to ensure the continuity of the faith, as personal experiences of God are tentative and easily dismissed.
2. Church membership is important and people are encouraged to become more engaged with each other and with congregational tasks.
3. Staff is focused on serving member needs and strengthening church membership.
4. Members are keen on meeting the volunteer needs of the congregation and coming to its aid during institutional crises.
5. Members are aware of the need of the congregation to grow stronger, add staff, and increase membership.

Spiritual Health
CHURCH UNIVERSAL

and

Institutional Health
INSTITUTIONAL CHURCH

1. Personal experiences of God are fragile and vulnerable and can be easily discounted.
2. Newcomers are not integrated with other church members. Church membership is not emphasized or talked about.
3. There is inadequate staff time for the institutional needs of the congregation.
4. The volunteer needs of the congregational are rarely met.
5. The church becomes an organizational disaster with little insight into how to structure itself for order and stability.

Fears = negative results from overfocusing on the left pole to the neglect of the right pole

1. Institutions, unconsciously, always seek first to survive, sometimes subverting their original reason for forming.
2. Getting people to join the church and support it becomes more important than having them surrender their lives to God.
3. Inadequate staff time for outreach to nonmembers or the spiritual needs of members.
4. There are frequent conflicts over the best ways to survive.
5. The spiritual transformation of members and the unchurched is rarely talked about. Members don't even know what this means.

Fears = negative results from overfocusing on the right pole to the neglect of the left pole

Declining Congregation

Deeper Fear from lack of balance

Map 3.1

It is a rare congregation that can balance the upper quadrants of this polarity and tap them both. Congregations that are able to balance them fairly well are the ones likely to be growing numerically and spiritually.

We can see this polarity played out in the book of Acts, when the apostles received complaints that the widows and orphans of the Gentile Christians were not receiving adequate care. The apostles concluded that they should not give up proclaiming the good news of Jesus Christ to serve tables, and they wisely appointed deacons to take care of this ministry on their behalf so that they could continue to focus on missionary outreach. The early apostles managed this polarity well.

The Upside of Spiritual Health

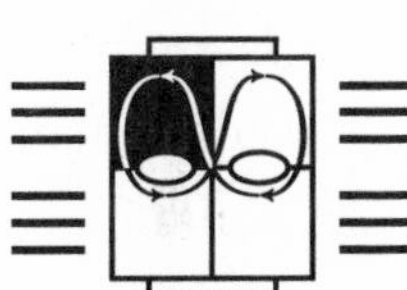

Upside Left

1. *In the upside of Spiritual Health, people's experiences of God are affirmed and explained, and they are supported in experiencing God more deeply and committing their lives to God.* Within any Christian congregation, members are at various levels of spiritual development. It is the task of every congregation to attend to members at every level of growth and to help them develop spiritually. Some of those attending a church may be "seekers," exploring whether they want a relationship with God and what it would entail. Regardless of their size, congregations need to have a process for these seekers to explore the Christian faith and to ascertain whether they want to surrender their lives to Christ and be baptized. These people may have had an experience in which they sensed the presence of the Spirit and may want to understand that experience more deeply. They need a safe environment within which to explore their questions about this God whom people worship. Many of these people do become converts. As they learn more about the Christian faith, they enter more deeply into a relationship with God. As they open themselves to the Spirit and experience the Spirit's presence at times, they experience a new joy and peace. This time can be euphoric for new Christians. They may feel as though their eyes have been opened and may begin to experience themselves and the world differently. Congregations need to support and assist people on this spiritual path.

A congregation includes many other members who have been committed Christians for a longer time. They also need support to remain continually open to the Spirit, which invites them to even deeper levels of surrender and faith. Still other members are part of an apostolic core in the congregation, and simply to be in their presence is to experience people of deep compassion who display the fruits of the spirit—love, joy, peace, patience, kindness, goodness, faithfulness, gentleness, and self-control. Those new to the faith gain much just by spending time with these people. Congregations need to be places where interaction between seekers and deeply committed Christians takes place. We might say that this is a primary reason for forming congregations.

2. *In the upside of Spiritual Health, programs that deepen and strengthen faith are encouraged.* In spiritually vital congregations, members are continually encouraged to engage in programs and projects that deepen their faith life. Becoming a member of a small group focused on Bible study and prayer is highly valued in such congregations. An alternative to offering small groups is to encourage members to sign up for something like the thirty-four-week Disciple Bible Study course.[1]

3. *In the upside of Spiritual Health, the staff focuses on the spiritual nurture of members and the unchurched.* The upside of this pole includes hiring staff for spiritual formation. In small-membership congregations, this step begins when the members call an ordained minister to be their pastor. Most often these congregations have called a pastor to provide them with spiritual nurture. Because the pastor will also need to provide leadership and administrative support, she will need to train lay volunteers to head other programs that offer spiritual nurture to church members. These volunteers may include Sunday-school teachers, music directors, youth advisors, and facilitators of small-group Bible studies. In large-membership congregations, governing boards will think about hiring additional staff members who specialize in some form of spiritual nurture. Congregational leaders sense when spiritual health is not being nurtured by existing programs and when current staff members are already carrying too heavy a load, and they hire one or more additional professionals with a reputation for developing quality and variety within an existing church program. For example, a congregation may have full-time staff members for children's ministries

and youth ministry, but when leaders notice that older members feel neglected, someone may be hired to focus specifically on the spiritual needs of older adults.

A rich spiritual life involves vigilance in three basic activities, often referred to collectively as a solid, three-legged stool. One leg is home rituals, including private prayer, grace at meals, activities that call attention to the liturgical year (lighting the candles on an Advent wreath or fasting during Lent or Holy Week), the laying on of hands and offering of prayers when a family member is sick, and occasional biblical or theological dialogue during a family meal. This leg is symbolized by the closet, recalling Jesus's admonition that we go into our closet when we pray.

The second leg of the stool that supports a vibrant spiritual life is membership in some small group where biblical and theological issues are studied and explored, and where prayers are offered. Such groups are also an excellent place for members to share their faith stories. Members develop greater spiritual depth when the composition of the group remains consistent over the course of several months and solid leadership is provided. (See appendix A, where we discuss four basic polarities that need to be managed well in small-group ministries.) This leg is symbolized by the living room, where a group can gather for face-to-face conversation.

The third leg of the stool is corporate worship, in which people at various levels of faith development and with diverse theological understandings of Scripture come together to worship God, united in their common offering of praise and thanksgiving. After listening to Scripture being read, they respond in unison, "Thanks be to God." The sharing of bread and wine in the Eucharist is symbolic of the way these members are bound together in the body of Christ.

When this polarity is well managed, seekers and longtime members alike are encouraged to nurture all three modes of spiritual activity to grow in their relationship with God. A congregation is fortunate if its staff members are able to support and encourage all three aspects of a growing, deepening spiritual life and are vigilant about their own spiritual nurture and growth.

4. *In the upside of Spiritual Health, members are keen on sharing their faith story with others and on being with others in times of spiritual crisis.* The

upside of this pole also addresses the transformational needs of members and nonchurchgoers. Within mainline denominations it is rare to find congregational members who talk about the exact time and place they surrendered their life to Christ. If they wrote out their spiritual autobiography, however, they would likely point to times when they had miniconversion experiences and their faith was deepened as a result. It is the task of every congregation concerned with the spiritual formation of its members to create experiences whereby members are drawn more deeply into grace and faith. As an important part of nurturing members, such congregations provide safe environments where members can share their faith journeys with one another. These experiences may range from a series of weekend retreats that include Scripture, silence, and prayer; work projects in a Third World country or a depressed area in this country; and small-group ministries. Clergy and members trained in pastoral care are coached to look for opportunities to help members move to a deeper level spiritually when they are experiencing a personal crisis.

5. *In the upside of Spiritual Health, members are aware of the need for spiritual transformation in themselves, other members, and those outside the church.* Personal spiritual transformation remains the focus of congregations centered on spiritual health. Some would say that congregations have lost their way when they forget that the church is in the business of transforming human lives. Whenever a spiritually healthy congregation engages in strategic planning, it always first reviews how the congregation is going to be revitalized spiritually in the coming years.

The upside of this pole also includes the congregation's reaching out to those not yet connected to a spiritual community and inviting newcomers and visitors to engage in one of the foundational courses offered by the congregation. These courses assume that individuals know nothing about the Christian faith and offer basic information on Christianity. We will talk more about this in the *Nurture AND Transformation* polarity.

We hope it is clear that a focus on Spiritual Health is essential to a thriving congregation. Now we will follow the normal flow of energy in a polarity, so that you can see what happens when a congregation overfocuses on Spiritual Health to the neglect of Institutional Health.

The Downside of Spiritual Health

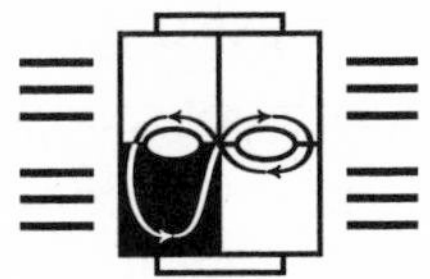

Downside Left

1. *In the downside of Spiritual Health, personal experiences of God can be fragile and fleeting.* Spiritual experiences can be tentative and easily dismissed. Over time we can begin to question the reality of those experiences, or we can begin to discount them or rationalize them away. For example, "That night when I sensed an unusual light in my bedroom and experienced a deep sense of peace—who knows, maybe I was just imagining things. It has never happened since, so I'm not sure I can trust it." Or: "That evening when we sat around a campfire and sang some of our old favorite hymns and I felt my heart was on fire for the love of God, maybe I just got carried away with sentimentality. These days, I can't seem to feel God's presence, ever. I wonder if God exists at all."

Over time our experience of Christ begins to fade, especially when we are not supported by other people. We need to spend concentrated time with people who share their experience of Christ's presence in their lives. Even when we do adopt home rituals and spiritual disciplines to support our faith, these practices can begin to feel hollow and meaningless. Without an ongoing spiritual community, we are not inspired to move deeper in the faith. In fact, we may lose our faith altogether. It is because personal spiritual experiences are vulnerable and fragile that we need an institution that guarantees the continuity of the faith. Without other congregational members to be with us during times of doubt or despair, we are likely to lose faith altogether.

2. *In the downside of Spiritual Health, church membership is seen as less important than one's spiritual journey.* When a congregation overfocuses on the spiritual health of individuals, building a cohesive church community becomes less important. Efforts are not made to integrate newcomers to the faith with long-term members. This integration takes hard work and may not be seen as necessary, or if it is seen as valuable, leaders and members may assume that this fellowship will develop on its own as people engage in church activities. Participation in a variety of worship experiences and in the church's study and fellowship programs is seen as the most important work

of individual members, and people are likely to be recruited to join a new or existing small-group study fellowship or to lead such a group. Members are not recruited to serve on the committees and task forces needed to support the congregation's infrastructure. In fact, few such committees function in this kind of church. The result is a congregation that is less healthy institutionally.

3. *In the downside of Spiritual Health, staff members do not have adequate time to care for the institutional needs of the congregation.* With so much emphasis on bringing people into a faith relationship with Christ, the organizational needs of the congregation can be overlooked. For example, establishing a capable group of people to focus on the needs of staff members may be seen as so much less important than worship, Bible study, and prayer that such a congregation does not even have a personnel committee. Staff members do the best they can, given what they understand their roles to be, and the senior pastor probably deals with the personnel issues of staff members individually. Few policies guide employees about their job descriptions, time off, and compensation.

Spirit-centered congregations often do not have adequate staff to support the institutional needs of the congregation. The bookkeeper of the congregation may be unable to keep up with her duties, but leaders will not consider hiring a part-time assistant bookkeeper. Instead, hiring a second music specialist to direct a youth choir, for example, would be given greater consideration. The church may always be short on custodial care.

4. *In the downside of Spiritual Health, the congregation's needs for volunteers to maintain the institution are not met.* When the roles that are prized within a congregation emphasize spiritual health and have to do with leading a Bible study, organizing a prayer group, or singing in the gospel chorus, it may be difficult to entice volunteers to work at some of the more mundane aspects of congregational life. The finance committee has few takers. The building-and-grounds committee is short on willing hands. No one clamors to serve on the governing board. These roles are not as highly valued as ones dealing with spiritual nurture.

5. *In the downside of Spiritual Health, the church becomes an organizational disaster with little insight into how to structure itself for order and stability.* Like one of the congregations cited at the beginning of this chapter, some

congregations need resource people outside the congregation to assist them in dealing with organizational issues that may not be obvious to those inside the congregation.

In a "spirit-filled" congregation, the church staff is usually stretched to the limit, but when chaos abounds, staff members usually see it as a sign of their failure. Their solution is often to work harder. They may think, "If only the congregation were more deeply committed to Christ, much of this chaos would not be happening." Staff members may even question their own commitment, because they don't have a clue as to how the congregation can work its way out of chaos.

As laudable as it is for a congregation to devote itself to spiritual health, the church pays a price for overfocusing on this pole. When experiencing the downside of Spiritual Health, a congregation may increasingly see the need to make a course correction and get to the upside of Institutional Health.

The Upside of Institutional Health

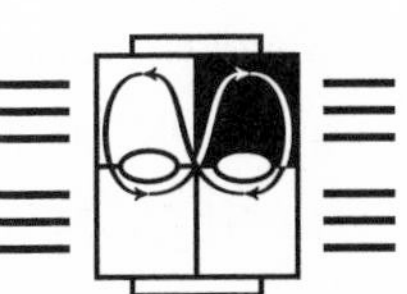

Upside Right

1. *In the upside of Institutional Health, the continuity of the faith is ensured.* After young parents bring their baby to church to be baptized or dedicated, that baby may be present in worship services with her parents. At some point in her development, she may begin to participate in Sunday school, vacation Bible school, church camp, and other church activities. When the congregation enjoys institutional health, the prayers that the child said with her parents at an early age are now supported by the whole infrastructure of the congregation as she grows in faith and grace. It is likely that parents appreciate their congregation more than ever at this stage in their child's development, because they don't feel capable of nurturing children's faith on their own and realize they need help if this child is to grow up as a person of faith.

Other people in the community may have never been inside a church except for a wedding or a funeral. They may have never learned a hymn or had instruction in the Christian faith. When a newcomer is brought to church, possibly by someone he is dating, and he expresses interest in becoming a Christian, the institutionally healthy church once again has something to offer, an orientation to the Christian faith. The congregation will initiate a seeker into a faith relationship with God. (Sometimes this initiation does not have the depth that is offered to the children of the congregation, but we will consider this matter in a later polarity—*Making Disciples: Easy Process AND Challenging Process.*)

In each case, the institutional church has built structures and programs; it has recruited, trained, and supported volunteers and staff who are able to nurture those new to the faith in their continuing growth in faith and grace, whether they are young or old. Without such an institution, it is hard to imagine how such growth in faith could take place or how someone who is not a Christian could be oriented to the faith and eventually desire to be baptized.

2. *In the upside of Institutional Health, people are encouraged to become engaged with each other and with congregational tasks.* Strong congregations have found ways of helping their congregants engage with one another in meaningful ways. Some of this bonding is both wide and deep. Congregants prize their membership in the church and are loyal to it through good times and bad. Such loyalty doesn't happen by accident, and these churches develop customs, norms, and programs that foster such commitment to their church.

When membership is so meaningful to members, they invite friends and family members to join their church. They want to share the riches their membership brings. When a visitor keeps returning to the congregation, it is not long before someone asks if she would like to become a member.

3. *In the upside of Institutional Health, the chief focus of the staff is serving members' needs and strengthening church membership.* One way a pastor can serve individual members' needs is through offering pastoral care in times of illness or crisis. Every time a person dealing with illness or crisis receives attentive pastoral care, his or her loyalty to the pastor grows stronger. Clergy can usually manage pastoral care by themselves when the congregation has an average worship attendance of one hundred or less. When attendance and membership increase, these clergy need the assistance of several lay callers trained by the pastor—lay members who are skilled at listening to people and praying with them. No matter what the congregation's size, the staff is concerned primarily with serving members' needs, either by doing it themselves or by training others in this art. Providing such care is one key way of strengthening church membership.

As seen on our polarity map, the work of staff members who specialize in some form of ministry appears on both upsides of this polarity. On the upside of the Institutional Health pole, a congregation hires a church administrator, a receptionist, or an additional custodian to ensure that the congregation has a well-functioning institution. On the upside of the Spiritual Health pole, a congregation hires someone who specializes in some aspect of spiritual growth, such as a director of religious education, a youth worker, or a director of evangelism and church growth. When a larger congregation is managing this polarity well, it will come up with the money to hire both a church administrator and a specialist in evangelism or a youth worker.

4. *In the upside of Institutional Health, members are keen on meeting the congregation's need for volunteers.* When members believe it is important to keep their church strong, they will make their volunteer energies available to the church, offering their best gifts. Church leaders will make clear which volunteer roles need to be filled if the church is to function well. They will see that the congregation's best leaders fill the roles central to the congregation's health.

5. *In the upside of Institutional Health, members are aware of the congregation's need to grow in some dimension—and at least to sustain its membership.* Loren Mead, in his book *More Than Numbers: The Ways Churches Grow,*[2] details four ways a congregation can move to greater vitality. One is to grow numerically, another is to grow spiritually, another is to grow in social-action or social-justice ministries, and finally, a congregation can grow in depth in the ways members care for one another. When a congregation is not growing in one or more of these four ways, members become nervous. They may begin to suspect that something is wrong with them.

This is likely the reason congregational members feel good when new people become members of the congregation. Some go out of their way to invite their friends and family members to become part of their church. Members also feel good when they hear that the youth group is going on a mission trip, or that the men's group had a great retreat, or that the church exceeded its budget for the year. These are all signs of life and vitality in the church, and members contribute their gifts and talents to support these activities. They are all part of maintaining a healthy institutional church.

The Downside of Institutional Health

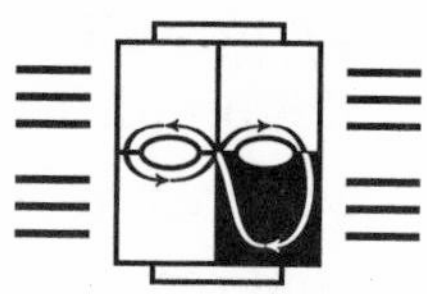
Downside Right

We have identified a few substantial upside results from tapping the pole of Institutional Health. We next look at what happens when a congregation overfocuses on Institutional Health to the neglect of Spiritual Health.

A congregation is not a gathering of saints but rather a gathering of sinners—forgiven sinners, but sinners nonetheless. Theologian Richard Rohr, a Franciscan monk, often comments in his many audiocassettes and CDs[3] that the worst fights happen between religious groups, often within the same church. Fights within religious circles are the most vicious because people think not only that they are right, but also that they have the moral duty to defend God on this point. Confrontational behavior on the part of some church members can disillusion other members. People new to the Christian faith may be especially disappointed by their experience in a Christian community. Some of the reasons we behave badly within a church have to do with our abandoning some religious values for the sake of institutional survival. Let's take a look at how this can happen in the downside of Institutional Health.

1. *In the downside of Institutional Health, congregations always seek first, even if unconsciously, to survive, sometimes subverting their original reason for forming.* Speak to any judicatory executive, and he or she will tell you how difficult it is to close a church. Even when only a handful of members are left, these few will struggle to keep their church alive. They will find a way to continue as a congregation. When this happens, almost all the members' energy goes into institutional maintenance. Members' behavior may have little in common with Jesus's expectations of his disciples, but their congregation will remain open. People may be mean to one another, gossip and backbite, and undermine one another—but they are going to remain together to keep their church doors open. Sometimes the church community may be made up of good people, but one or two ill-tempered cranks spoil it for everyone and turn off any visitors who drop in. To be sure, congregations like this are an exception, but they do exist.

Another example of congregations' commitment to survival can be seen in a congregation that decides to start a soup kitchen to offer at least one hot meal a week to the homeless people in the area—a commendable venture. They realize they can afford ten thousand dollars for the project and are willing to spend it on this ministry. Along the way, however, the property committee discovers that the church roof just sprang a leak and that the seeping water is starting to damage the church interior. The governing board must now decide: Do we spend our ten thousand dollars on the soup kitchen or do we use it to repair the roof? In our experience, the roof always wins.

It is true that we need an institutional church to ensure the continuity of the Christian faith. In the process of ensuring that continuity, however, the institution eats up enormous resources just to extend its own life. Sometimes a congregation is what we call "building poor." At one point in its history, it had many members, but over time membership has greatly diminished. The cost of keeping up a huge facility does not leave money for outreach, social-justice ministries, or well-planned religious education for children and youth.

In addition to building and maintaining church buildings, congregations need to pay salary, benefits, and housing costs for the church professionals who serve them. They are expected to support regional bodies—to send a given amount of money to their diocese, synod, presbytery, conference, or district. These regional bodies in turn send money to support the national church and its administrative and program costs. Then there are seminaries to support so that the church can have professionally trained clergy. Seen as a whole, the work of maintaining institutional structures requires huge sums of money. This is the price we pay when institutional survival is at stake.

2. *In the downside of Institutional Health, getting people to join the church and support it becomes more important than leading them to surrender their lives to God.* As church membership continues to decline in mainline denominations, especially among smaller congregations, efforts are made to attract new members. In the past few years, some congregations thought they could increase their membership by starting a "contemporary" service. They saw that this strategy had brought new members to other congregations, so they invested in a band that could bring popular music into the church. The problem was that some congregations simply used the music as a way to bring in new people. They did not seem to have genuine concern for the spiritual welfare of those they were trying to attract. Most people can

smell an underlying motive a mile away. Whatever tactic is used to gain new members, genuine caring for people without a church home needs to be part of it, or the effort will fail.

There is a spiritual hunger out there. People are searching for genuine community, but in the stark individualism of North America, many do not see themselves as connected to a larger story that helps them understand themselves and their place in history. Being a Christian is a larger way to define oneself than just living with the ups and downs of life. Whatever means are used to attract people into a church, the congregation needs to welcome them with warmth and offer food to satisfy hungry souls. In short, the congregation needs to have compassion for those who are drifting in society without a spiritual base. Unfortunately, when institutional survival becomes the primary concern of congregational leaders, the emphasis becomes getting new members rather than inviting them into a transformational process that will bring them peace and joy.

3. *In the downside of Institutional Health, inadequate staff time is available for outreach to nonmembers or attention to the spiritual needs of members.* Strong, well-administered congregations are going to ensure that there will always be adequate staff to maintain the building and tend to the financial and administrative tasks of the church. They may, however, lack staff to nurture the spiritual life of children, youth, young adults, young families, and older members. We may assume that well-run churches automatically take care of the spiritual needs of members. But that assumption is valid only if the congregation makes an ongoing effort to support the Spiritual Health pole.

4. *In the downside of Institutional Health, frequent conflicts arise about the best way for the church to survive.* When a congregation is struggling to maintain its membership or to reverse a decline, conflicts often break out as members disagree about the best way to gain new members. Some would say that the church needs a new preacher. Others insist that it needs to appeal to youth and that it should go out on a limb and hire a youth director. Still others place the emphasis on strong music and argue that the church should install a new pipe organ or invest in an electronic sound system. Some favor selling the building and moving to an area with a growing population.

Overall, the most vulnerable people in a slowly declining congregation are the staff. It is simply too convenient for church members to think that all their problems would be solved and that they would begin to grow again if they had a different staff. Staff members know this and often overextend themselves trying to prove their worth, sometimes burning out in the process. Trying to grow a church with burned-out staff members is a real challenge, so we can see a vicious cycle developing here. It takes a wise and discerning governing board to ensure that the congregation has good staff members who do not consistently overextend themselves. A church board that wants to manage this polarity well needs to develop strategies that will help the congregation reverse its declines with its current staff.

5. *In the downside of Institutional Health, the spiritual transformation of members and the unchurched is rarely talked about.* Whenever Roy leads a congregation through a strategic planning process, he has the planning task force and governing board consider this polarity while on retreat. He divides the leaders into work groups of four or five and gives them a block of time to come up with ways to spiritually revitalize the congregation in the next four years. Their recommendations usually involve the development of small groups, including groups that focus on Bible study and prayer. Other suggestions may include holding a variety of weekend retreats focused on renewing one's faith, starting a series of adult sessions on contemplative prayer, sharing dreams in a dream group, supporting families in using home rituals that remind them of their baptism, beginning a Taize service[4] on Sunday evenings, finding spiritual mentors for confirmands, sponsoring an Alpha course of Bible study,[5] holding Cursillo weekend retreats,[6] starting a yearlong catechumenate for adults new to the faith, or sponsoring mission trips to a Third World country.

In other retreat groups, Roy finds that some small groups do not even know what outcome they are expecting from spiritual revitalization. The group recommendations have to do mainly with institutional renewal. Members want to go from the downside of this pole to the upside of the same pole. Such a congregation assumes that spiritual renewal "just happens" as a result of members' keeping the church running.

In a sense, congregations like this have lost their way. They have forgotten the reason for their existence as a Christian church. They are focused totally on institutional maintenance and are not aware that they have forsaken their founding mission.

Managing the Polarity Poorly: Early Warnings

Even with the best efforts to stay in the upsides of both poles, it is helpful to know when you are getting into one downside or the other. It is here that the Early Warnings are helpful.

Early Warnings for the Downside of Spiritual Health

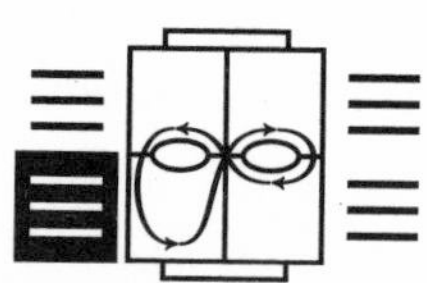

Early Warnings Left

These are indicators that your congregation has overfocused on Spiritual Health to the neglect of Institutional Health.

1. Even though the sanctuary looks shabby and the use of space is poor, the governing board refrains from asking an architect to help reconfigure the space to make it more attractive.
2. When a congregation is interviewing a potential new senior pastor, search committee members do not inquire about skills in congregational administration.
3. The congregation refuses to help raise funds for the church camp owned by the middle judicatory. Consequently, children and adults do not have a place to retreat for spiritual enrichment and faith development.
4. Because of the lack of adequate administrative staff, when members place a call to the church office, they get the sense that the office is in chaos most of the time.
5. The governing board fails to offer staff members raises and cost-of-living increases; the result is a demoralized, discouraged staff.
6. The board continues to function with twenty or more members, though leaders know that it is too large and that its size inhibits it from making intelligent decisions.

Early Warnings for the Downside of Institutional Health

Congregations should watch for these warning signs indicating that they have overfocused on Institutional Health to the neglect of Spiritual Health.

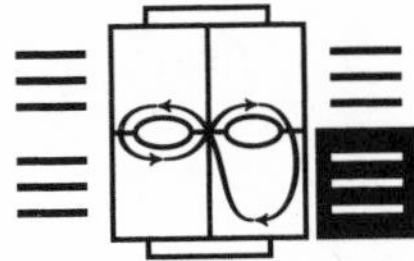
Early Warnings Right

1. Staff meetings at the church no longer include prayer or Scripture reading but focus solely on keeping programs going and serving parishioners' needs.
2. Staff members take no individual time for personal spiritual renewal, and no one inquires about their need for spiritual renewal time, even though their contract with the church calls for a personal spiritual retreat of one day or more each year.
3. Even when the church's board meetings open with Scripture and prayer, the rest of the meeting is conducted like that of any secular decision-making body. Board members have forgotten to take time for silence and discernment when considering key decisions for the congregation.
4. Members have lost their zeal for being living witnesses to their faith. As a result, the congregation has had no adult baptisms for the past three years.
5. The congregation does not host an annual banquet to celebrate all the new members who have become committed to Christ and to the congregation.
6. Exit interviews indicate that people are leaving the church because of a lack of spiritual nurture within the congregation.

Managing the Polarity Well: Action Steps

To manage this polarity well over time, we need to maximize the upsides of both poles and to minimize the downsides. Let's look at possible Action Steps to gain or maintain the upsides of the poles.

Action Steps for Spiritual Health

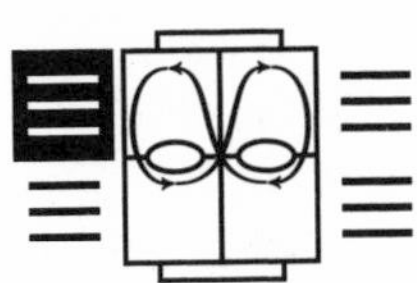
Action Steps Left

1. Provide members with resource material to support home prayer rituals, Bible reading, blessings before meals, the laying on of hands with prayers

for healing when a family member is not well, and the interpretation of dreams.

2. Encourage all members to become part of a small group that studies Scripture, discusses theology, prays, and offers pastoral care to any of its members who are experiencing a crisis.
3. Ask the governing board and all committees to engage in a spiritual audit once a year. The key question: "How have we been faithful to the call of Christ to move deeper into faith and service?"
4. Ensure that all program staff of the congregation are given financial support and time away for spiritual renewal.
5. When engaging in a strategic-planning process, include ways the congregation might enrich its spiritual life over the next few years.

Action Steps for Institutional Health

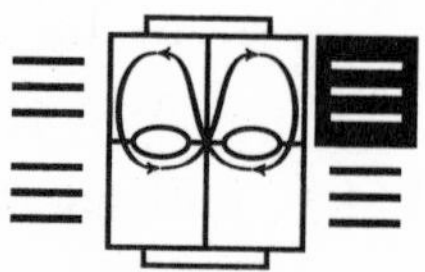

Action Steps Right

To ensure that the organizational structures supporting the church remain strong, these steps might be taken:

1. Members are encouraged to give sacrificially to support not only the staff and church building but also the denominational structures that provide resources for the church.
2. When the congregation has reached an impasse in a conflict that threatens to split the church, leaders readily invite in an outside conflict specialist to assist them in addressing the challenge.
3. There is excellent signage to guide visitors, both inside and outside the church. A sign next to the church's busiest street has a message that changes every week, ensuring that passers-by will always notice it.
4. When the church property has no space left for building expansion, there is no possibility of buying adjacent property, and parking is clearly inadequate, the congregation enters a discernment process about such options as moving to a new location that could handle its membership growth or starting a new mission or satellite church in another location.
5. The congregation is vigilant about electing its more capable leaders to boards and committees to ensure congregational health.

6. The congregation has an astute personnel committee that sees to it that all church staff members are adequately paid and that staff morale remains high.
7. Leaders devise a process that monitors members' worship attendance patterns and designates someone to call members when those attendance patterns are broken to inquire if anything is wrong.

POLARITY PRINCIPLE 10

When your Early Warnings indicate that you are getting into the downside of a pole, revisit your Action Steps for the upside of the opposite pole. If you are doing the planned Action Steps and are still getting the Early Warnings, you may need to identify additional Action Steps for a course correction and to minimize the downside of the pole.

Summary

A healthy, thriving congregation will spend most of its time in the two upper quadrants of this polarity. (See map 3.2 on pages 72–73.) Managing this polarity well requires wise leaders. Congregational leaders need continually to ask: "How well are we transforming the lives of our visitors and members AND continuing to develop an inspiring place for worship and study?" The way to address this polarity is to empower both poles over time. Leaders need to fill out a map to appreciate the upsides and downsides of each pole, agree on a Greater Purpose and a Deeper Fear, create Action Steps to get the upsides of each pole, and identify warning signs that will let them know early that the congregation is moving out of balance.

There is no question that congregations need to maintain a healthy organizational structure and a well-managed operation. Congregations need not become slaves to the business practices of secular organizations, but they cannot ignore sound practices that would clearly enhance congregational life. In this regard, they need to hire well-trained clergy and laity who know how to maintain a healthy institution. They need to have sound fiscal policies in place. With every major shift in worship attendance, they need to evaluate whether the congregation's current organizational structure is

Action Steps

How will we gain or maintain the positive results from focusing on this left pole? What? Who? By when? Measures?

1. Members are provided resources of home ritual of prayer and Scripture reading.
2. Members are encouraged to become part of a small study or prayer group.
3. Board members and committees are encouraged to engage in a spiritual audit once a year.
4. Staff is provided with financial support and time away for spiritual renewal.
5. Strategic planning in the congregation always involves ways to renew the congregation spiritually in the next few years.

Early Warnings

Measurable indicators (things you can count) that will let you know that you are getting into the downside of this left pole.

1. Even though the sanctuary looks shabby and the use of space poor, the governing board does not take action to improve the situation.
2. When looking for a new pastor, the search committee does not inquire about administration skills.
3. The congregation refuses to raise funds for the denomination's church camp, thereby depriving their children and adults of spiritual enrichment outside the congregation.
4. The church office seems to be in chaos most of the time.
5. The governing board fails to adequately support church staff, resulting in a demoralized, discouraged staff.

Polarity Management®

Greater Purpose Statement (GPS)

Thriving

Values = positive results from focusing on the left pole

1. People's experiences of God are affirmed and explained. People are supported in experiencing God more deeply and committing their lives to God.
2. Engaging in programs that deepen and strengthen faith is encouraged.
3. Staff is focused on the spiritual nurture of members and the unchurched.
4. Members are keen on sharing their faith story with others and being with others at times of spiritual crisis.
5. Members are aware of their needs for spiritual transformation in their lives, other members, and those outside the church.

Spiritual Health

CHURCH UNIVERSAL

and

1. Personal experiences of God are fragile and vulnerable and can be easily discounted.
2. Newcomers are not integrated with other church members. Church membership is not emphasized or talked about.
3. There is inadequate staff time for the institutional needs of the congregation.
4. The volunteer needs of the congregational are rarely met.
5. The church becomes an organizational disaster with little insight into how to structure itself for order and stability.

Fears = negative results from overfocusing on the left pole <u>to the neglect</u> of the right pole

Declining

Deeper Fear from

Map

Why balance this polarity?

Congregation

Values = positive results from focusing on the right pole

1. People need an institution to ensure the continuity of the faith, as personal experiences of God are tentative and easily dismissed.
2. Church membership is important and people are encouraged to become more engaged with each other and with congregational tasks.
3. Staff is focused on serving member needs and strengthening church membership.
4. Members are keen on meeting the volunteer needs of the congregation and coming to its aid during institutional crises.
5. Members are aware of the need of the congregation to grow stronger, add staff, and increase membership.

and

Institutional Health

INSTITUTIONAL CHURCH

1. Institutions, unconsciously, always seek first to survive, sometimes subverting their original reason for forming.
2. Getting people to join the church and support it becomes more important than having them surrender their lives to God.
3. Inadequate staff time for outreach to nonmembers or the spiritual needs of members.
4. There are frequent conflicts over which are the best ways to survive.
5. The spiritual transformation of members and the unchurched is rarely talked about. Members don't even know what this means.

Fears = negative results from overfocusing on the right pole to the neglect of the left pole

Congregation

lack of balance

Action Steps

How will we gain or maintain the positive results from focusing on this right pole? What? Who? By when? Measures?

1. Members are encouraged to give sacrificially to support their church and denomination.
2. When serious conflict occurs, church leaders readily ask for an outside conflict specialist to assist them in dealing with the conflict.
3. There is excellent signage both inside the church and outside it.
4. The congregation is vigilant in electing its most capable leaders to serve on boards and committees.
5. The congregation has an astute personnel committee that sees to it that staff morale remains high.

Early Warnings

Measurable indicators (things you can count) that will let you know that you are getting into the downside of this right pole.

1. Staff meetings no longer begin with Scripture and prayer.
2. Staff members no longer take time for personal spiritual renewal.
3. Church board meetings reflect secular decision-making bodies, rather than spiritual discernment.
4. Members have lost their zeal for being living witnesses to their faith.
5. The congregation does not host an annual banquet to celebrate all the new members that have joined.

Map 3.2

serving it well. At the same time, members need to return frequently to the basic questions: "What is our primary reason for existing? Why do we need a healthy church?" These questions usually lead us to look to the upside of spiritual health.

Often a governing board assumes that the clergy are taking care of the spiritual life of the congregation, and that the board should focus only on the institutional side of congregational life. Even when clergy are attentive to a congregation's spiritual health, however, they cannot take care of the Spiritual Health pole of this polarity by themselves. They need support and encouragement. Lay leaders need to ask, "How can we continue to revitalize our congregation spiritually while at the same time maintaining excellence in institutional health?" Asking this question will support clergy in doing the same. In the end, there should be as many goals that deal with the spiritual enrichment of members as there are goals to strengthen the administrative side of the congregation.

CHAPTER 4

Management AND Leadership

There is a major difference between management and leadership. We hope those in responsible roles within a congregation will possess the skills to do both, though it is rare that any individual is equally competent in these two arenas. People are usually better at one than the other. For this reason a thriving congregation's governing board or a committee or task force will include some people who have leadership skills and others who have management skills. In this polarity, faith communities hold something in common with the corporate world. *Management AND Leadership* is a polarity that has been shown to make a difference in well-run organizations. A variety of books written for corporate America lend great insight into this polarity. One has the fascinating title *Mind of a Manager, Soul of a Leader.*[1]

A Manager and a Leader

Jason Carothers and Sally Wallford were clergy who served neighboring congregations of different denominations. The congregations were about the same size, averaging between eighty and one hundred in worship each Sunday. Both pastors were considered by their middle-judicatory executives as failing to lead their congregations toward numerical growth. Jason had served his congregation for eight years and Sally had served hers for ten, yet both congregations were smaller now than when these pastors arrived.

In the view of his peers, Jason was a plodder. He did everything according to denominational protocol. He was a loyal, faithful servant of his people. No one was ever in the hospital without Jason's showing up to pray with them. His sermons were down-to-earth and practical. He tended to be on the conservative side theologically. From time to time members of Jason's congregation would come to see him about trying some new ways of attracting new members. He would listen intently, but at some point he would interject that their ideas were impractical and would not work in this congregation. He was especially opposed to compromising the excellent traditional worship style by adopting elements of a contemporary style. He called that "dumbing down" the faith. In the long run, he thought, by changing its worship style the congregation would lose its solid faith tradition for the sake of gaining a few new members.

Sally was quite the opposite. She was always excited about some new idea and often came to governing board meetings with suggestions for how the congregation might gain members. Yet nothing ever seemed to happen once the ideas were discussed. Sally certainly had great fun exploring these proposals with others, but somehow she didn't know how to put a foundation under them so that they could come to fruition. She did not delegate well, nor did she know how to equip others to manage aspects of the congregation's life. Members had come to regard her as disorganized and inconsistent. She tended to jump from one idea to another and often abandoned a project and the people who had initiated it, expecting them to make things happen on their own, even though she had initially supported the idea. Sally had wowed the search committee when it first interviewed her; the group was determined to find someone who was open to new visions. When she had spoken about all the things she thought the congregation might do to grow, the search committee had thought she was definitely what the church needed. Yet here it was, ten years later, and the congregation was a little smaller than it had been before.

The Polarity to Be Managed

Sally and Jason represent opposite poles in the *Management AND Leadership* polarity. Jason was a manager who lacked visionary skills. Sally was a visionary who lacked managerial skills. Neither knew how to engage those in the congregation skilled in the pole in which they were weak. In short, neither knew how to manage this polarity well.

A well-managed congregation is dependable; it has a workable order and structure. When someone has a creative idea that will clearly help the

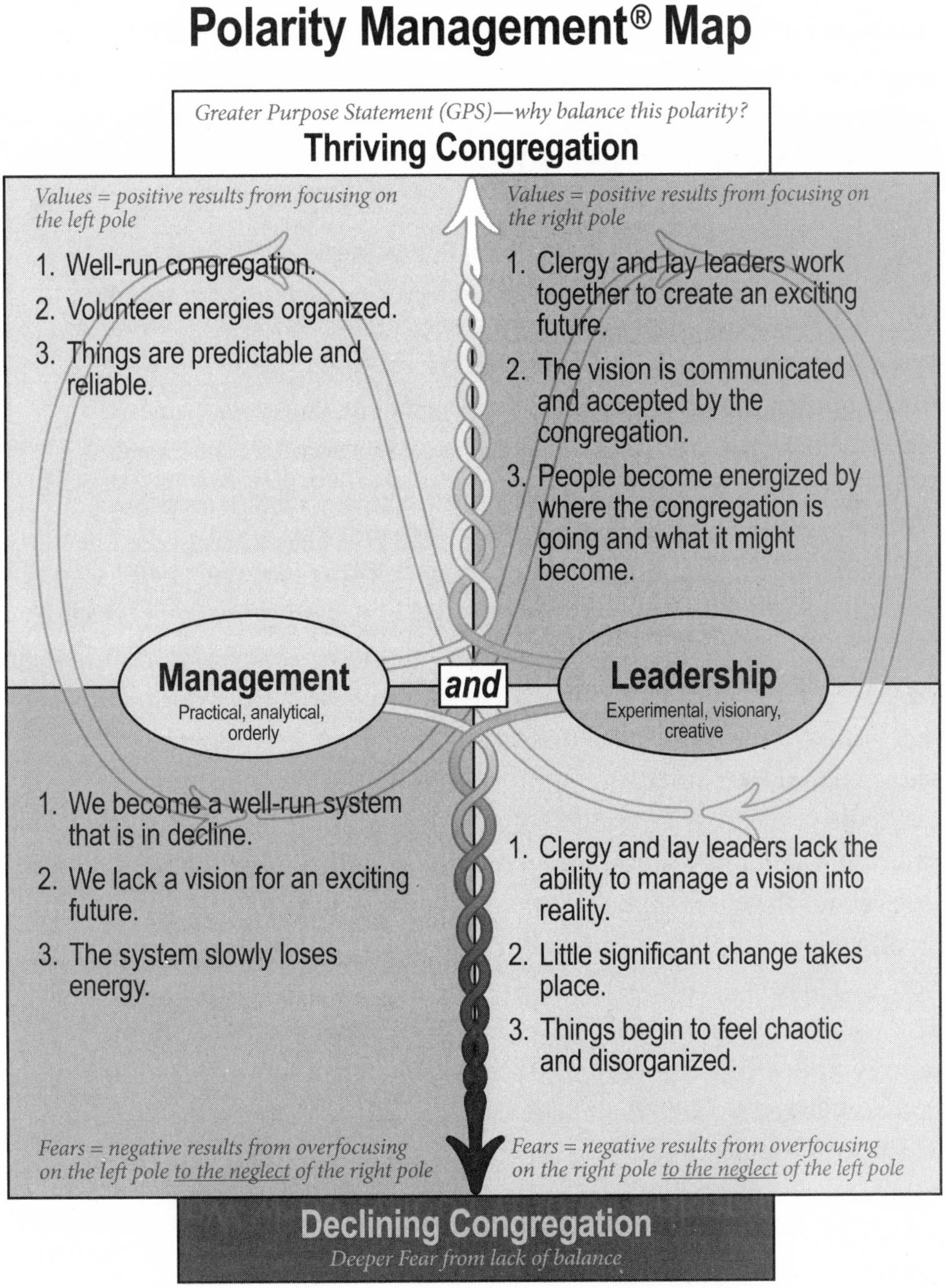

Polarity Management® Map

Greater Purpose Statement (GPS)—why balance this polarity?

Thriving Congregation

Values = positive results from focusing on the left pole

1. Well-run congregation.
2. Volunteer energies organized.
3. Things are predictable and reliable.

Values = positive results from focusing on the right pole

1. Clergy and lay leaders work together to create an exciting future.
2. The vision is communicated and accepted by the congregation.
3. People become energized by where the congregation is going and what it might become.

Management
Practical, analytical, orderly

and

Leadership
Experimental, visionary, creative

1. We become a well-run system that is in decline.
2. We lack a vision for an exciting future.
3. The system slowly loses energy.

Fears = negative results from overfocusing on the left pole to the neglect of the right pole

1. Clergy and lay leaders lack the ability to manage a vision into reality.
2. Little significant change takes place.
3. Things begin to feel chaotic and disorganized.

Fears = negative results from overfocusing on the right pole to the neglect of the left pole

Declining Congregation

Deeper Fear from lack of balance

Map 4.1

system, there are others who know how to put a foundation under that idea and make it a reality. Unfortunately, too many congregations are well managed but are being managed into extinction. The vision to make them into turnaround congregations is lacking. The reverse can also be true. A congregation may have a vision of what would make it a thriving congregation but lack the management capacity to make that vision a reality.

The Upside of Management

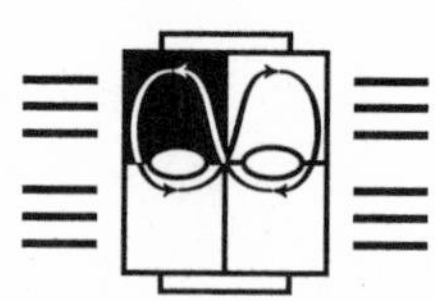

Upside Left

1. *In the upside of Management, the congregation is well run.* Have you ever visited a congregation and right from the beginning sensed it was a well-run place? As you entered the building you could discern the plan and order. When you walk into such a congregation on a Sunday morning, volunteers are in the narthex to greet you. As you move into the sanctuary, you are handed a bulletin. As you find a place to sit and scan the bulletin, you find the order of the service as well as announcements that give you an overview of the activities sponsored by the congregation. It is clear where you could go for more information about the congregation. As part of that Sunday morning experience, the congregation may manage to get your name and address so that members can follow up on your visit. Someone may even come to your home that afternoon, bringing a freshly baked loaf of bread, thanking you for your visit, and inquiring if you have any questions about the congregation or the Sunday-morning experience.

As you reflect on your initial encounter with a well-managed congregation, you become aware of the organization that supported your experience. The volunteer greeters and ushers had been trained. Other volunteers had been recruited to make the follow-up visits with loaves of bread. Someone had been asked to bake the bread so that it would be fresh for that Sunday. Much work went into putting the bulletin together. Many individuals contributed items for the bulletin. All these efforts were organized as a package for your hour-plus encounter with the congregation. A well-run congregation takes a lot of hard work.

2. *In the upside of Management, volunteer energies are organized.* A poorly run congregation would not likely be supported by the numbers of

volunteers described above, because busy people cannot be bothered to fit into a chaotic, disorganized system. Working with church volunteers requires discipline and dedication. The people who coordinate volunteers need to enjoy continually recruiting new people, often to take on small tasks. Beyond Sunday morning, volunteers must be recruited, trained, and supported to serve on boards, committees, and task forces—to crank out the decisions that keep a congregation running smoothly.

A well-run congregation also keeps an optimal ratio of paid staff to volunteers. From years of experience with congregations, Alban consultants have concluded that for every one hundred people in worship each week, the congregation needs the equivalent of one full-time program staff person. When a congregation tries to run a complex operation using only volunteers, the wheels keep falling off. When a volunteer gets sick or moves, someone needs to find a replacement. Without adequate staff to do such tasks, the responsibility inevitably falls into the lap of the pastor, who then needs to drop what he or she is doing and find that replacement—a task that is probably not be the best use of the pastor's time. A congregation that is managed well finds the resources to keep the staff-volunteer ratio at a reasonable level.

3. *In the upside of Management, congregational life is predictable and reliable.* Predictability and reliability are important ingredients in a well-managed congregation. Members need to know what they can count on and expect as part of their membership. They want to know whether someone will be there for them if they encounter a crisis. Should they volunteer for a specific role, they want to know what kind of backup they will receive if they run into difficulty. They need to know that they will not be abandoned in a specific role.

Predictability and reliability need to flow the other way as well. For a congregation to remain well managed, it needs to be able to count on its members to support the congregation with their money, time, and participation, as well as emotionally and spiritually. In a well-managed system, these expectations are put forward in a gentle yet persistent way.

Congregations clearly need the benefits of good management. A congregation can, however, overfocus on being well managed to the neglect of being well led, and thus experience the downside of this pole. Let's now shift our attention to this downside quadrant.

The Downside of Management

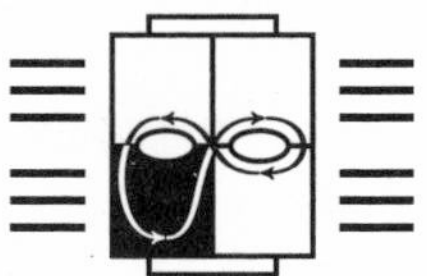

Downside Left

1. *In the downside of Management, the congregation can become a well-run system that is in slow decline.* Good management does not ensure that a congregation is going to continue to grow—numerically, spiritually, financially, or in a deepening fellowship. Growth in these arenas may require vision and leadership, which are not part of the management function. Unfortunately, many well-managed congregations are not growing in any significant area of congregational life. Volunteers keep showing up for their responsibilities, but to their dismay, the organization they support is not going anywhere.

2. *In the downside of Management, the congregation lacks a vision for an exciting future.* The Old Testament says, "Where there is no vision, the people perish" (Prov. 29:18, KJV). For us, this means that a congregation can become so attached to its way of doing things that any departure from order and structure is experienced by the congregation as a death wish. In fact, evidence of a death wish is staying with the old familiar patterns, a course that will inevitably lead to decline and death.

3. *In the downside of Management, the system slowly loses energy.* When clergy and volunteers continue to offer their time and energy to the church, yet see that they are not producing the desired results, discouragement follows. Members begin to lose their enthusiasm for their congregation and the roles they play. A downward spiral can begin. The more clearly members see their congregation in a slow decline, the less enthusiasm they maintain for performing their roles. They do not continue to offer their best. Visitors to the congregation discern the lack of gusto and may decide not to stay around because they sense an atmosphere of depression. When visitors fail to return, members are discouraged even more. They begin to doubt that their church will ever be able to pull out of this downward spiral. Something needs to happen to put energy back into the system.

As a congregation anticipates or experiences the downside of Management, it makes a natural self-correction to get the benefits of effective leadership. The energy now moves from the downside of managing to the upside of leading.

The Upside of Leadership

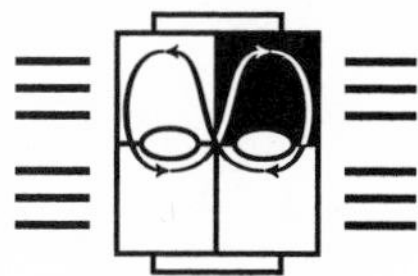

Upside Right

1. *In the upside of Leadership, clergy and lay leaders work together to create an exciting vision.* The upside of Leadership involves generating a vision that captures the imagination of congregation members. But then leaders must get out in front and lead the charge. Anything that has the potential to turn the congregation around will carry some risk, and those who believe it's safer to stay with what worked in the past will resist trying something new. Leadership involves persuading congregational members that the potential rewards of doing something new outweigh the risks. It also involves respecting and upholding tradition and stability while promoting change.

2. *In the upside of Leadership, the vision is communicated to and accepted by the congregation.* In his book *Leading Change,* Harvard business professor John Kotter identifies the first step in creating major change in an organization: "Establishing a sense of urgency."[2] Effective church leaders help members see and feel a sense of urgency about the need for change. They also point out the positive things that could be done to alleviate what is not working. The second step is building the right coalition of people who will make change happen. Step three is developing a vision that captures the enthusiasm and interest of people. Step four of the eight-step process is communicating that vision by a factor of ten.

These first four steps toward transformation point to what effective leaders do well. Good leaders communicate the urgency for change in a way that people can understand but that will not leave them feeling overwhelmed. They mobilize credible people in the system to work for the needed change. These are people who have the trust of the membership. Members begin to realize that if these people are behind an effort, things are going to happen. Leaders then engage members in shaping an exciting vision of change. Visionary goals are going to have much greater support if people believe they have had a hand in shaping those goals.

Leaders, however, do not stop there. They know that undercommunicating the vision could be a serious mistake. Strategies are developed to bring these goals to people's attention in a variety of ways. Leaders talk to congregation members about the vision every chance they get. They write newsletter articles about the goals. They talk to groups about the goals and the ways a group might support them. They are never too busy to sit down with a member and explain the vision. In this way, members are convinced that these are the things "that we just need to do."

3. *In the upside of Leadership, people are energized by where the church is going and by what it might become.* When a vision has captured the imagination of members, an air of excitement pervades the congregation. Members feel the sense of urgency that the congregation must do something to reverse its decline, but they have confidence that the vision they have set is going to work.

Energy abounds when an exciting vision for the congregation has been caught by members. New energy translates into people who want to be on task forces to implement new goals. Members are likely to increase their giving to ensure that the new goals are supported financially. Energy also translates into members' inclination to talk about their church to friends and family members. It may even result in an invitation to these outsiders to "come and see the exciting things we are doing in my church."

Visionary leadership is powerful and essential. And it is not enough. When an energized congregation overfocuses on leading to the neglect of managing, it will find itself on the downside of this pole.

The Downside of Leadership

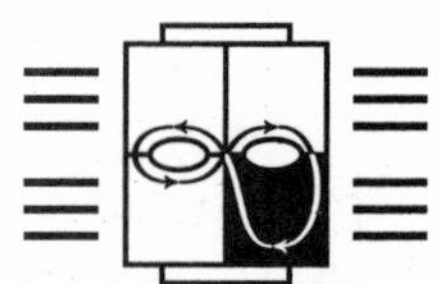
Downside Right

1. *In the downside of Leadership, clergy and lay leaders lack the ability to manage the vision into reality.* It is tragic when a congregation gets excited about a new vision and then nothing happens. This failure may result because congregational leaders had visionary leadership capacity but lacked the managerial ability to turn great ideas into a reality.

At a clergy workshop Roy was leading, the subject of alternative worship forms came up. Some participants suggested that a contemporary worship service could be the key to involving new younger families. At one point a participant responded, "We tried that and it didn't work." Upon analysis it became clear that management skills to ensure the success of such a service were lacking. Little preparation had been made to publicize the contemporary worship to the surrounding community. The congregation had not identified the target audience for such a service or devised a strategy to let that audience know about the worship opportunity. In addition, members were not asked to attend the alternative worship service to get it launched.

Controversy is bound to erupt when a new vision is proposed for a congregation. More controversy ensues when it comes time to implement agreed-upon goals. Members may have approved certain goals in principle as desirable, but putting those goals into practice involves a concrete change in the way a congregation functions. When it becomes clear to members that one of their favorite activities is going to change, they erect a wall of resistance. Congregational leaders may simply not know how to deal with this kind of opposition. We will talk about respecting and taking advantage of resistance later in this book.

2. *In the downside of Leadership, little significant change takes place.* Over time, when goals are left to stagnate rather than being implemented, a new lethargy sets in. Members become pessimistic about the vision and come to see it as a pipe dream. As a result, little change of significance takes place. The congregation is back to square one, but this time the members sink into even greater despair. They continue to lose confidence that the congregation is able to do anything of import to help itself thrive and grow.

3. *In the downside of Leadership, congregational life becomes chaotic and disorganized.* When visionary leaders don't know how to manage good ideas into reality, they often begin to question the vision and to cast about for a new vision. Roy has noticed that some of his highly intuitive clergy colleagues throw out a creative idea and, when it doesn't take hold, throw out another idea. When that one doesn't take, they throw out yet another idea. Over time, members begin to sense that their congregation is becoming disorganized and chaotic.

In situations where new ideas are implemented and more new ideas are explored, the rate of change is faster than some members can tolerate. They begin to believe that there is little they can count on to remain stable and secure. Such a situation arises when leaders want to see more new and creative things happening. Some people will be thrilled with continual changes in the congregation and voice their excitement. Leaders, hearing their enthusiasm, assume that it's time to press the accelerator to the floor. On the other hand, some people will always resist change and think that congregational life is becoming chaotic when the ground beneath their feet continues to shake.

POLARITY PRINCIPLE 11

A polarity can exist within one or both poles of a larger polarity. For example, to support both *Spiritual Health AND Institutional Health*, a congregation needs both *Management AND Leadership*.

Managing the Polarity Poorly: Early Warnings

We now have a more complete picture of this polarity. We need to shift to managing it well over time. We will identify possible Action Steps for each upside and possible Early Warnings that signal the onset of falling into a downside. (See map 4.2 on pages 86–87.)

When a congregation anticipates or experiences the downside of Leadership without enough Management, the natural thing to do is to follow the infinity loop to the upside of Management to tap its contribution to this polarity. But how will you know if you have overfocused on Leadership and are moving into the downside? Below are some possible Early Warnings.

Early Warnings for Leadership

Early Warnings Right

1. New ideas are not challenged to test whether they fit with the mission of the congregation.
2. Clergy with strong leadership skills are not given administrative backup.

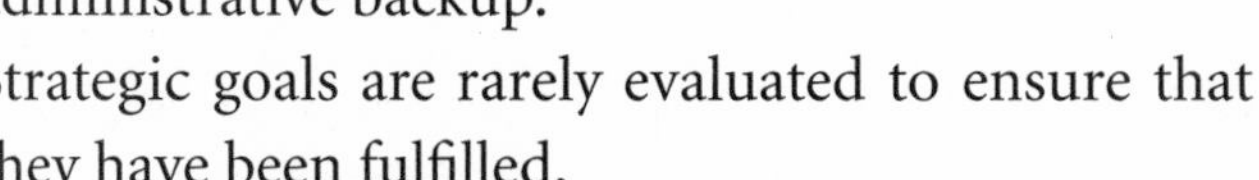

3. Strategic goals are rarely evaluated to ensure that they have been fulfilled.

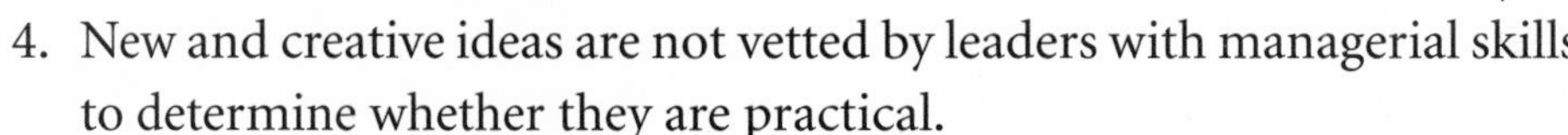

4. New and creative ideas are not vetted by leaders with managerial skills to determine whether they are practical.
5. When a new idea fails, the causes of failure are not evaluated. Members simply move on to another creative idea.

On the other side of the coin, let's look at how you can know that you are in the downside of Management.

Early Warnings for Management

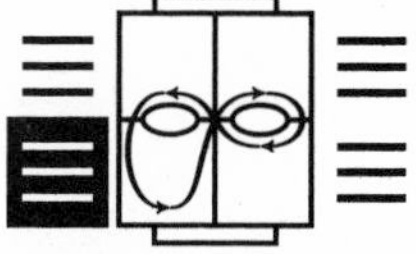
Early Warnings Left

1. Members repeatedly complain about the lack of vision or direction.
2. Members grumble incessantly about a lack of spirit and excitement in the congregation.
3. Volunteers are micromanaged and are not given the freedom to execute their roles in their own way.
4. The governing board is stacked with "management types" who are skilled at shooting down creative ideas—people whose idea of fun is blasting innovative proposals as impractical.
5. Members with creative ideas are seen as disparaging existing church programs and are shunted aside when committee appointments are made.

Managing the Polarity Well: Action Steps

Because the two poles are interdependent, congregations need to balance actions to support Management with equally important actions to support Leadership. Here are some possibilities.

Action Steps for Management

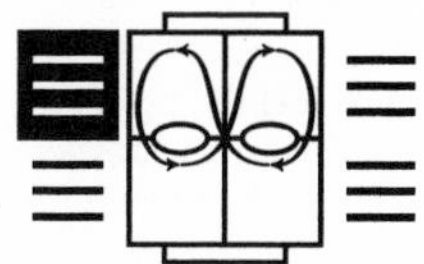
Action Steps Left

1. If a congregation engages in a strategic planning process every four years, at the end of those four years the governing board takes time to critique the way the last plan was managed, looking for ways church leaders can better manage a great idea into reality.
2. The congregation has an active personnel committee that maintains solid policies for church employees, and annual evaluations are conducted to review their performance.
3. Weekly staff meetings are held to review how things were managed last week and to plan how they will be managed this coming week, including next Sunday morning.

Action Steps

How will we gain or maintain the positive results from focusing on this left pole? What? Who? By when? Measures?

1. Before engaging in a new strategic plan, the governing board evaluates the old plan looking for ways to better manage an idea into reality.
2. The congregation has an active personnel committee that maintains solid policies for church employees.
3. Weekly staff meetings are held that review how things were managed last week and to plan how they will be managed this week, including next Sunday morning.
4. All church committees have a clear job description that is reviewed annually by the governing board.
5. The governing board has a clear sense of its oversight responsibilities with the congregation.

Early Warnings

Measurable indicators (things you can count) that will let you know that you are getting into the downside of this left pole.

1. Members repeatedly complain about the lack of vision or direction.
2. Members grumble incessantly about the lack of spirit and excitement in the congregation.
3. Volunteers are micromanaged and not given the freedom to execute their roles in their own way.
4. The governing board is stacked with "management types" who are skilled at shooting down creative ideas.
5. Members with creative ideas are seen as disparaging existing church programs.

Polarity Management®

Greater Purpose Statement (GPS)

Thriving

Values = positive results from focusing on the left pole

1. Well-run congregation.
2. Volunteer energies organized.
3. Things are predictable and reliable.

Management

Practical, analytical, orderly

and

1. We become a well-run system that is in decline.
2. We lack a vision for an exciting future.
3. The system slowly loses energy.

Fears = negative results from overfocusing on the left pole to the neglect of the right pole

Declining

Deeper Fear from

Map

Why balance this polarity?

Congregation

Values = positive results from focusing on the right pole

1. Clergy and lay leaders work together to create an exciting future.
2. The vision is communicated and accepted by the congregation.
3. People are energized by where the congregation is going and what it might become.

and

Leadership

Experimental, visionary, creative

1. Clergy and lay leaders lack the ability to manage a vision into reality.
2. Little significant change takes place.
3. Things begin to feel chaotic and disorganized.

Fears = negative results from overfocusing on the right pole to the neglect of the left pole

Congregation

lack of balance

Action Steps

How will we gain or maintain the positive results from focusing on this right pole? What? Who? By when? Measures?

1. Every four years the congregation engages in a strategic planning process to establish goals that are to be the focus of the congregation's energy and resources for the next four years.
2. Church committees are asked annually to share their vision of what they would like to accomplish in the next twelve months.
3. Visionary leaders are sought out to head committees or tasks that appear to be stuck.
4. The church staff goes on an annual overnight retreat to map out the ideas that they believe will help their congregation thrive.
5. Search committees seek out clergy with a proven track record of leadership in congregations they have served.

Early Warnings

Measurable indicators (things you can count) that will let you know that you are getting into the downside of this right pole.

1. New ideas are not challenged as to their practical nature.
2. Clergy with strong leadership skills are not given administrative backup.
3. Strategic goals are rarely evaluated as to their fulfillment.
4. New and creative ideas are not vetted by leaders with managerial skills to determine whether they are practical.
5. When a new idea fails, the causes of failure are not evaluated Members simply move on to another creative idea.

Map 4.2

4. Each church committee has a clear job description that is reviewed annually by the governing board.
5. The governing board has a clear sense of its oversight responsibilities with the congregation.

POLARITY PRINCIPLE 12

Sometimes when thinking of Action Steps to get to the upside of one pole, a group realizes that the Actions Step for one pole could also support the upside of the other pole. We call these High-leverage Action Steps and list them for both upsides.

Action Steps for Leadership

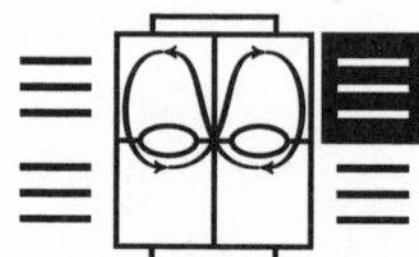

Action Steps Right

1. Every four years the congregation engages in a strategic planning process to establish goals that are to be the focus of the congregation's energy and resources for the next four years.
2. Church committees are asked annually to share their vision for what they would like to accomplish in the next twelve months.
3. Visionary leaders are sought out to head committees or task forces that appear to be stuck.
4. Church staff members go on an annual overnight retreat to map out the ideas they believe will help the congregation thrive.
5. Search committees seek out clergy with a proven track record of leadership in the congregations they have served.

Managing AND Leading are both essential to a thriving congregation. If the Action Steps you have decided on to get to the upside of Management and avoid the downside of Leadership are not being implemented, you need to understand why and either begin doing them or find other Action Steps that will work. If the Action Steps are already being done, maybe additional ones are needed.

CHAPTER 5

Strong Clergy Leadership AND Strong Lay Leadership

Having a strong, effective pastor is not enough. Unless strong pastoral leadership is matched by strong lay leadership, congregational life will not thrive. When there is no match in leadership strength, the first task of an effective pastor is to recruit and develop a strong lay team.

On the other hand, a strong group of lay leaders who have called a young or inexperienced clergy leader can simply overwhelm their new pastor. Little of significance will take place in this case either. We often see this phenomenon in congregations that have a worship attendance of fifty or fewer and that experience high clergy turnover. In such congregations, a patriarch or matriarch has usually taken over the leadership reins and is reluctant to surrender them to the incoming pastor. Congregations of any size that have been burned by clergy in the past may try to micromanage their pastor so that they won't get burned again. When a pastor discovers that he or she will be little more than the "flunky" for a ruling matriarch or patriarch, he or she will soon look for a call or placement elsewhere.

Why Shared Leadership Is Important

John and Brigetta were pastors of neighboring congregations. Even though they represented different denominations, their congregations were quite similar. Both had approximately 110 members attending Sunday worship, and both congregations had been stuck at that number for the past eight years. John and Brigetta knew each other well, as they belonged to the same clergy support group, yet their leadership styles differed greatly.

Brigetta was a tough-thinking woman who made most of the decisions at Good Samaritan Church. She had a strong, driven, Type-A personality.

Brigetta had a clear vision of where the congregation should be headed, and she worked tirelessly at getting laypeople to carry out her vision. Although she had great ideas, she continually encountered lackluster support for these proposals from the board and committee members. Some lay leaders had tried to revise some of her ideas to make them more relevant to congregational needs, but she insisted on their doing things her way. Brigetta repeatedly rebuffed their attempts to gain some ownership of her plans by incorporating some of their own, and in the end, they acquiesced to her. Over time, members who had leadership capacities simply stopped serving on congregational boards and committees. Brigetta had not noticed that lay leaders lacked enthusiasm because they felt they were treated as lackeys whose purpose was to carry out her vision. She, on the other hand, complained to her colleagues that she wished she had just a few capable lay leaders who wanted to do something to make the congregation thrive.

John was laid-back and easygoing. He also had a natural proclivity to pursue peace at all costs. Early in his tenure at St. John's, he had tried exercising leadership but had found himself quickly overruled by strong-willed lay leaders who disagreed with the changes he wanted to make. After several attempts with the same results, he decided to offer the congregation excellent pastoral care and leave the leadership of the congregation in the hands of the strong lay leaders. He saw himself as carrying out the directions his lay leaders set for him, and he seemed willing to pay this price to keep the peace. Besides, these lay leaders were an intimidating bunch. They were tough, successful executives in their corporate settings, and in their opinion John knew little about either leadership or management. Sometimes he knew that what they were proposing would not work, because he was in touch with a much broader segment of the congregation. But he would bite his tongue and go along with their proposals, though his heart was not in them, and he gave only token support to implementing their ideas.

The Polarity to Be Managed

Here were two congregations going nowhere. In each case, there was no partnership between clergy and lay leaders. The congregations were stuck on alternate poles of this polarity, and both were experiencing more and more

Polarity Management® Map

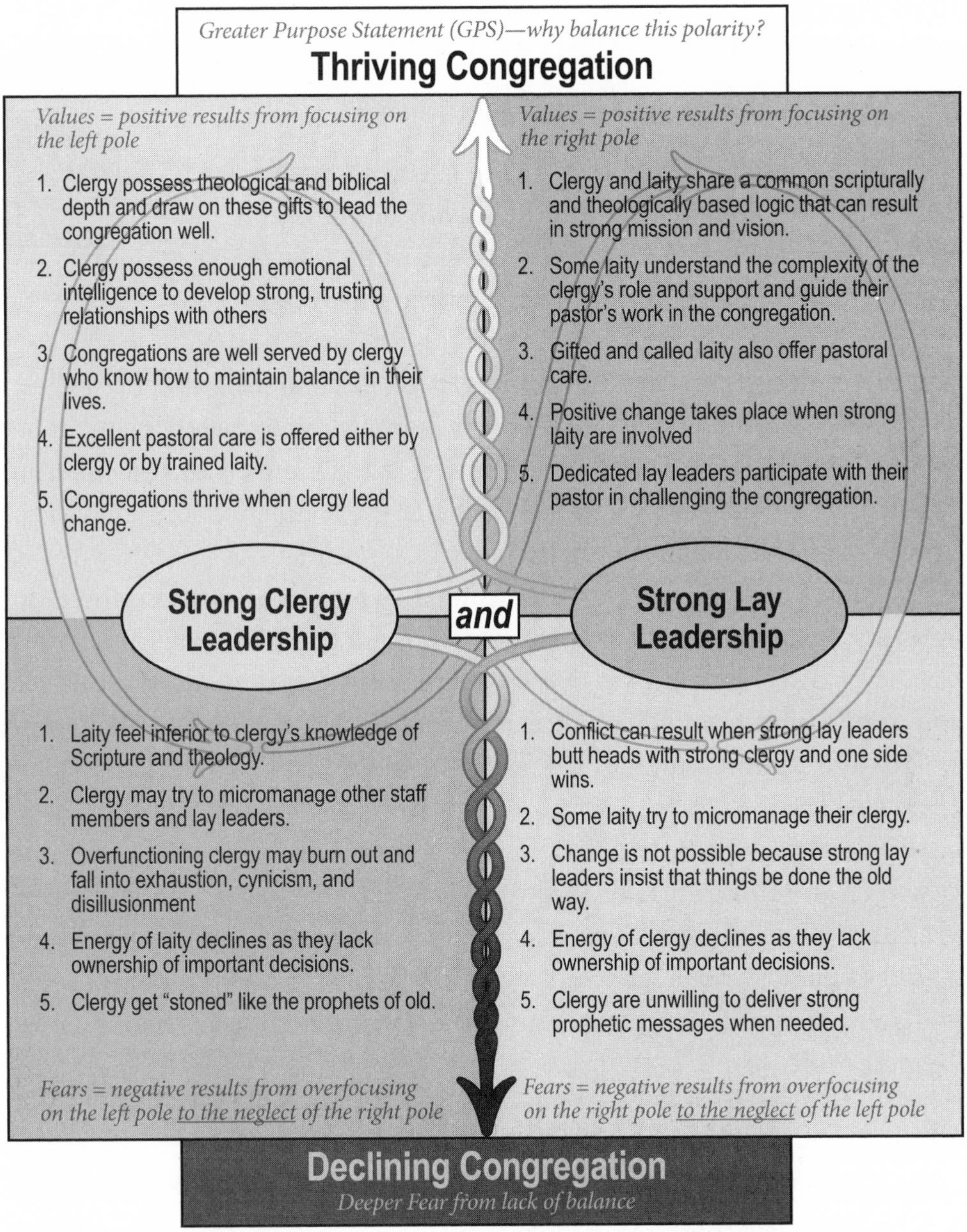

Greater Purpose Statement (GPS)—why balance this polarity?

Thriving Congregation

Values = positive results from focusing on the left pole

1. Clergy possess theological and biblical depth and draw on these gifts to lead the congregation well.
2. Clergy possess enough emotional intelligence to develop strong, trusting relationships with others
3. Congregations are well served by clergy who know how to maintain balance in their lives.
4. Excellent pastoral care is offered either by clergy or by trained laity.
5. Congregations thrive when clergy lead change.

Values = positive results from focusing on the right pole

1. Clergy and laity share a common scripturally and theologically based logic that can result in strong mission and vision.
2. Some laity understand the complexity of the clergy's role and support and guide their pastor's work in the congregation.
3. Gifted and called laity also offer pastoral care.
4. Positive change takes place when strong laity are involved
5. Dedicated lay leaders participate with their pastor in challenging the congregation.

Strong Clergy Leadership **and** **Strong Lay Leadership**

1. Laity feel inferior to clergy's knowledge of Scripture and theology.
2. Clergy may try to micromanage other staff members and lay leaders.
3. Overfunctioning clergy may burn out and fall into exhaustion, cynicism, and disillusionment
4. Energy of laity declines as they lack ownership of important decisions.
5. Clergy get "stoned" like the prophets of old.

Fears = negative results from overfocusing on the left pole to the neglect of the right pole

1. Conflict can result when strong lay leaders butt heads with strong clergy and one side wins.
2. Some laity try to micromanage their clergy.
3. Change is not possible because strong lay leaders insist that things be done the old way.
4. Energy of clergy declines as they lack ownership of important decisions.
5. Clergy are unwilling to deliver strong prophetic messages when needed.

Fears = negative results from overfocusing on the right pole to the neglect of the left pole

Declining Congregation

Deeper Fear from lack of balance

Map 5.1

of the downside of their respective poles. Map 5.1 on page 91 shows how the situations look on a polarity map.

In the context of map 5.1, let's look at each of the quadrants in more detail.

The Upside of Strong Clergy Leadership

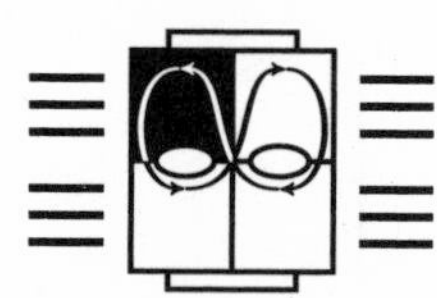

Upside Left

1. *In the upside of Strong Clergy Leadership, clergy possess theological and biblical depth and draw on those gifts to lead the congregation well.* There is a clear rationale for our wanting seminary-trained clergy to lead our congregations. Without this trained leadership, congregations would wander all over the biblical and theological landscape, moving from one questionable dogma to another. For example, some members might begin exploring new-age practices and esoteric rituals and encourage others to follow. There would be no one to challenge these practices on the basis of Scripture and the denomination's theological foundations.

A congregation may have an occasional layperson preach a sermon, but most members insist that their ordained pastor offer them spiritual guidance every week through sermons. In this way, clergy guide parishioners into sound biblical and theological thinking. As clergy work informally with boards and committees, they can offer guidance to the people who meet in these small groups.

Effective pastors are hard to find, in part because clergy need to be competent in an extraordinarily wide range of skills. No pastor can give a congregation all it thinks it needs in a spiritual leader, but congregations hope to call someone who is "good enough" with regard to most of the skills and traits they desire in a pastor. Training in Bible and theology is high on most congregations' list.

2. *In the upside of Strong Clergy Leadership, clergy possess enough emotional intelligence to develop strong, trusting relationships with others.* Clergy who exhibit high emotional intelligence possess the people skills to build trust and unity within the congregation.

Because being a pastor in a congregation requires immense involvement in people's lives, every congregation wants its pastor to score high in emotional intelligence—a term that has been variously defined.[1] Researcher Daniel Goleman says it is "the capacity for recognizing our own feelings and those of others, for motivating ourselves, for managing emotions well in ourselves and in our relationships."[2] John D. Mayer and his colleagues, also key researchers in this field, define it as "the ability to monitor one's own and others' emotions, to discriminate among them, and to use the information to guide one's thinking and actions."[3] The underlying polarity within emotional intelligence is recognizing and addressing our own emotions AND recognizing and addressing others' emotions in the service of a Greater Purpose that could be termed "Enhanced Relationships."

Emotional intelligence is especially important for clergy and religious leaders because they often have to manage stressful situations in congregational life or other settings. In the process, they have to manage their own emotions, which others may want to exploit. And they have to understand the emotions of their supporters and detractors. According to the research of Alban Institute consultant Speed Leas on the involuntary termination of clergy,[4] clergy are fired not because their theology is lacking or in error. Nor is the usual problem their ethics or spirituality. According to Leas, such pastors simply lack the capacity to develop the kinds of relationships with congregants that result in confidence and effectiveness in ministry. They are deficient in the people skills needed to be good pastors.

3. *In the upside of Strong Clergy Leadership, congregations are well served by clergy who know how to maintain balance in their lives, thus remaining vital and healthy while playing a demanding role.* Clergy burnout is epidemic and can be cited as one reason congregations lack the vitality and leadership needed to grow. Clergy continue to be invited to overextend themselves; pastors often work sixty-hour weeks, seldom taking a day off. To be sure, some weeks bring enough crises that clergy have no choice but to work overtime. When overwork becomes the norm, however, the pastor is bound to end up exhausted, cynical, disillusioned, and self-deprecating—characteristics of burnout. It is difficult for a congregation to thrive and grow when its pastor is burned out.

Congregations thrive when their clergy are able to lead a balanced life in the midst of church demands, finding time for family and friends, exercise, spiritual nourishment, hobbies, and rest. This balance is most likely to be achieved when the pastor has a pastor-parish relations committee or mutual ministry committee that carefully monitors the demands placed upon her and runs interference when other church leaders invite the pastor to overextend.

4. *In the upside of Strong Clergy Leadership, excellent pastoral care is offered, either by clergy or by trained laity.* Most congregants want a pastor who will take a personal interest in them. When congregants believe that they are known and accepted by their pastor, they are much more open to receiving spiritual guidance from him or her. Personal attention is most critical when parishioners experience personal crisis. This concern is often a key reason people join a congregation. They want to be part of a resourceful community that knows them well. They want to know that when they are down and out, they can expect someone from the congregation to come and be with them, perhaps simply to listen to their story and pray with them. Within smaller congregations, clergy do most of the pastoral care. Within larger congregations, church members who feel called may exercise a "ministry of presence" with other church members who are in distress. Every thriving congregation works hard to see that people receive pastoral care in a crisis. Effective pastoral care of members happens best when clergy have a passion for it. In larger congregations where lay members provide much of the pastoral care, they need to be trained well by a pastor with a passion for this ministry.

5. *In the upside of Strong Clergy Leadership, congregations thrive when clergy lead congregational change.* Within the past thirty years, congregations have increasingly sought clergy who are organizational change agents. At a time when the majority of mainline churches are in numerical decline, congregations desire clergy who can lead change that will result in membership gains. Of course, many congregations resist the changes they will have to make to attract new members, but current members want a pastor to be the kind of change agent who will make the congregation attractive to outsiders without creating too much conflict in the process.

There is no question that conflict will ensue as a congregation decides to do what is needed to grow numerically—an action that sometimes results in some members' leaving the congregation. (We deal with this phenomenon in the *Tradition AND Innovation* polarity in chapter 2.) Clergy who survive these conflicts work to garner support from a cadre of strong lay leaders for any change effort and know when they have enough support to initiate a change process. They also have an intuitive appreciation that change is one pole of a polarity and that there is wisdom to be tapped within the values and fears of those who resist change. These clergy are in fact *"Stability AND Change"* agents. Ideally, such pastors have a solid clergy support group where they can vent their feelings and find courage to maintain the unpopular stands that will ensure change and growth while maintaining adequate stability.

6. *In the upside of Strong Clergy Leadership, strong prophetic messages are delivered when necessary.* Most congregants expect that their pastor will make them feel uncomfortable at times to help them grow spiritually. The pastor needs the courage and skill to help the congregation grapple with issues of life and faith. This is the prophetic role of spiritual leaders, a tradition that is clearly part of both Christianity and Judaism.

The Bible is different from many history books in that the flaws and mistakes of God's people are made obvious. Congregational clergy are called upon to follow that tradition and to preach a strong prophetic message when they believe the congregation is clearly forsaking the truth of Scripture in word and deed. Such preaching calls members to grapple with tough issues, to explore how Scripture and the sociopolitical issues of the day collide. The desired result is change in both the attitudes and behavior of members.

The Upside of Strong Lay Leadership

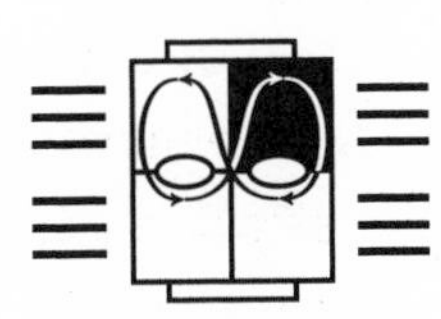

Upside Right

Strong clergy are essential, but they are not enough. Thriving congregations thrive in part because they also have strong lay leaders. Let's look at the positive things that happen in a congregation with strong, empowered laity.

1. *In the upside of Strong Lay Leadership, clergy and laity share a common scripturally and theologically based logic that can result in strong mission and vision.* In such mutual leadership, clergy and lay leaders decide together on both congregational direction and structure; as a result, both clergy and lay leaders are invested in outcomes. The consequence is high energy from both as they move to implement what they have decided upon together.

Often, when some change effort is decided on, a relevant theological or biblical understanding needs to change within a congregation. (We make reference to this point in the *Inreach AND Outreach* polarity in chapter 6.) For significant outreach to take place, congregational members need a solid biblical and theological grasp of what it means to be a person of faith. Lay leaders become vital in such a change effort in their familiarity with congregational members who hold an outdated or flawed biblical or theological stance. These lay leaders are often more effective than clergy in changing the perspective of resistant congregational members. The lay leaders will likely have known these resistant members longer and will also know who has their ear. They can then mobilize those who have the respect of these resistant members and who respect the resisters' values and fears.

2. *In the upside of Strong Lay Leadership, some laity understand the complexity of the clergy's role and support and guide their pastor's work in the congregation.* When lay leaders work with clergy over time, they realize that there is much more to the pastoral role than they first thought. Some lay leaders wish they better understood the load their pastor seems to carry, including the way the pastor is treated by certain congregational members. Special lay leaders sense the trials and tribulations of their pastor and try to support him or her in a one-to-one relationship.

Some denominations recommend that congregations establish a special committee whose sole responsibility is to see that the pastor-parish relationship, the most important one in the congregation, continues to be healthy. This committee will spend much of its time trying to comprehend what the pastor goes through from day to day. Such a committee will often ask pastors to keep a log of their time, in thirty-minute blocks, for a week or two. Sometime this discipline is instructive to clergy themselves. It is only in this way that lay leaders can see that their pastor is often consumed by congregational demands. They then come to realize why the pastor has a hard time keeping his or her workweek at fifty or fewer hours, and they can help the pastor maintain physical, emotional, social and interpersonal, vocational, intellectual, and spiritual well-being.

This committee will also surface congregation members' complaints about the pastor. That is the other side of ensuring that this relationship remains healthy. Committee members need to be sure that the pastor does not spend excessive time trying to appease everyone who has a complaint. However, they also need to recognize when the pastor is alienating a larger majority of the congregation and to bring up legitimate concerns. People who care deeply about their pastor do not want him or her to self-destruct or stir up negative feeling that will diminish pastoral effectiveness. Wise and discerning lay leaders know which issues to raise at these meetings and which to screen out.

The way this committee is formed profoundly affects its ability to function as a positive resource to the pastor. When there is any committee member whom the pastor cannot trust, it is unlikely that material will be shared with the group about which the pastor feels vulnerable. The trust level needs to be such that the pastor can be confident that the material explored in these committee meetings will remain with the committee. For this reason we recommend that the pastor select the committee members. Some members may protest that if a pastor names "favorite people" to this committee, it will not raise important issues with the pastor. We don't believe this to be true. If people really care about their pastor, they will want him or her to succeed, and they will not refrain from raising difficult subjects.

When such a committee focuses energy on understanding the complexity of the pastor's role and broaches issues or behaviors that are alienating some members, the committee will have a positive impact on the pastor and the whole congregation. Every parish pastor should have such a dedicated group of people in his or her corner.

3. *In the upside of Strong Lay Leadership, gifted and called laity also offer pastoral care.* As the congregation continues to grow, the increased load of pastoral care is not seen as totally the pastor's responsibility. Strong lay leaders are in touch with the members of the congregation who have a special gift of listening to people in crisis and praying with them. These lay leaders begin working to structure training events that help prepare lay pastoral callers for this task. With training, a strong partnership can develop between clergy and lay leaders as together they take on the pastoral needs of the congregation. The results are noticeable. When members feel cared for, especially in times of crisis, the morale of the whole congregation is raised. Research shows that people who belong to a congregation live longer than those who don't, just as people who belong to a support group live longer

than those who don't. Their congregation is their community of support and guidance. For some people, the congregation is the only place where they are accepted as they are.

4. *In the upside of Strong Lay Leadership, positive change takes place in a congregation when strong lay leaders are involved.* All of us become more deeply invested in decisions when we have a role in formulating them. That is one reason this polarity needs to be managed well within a congregation. When congregational life is dominated by clergy without a complementary group of strong lay leaders, the congregation's energy dissipates. Lay leaders need to become invested in congregational life, and they will become invested when they participate in decisions related to change. The congregation's finances also depend upon this dynamic. A congregation's highest financial contributors are those members who are most active in congregational life and who have had a major role in shaping the direction of the congregation.

5. *In the upside of Strong Lay Leadership, dedicated lay leaders participate with their pastor in challenging the congregation.* At times a pastor can present a theological or biblical principle, but it is lay leaders who spell out how the principle can best be played out within the congregation. A pastor can, for example, preach a great sermon telling how Jesus consistently identified with the poor in the community. The lay leaders may say to the pastor, "You know, this thing you talked about in your sermon Sunday about identifying with the poor? Well, a few of us have been talking about the fact that our congregation has no involvement with the people living on the east side of town. We want to put together a task force to explore how our congregation can become involved there. A few of us have had this concern for some time now, but your sermon brought it to the forefront of our thinking again."

The prophetic tradition continues to be a strong aspect of Judaism and Christianity. Yet more important than prophetic preaching is prophetic congregations. Prophetic preaching can get things started, but it takes strong lay leaders to find ways the whole congregation can take a prophetic stand on social issues. This activity involves considerable time and energy, but the impact can be far-reaching.

An example of this dynamic at work is found in Pullen Memorial Baptist Church in Raleigh, North Carolina, a Southern Baptist congregation whose pastor, Mahan Siler, was loved and respected.[5] A gay couple came to Siler and asked if he would perform a holy union ceremony for them. He responded that he couldn't, but added that he would have his congregation search the Scriptures for an appropriate response. For the next two years the entire congregation engaged in small-group Bible studies. During these studies, Siler did not try to persuade his congregation to take a particular stand on the matter. He simply let the lay leaders lead the small-group Bible studies. At a congregational meeting two years later, the congregation voted unanimously to permit the pastor to proceed with this ceremony.

After this vote, the pastor did perform the ceremony, and the week after this act, the congregation was dismissed from its denomination. The long-term results of this action were not particularly negative, however, as the congregation became united with many other congregations that admired its prophetic stance, and a new denomination was formed. This denomination, the Cooperative Baptist Fellowship, is now strong enough to support two seminaries, as well as a staff to manage regional and national administrative issues.

The Downside of Strong Clergy Leadership

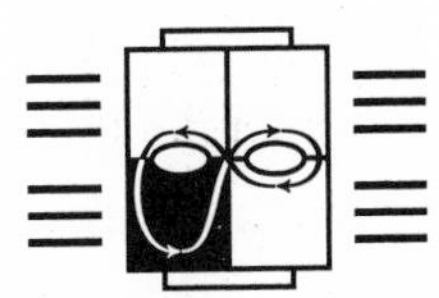
Downside Left

As we can see, strong lay leadership, like strong clergy leadership, is essential. We have seen both upsides of this polarity. Now let's look at how problematic it becomes when a congregation overfocuses on one pole to the neglect of the other.

1. *In the downside of Strong Clergy Leadership, laity can feel inferior to clergy in their knowledge of Scripture, theology, and congregational life.* When strong lay leadership is absent, clergy can get out of hand. They can begin to feel superior to their lay members and start talking down to them. This condescension is quickly sensed by the laity, who begin to resist ideas and efforts their clergy recommend. A passive codependence can develop.

The clear downside to this arrangement is that over time the energy lay leaders devote to their congregation dwindles. They become less and less invested in congregational work because they were not part of creating the mission and vision of the congregation. Their work has been preempted by the pastor. This lack of lay ownership of key congregational decisions can be deadly, because laypeople begin to feel that the congregation is no longer theirs but the pastor's. Lay leaders may come to feel that they are too uninformed or ignorant to make key congregational decisions—not the way we want congregational members to feel.

Clergy exploitation of lay leaders' feelings of inferiority can cause deep wounds. For example, if in any public setting a pastor becomes irate and humiliates an individual or group for doing something the pastor feels is wrong or ill-advised, the ripple effect goes out to other congregational leaders. Intimidated lay leaders are unlikely to take initiative within the congregation, fearing they will be publicly embarrassed by the pastor. When there are no strong lay leaders who will confront the pastor on such behavior, the abuse may continue. A passive-dependent congregation is unlikely to have a positive impact on its community.

2. *In the downside of Strong Clergy Leadership, clergy may try to micromanage other staff members and lay leaders.* Clergy with a strong need to be in control may insist that everything be done their way. Staff members and lay leaders are no longer free to complete a task or project in their own way. The pastor keeps everyone with responsibility in the church on a tight leash.

The result is that creative lay leaders begin to back off and resist taking on leadership roles in the congregation. If people serving on the church staff are micromanaged by the pastor, they will either capitulate to keep their jobs, or they will try to find work in another congregation where their job may be more satisfying. Either way, the congregation loses. A congregation whose pastor dominates everyone around him or her is unlikely to grow as visitors to the church observe an unhealthy interaction between the pastor and lay leaders.

3. *In the downside of Strong Clergy Leadership, overfunctioning clergy may burn out and fall into exhaustion, cynicism, and disillusionment.* Clergy burnout is a well-known dilemma within denominations. Almost 25 percent of clergy score high on a clergy-burnout inventory. Another 25 percent are on the borderline, already experiencing some symptoms of burnout. Burnout may be less likely if there is a balance between strong clergy leadership and strong lay leadership.

The more clergy overfunction, the more likely it is that laity will underfunction. Soon lay leaders simply expect that responsibility for congregational life and health belongs to clergy. When clergy overfunction, they create a norm that continues to affect the clergy who follow them. When a new pastor arrives, laity automatically expect him to dominate congregational life. If the new pastor does not buy into this notion of congregational life, he will be accused of not giving the congregation the service and leadership it needs. In fact, effective leadership is almost impossible in such situations, because the pastor is so busy meeting everyone's expectations that there is no time to do the work that might lead to growth in numbers or spiritual depth.

Clergy overfunction to the detriment of their family life, physical well-being, and spiritual life. Overfunctioning creates a downward spiral: as the personal life of clergy begins to suffer, they become less effective leaders of their congregations. The body and life of a pastor constitute the medium of his or her message. When there is a disjuncture between what comes out of a pastor's mouth and everything else that congregants see in their pastor, clergy lose credibility. When clergy become overweight because they do not rest, exercise, or eat properly, and they continually look haggard, the message they hope to bring to the congregation lacks integrity. You can almost hear laity saying to themselves about their clergy, "Hold the phone a minute, Pastor. You want me to make a deeper commitment to Christ and become like you? Why am I not jumping up and down with excitement about what you are saying?"

The baneful effects of a clergyperson's overfunctioning can be difficult to address in a congregation. When everyone knows that the relationship members have with their pastor is not working well, no one seems to know how to raise the issue. If anything, members begin to talk about what their pastor is not doing to bring about numerical growth, a concern that only drives clergy to try harder and work even longer hours. When clergy overfunction, laypeople over time come to believe that congregational life is all about clergy and not about a joint effort of clergy and lay leaders.

4. *In the downside of Strong Clergy Leadership, lay leaders' energy declines because they lack ownership of important decisions.* When clergy dominate congregational life, lay leaders become less and less involved. Clergy burn out, and laity find they have less energy for congregational work. Clergy

engage in wrongheaded thinking if they assume that the harder they work, the more invested congregants will become in the congregation. Usually the opposite happens. Laity begin to feel that church life is all about clergy and how they perform; the lay members back off and let the pastor do it all. As this process is prolonged, the congregation will continue to have financial difficulties, since uninvolved members contribute less. Lay leaders may also believe that the gifts and talents they have to offer their congregation are not welcome, and they may become even less invested in the congregation. When a congregation appears to have low energy, could the root of the problem be that gifted lay leaders are not being challenged to take on responsible roles? This question reflects a vicious circle, an attribute of polarities that are poorly managed.

POLARITY PRINCIPLE 13

The overfocus on one pole will eventually lead to the downside of both poles. If we overfocus on one pole—because we value that pole and fear the downside of the opposite pole—we will first move to the downside of our preferred pole.

In this case, an overfocus on strong clergy leads to weak laity. Next, we get the very thing we were afraid of—the downside of the opposite pole. In this case the downside of weak laity leads to overextended and increasingly weaker clergy. The overfocus on one pole always leads eventually to the downside of *both* poles. In this case, it leads to weak laity *and* weak clergy. The same outcome will occur with an overfocus on strong laity as well.

5. *In the downside of Strong Clergy Leadership, clergy are, so to speak, stoned to death like the prophets of old.* As mentioned earlier, clergy are often called upon to preach a strong, prophetic message to the congregation. The majority of members may accept the message as something the congregation needed to hear to help them move toward spiritual maturity, but a minority may take offense and may even look for ways to strike back at the pastor. One difference between the prophets of old and modern clergy is that the prophets of old came to proclaim their controversial message and then went

back to, say, trimming sycamore trees. They did not need to face a congregation week after week. This can be one hazard of strong clergy leadership. When clergy still bear the scars of the last controversy they took on, they may be reluctant to take on another one. At other times they cannot with integrity hold back and will go ahead and say the things that may cause the congregation to ask them to leave. Biblical history consistently tells us that the people of God often stone their prophets and crucify their leaders. We will deal with this phenomenon in more depth when we pursue the *Nurture AND Transformation* polarity in chapter 7.

The Downside of Strong Lay Leadership

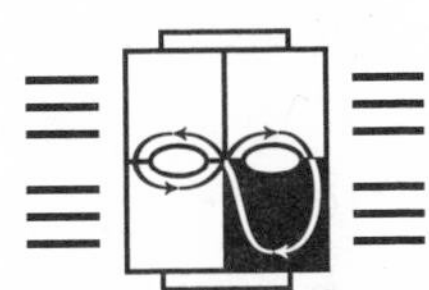

Downside Right

The downside of strong clergy leadership is a truly sad state of affairs. It is matched only by the sad state of affairs in the downside of the other pole, strong lay leadership.

1. *In the downside of Strong Lay Leadership, conflict can result when strong lay leaders butt heads with strong clergy, and one side wins.* In some congregations significant theological and biblical conflict simmers between clergy and lay leaders. In some cases, the search committee recommended a certain pastor, and the board and congregation approved, but it became clear very shortly that it was a mismatch. The congregation hired a pastor who was theologically either much more liberal or much more conservative than the core of the congregation. When there is a disagreement between strong clergy leaders and strong lay leaders, combined with either/or thinking, sparks will fly.

Clergy and laity may see their differences as an opportunity for open dialogue on these issues. They may also agree that they have reached an impasse and that they need to call in an outside consultant to help them deal with their differences. Those would be mature ways of dealing with the conflict at hand. A less mature way would be for strong lay leaders to pressure their pastor either to change his or her position on a social or biblical issue or to leave. It is not uncommon for strong lay leaders to want weak clergy whom they can control. In such cases, the congregation has continually had weak clergy whom laity could dominate.

Such situations are exacerbated when the pastor is abusive to congregants who hold a theological position that differs from the pastor's. One immature way strong clergy may respond is to threaten members with excommunication if they do not fall into line. Another bad scenario is played out when both the pastor and the lay leaders are over their heads in this conflict but do not call in outside consultation to help them resolve their differences. The worst-case scenario when clergy and congregation do not match is that strong lay leaders begin soliciting support from other laypeople and the pastor begins rallying his own supporters. This kind of showdown can only wound congregational life. Members begin leaving because they can't believe how badly both clergy and lay leaders are handling their disagreement.

2. *In the downside of Strong Lay Leadership, some laity try to micromanage their clergy.* When a congregation has been wounded in some way by former clergy, leaders may want to micromanage the current pastor. The likelihood that such attempts will have a positive outcome is slim. The pastor is constantly humiliated by lay leaders trying to tell him or her how to handle daily tasks and serve the congregation. It is not unusual for the pastor to adopt a passive-aggressive stance toward these leaders. Unless the lay leaders abandon their approach, it is unlikely that the pastor will stay around for long.

Just as lay leaders lose energy for congregational ministry when they have little or no input into the shape of the congregation's ministry, clergy function halfheartedly when they believe they can only carry out the dictates of strong lay leaders. A pastor new to a congregation may encounter certain lay leaders who have such influence in the congregation that the pastor has little choice but to do their bidding. We often see this scenario develop when a newly ordained pastor is called to a small-membership congregation that has been run for years by a patriarch or matriarch. Especially when the congregation experiences high pastoral turnover and long interims between clergy, someone in the congregation has to lead while the congregation is without a pastor. These interim leaders may continue to hold onto this leadership role, even when a pastor has been called and is on the scene. In addition, because of high clergy turnover, the patriarch or matriarch will seek to maintain control to prevent the congregation from being jerked in different directions with each new pastor. Such a situation tends to perpetuate itself, because clergy forced to acquiesce to the leadership of a matriarch or patriarch leave the congregation as soon as they can get a call elsewhere.

3. *In the downside of Strong Lay Leadership, change is not possible because strong lay leaders insist that things be done the old way.* For a congregation to survive, it must continually adopt new forms of service and ministry, creating new worship opportunities and programs that appeal to a new generation. The flexibility needed to do this is not possible when a cadre of strong lay leaders insist on staying with long-held practices. In some cases, such lay leaders may hold a congregation hostage because they are the biggest financial supporters, and the congregation cannot afford to lose them and their financial contributions.

A particular challenge arises when a congregation grows from pastor-size (50–150 in attendance) to program-size (150–250 in attendance). For a change in the appropriate style of leadership to take place, the pastor needs to do less pastoral care and to devote more energy to creating programs that will meet the spiritual needs of members. Lay members who feel a call to a ministry of pastoral care need to take over that aspect of congregational life. It is not unusual in such a situation for controversy to develop when strong lay leaders are insistent that pastoral calling is the sole responsibility of the ordained pastor. They themselves will refuse the ministry of other lay callers and sometimes try to garner support from other lay leaders to demand that the pastor either do all the pastoral calling or leave. This is another occasion for a congregational rift.

4. *In the downside of Strong Lay Leadership, the energy of clergy declines as they lack ownership of important decisions.* In the opening of this chapter we described John, pastor of St. John's Church. We depicted him as a passive-aggressive person who believed it was dangerous for him to take any initiative that would set a new direction for the congregation. He had been burned too many times by strong lay leaders and had decided to engage only in pastoral care and congregational maintenance. By making this decision, he had consigned the congregation to a status-quo ministry, with little direction from him. He had in essence robbed the congregation of an important function—namely, his leadership as the congregation's biblical and theological specialist. He was not leading the congregation to examine the implications of biblical truth for the issues of the day or its community.

Instead, he allowed the congregation to remain in the hands of a few strong lay leaders, who likely held to a singular and narrow biblical and theological perspective. He often found he had little energy to carry out the wishes of this group of powerful lay leaders. John is a perfect example of the downside of the strong lay leadership pole.

5. *In the downside of Strong Lay Leadership, clergy are unwilling to deliver strong, prophetic messages.* In John we also see a pastor who is not likely to present the congregation with a challenge. When he tried that in the past, he got his knuckles rapped; he was not willing to risk such a move again. John also was not about to confront this group of strong lay leaders on the shortcomings of their biblical and theological stances. The strong prophetic figures we find in Scripture constantly addressed the unfaithfulness of the children of Israel and their lack of obedience to the covenant they had with God. John had turned his back on that rich tradition in Scripture.

Just as not every leader in the Old Testament was called to be a prophet, so not every pastor today is called to be prophetic. However, we might understand the prophetic role more broadly as a pastor's responsibility to encourage the congregation to grow spiritually. Without some type of prophetic voice, a community will continue to reside in status-quo thinking. Rather than rising to greater faithfulness and service, the congregation will allow its accustomed norms to prevail. As a result, the congregation is denied a new source of energy that usually emerges when a congregation embraces an exciting vision for itself. Further, because money is energy, a congregation stuck in a status-quo mentality usually has difficulty meeting its budget. In addition, without new and exciting things taking place in the congregation, few laypeople are motivated to invite their friends to church. Such a congregation will continue in a membership decline caused by natural attrition.

Managing the Polarity Poorly: Early Warnings

We've looked at both the upsides and the downsides of this polarity. Now how do we minimize the downsides? What Early Warnings might we build in to help us self-correct?

Early Warnings for Strong Clergy Leadership

Early Warnings Left

1. The pastor stops asking for the perspectives of lay leaders on some of the tough issues she is facing. It may be that the pastor simply does not respect the perspectives of lay leaders but rather consults with her peers in ministry.
2. Clergy are so convinced that they alone know what needs to be done that they impose their will on lay leaders. Their style disempowers lay leaders, who then become less motivated to try to find ways to work with the pastor.
3. Lay leaders think clergy "have it easy," so there is little support for sabbaticals and days of retreat, or for limiting the pastor's work in the congregation to fifty or fewer hours a week. Clergy may simply take matters into their own hands and demand more time off, sabbaticals, and the like.
4. Clergy are underpaid and underappreciated; they become cynical and disillusioned, possibly to the point of deciding to leave the ordained ministry. Or strong, dictatorial clergy demand that lay leaders pay them more money as they do less and less for the congregation.
5. The congregation appears to be always in a financial crisis, a situation due largely to the lack of involvement of laypeople in congregational decisions and actions. Members continue to allow their pastor to make most decisions related to congregational life.
6. Lay leaders systematically withdraw from the congregation. This phenomenon can be monitored by observing how many lay leaders disengage from church activities after serving a term on the governing board. They may have become cynical and disillusioned with the church in general, having lost their investment in congregational life and health.

Early Warnings for Strong Lay Leadership

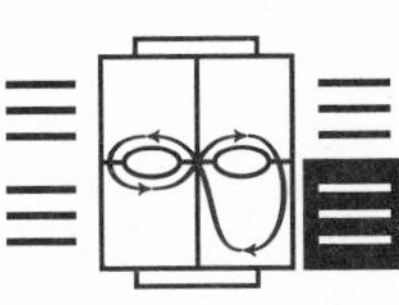
Early Warnings Right

1. Lay leaders rarely set aside time to come to some mutual understandings with their clergy on the goals of the congregation and its mission.

2. Lay leaders increase demands that clergy account for how they spend the hours of each day.
3. Lay leaders are unwilling to negotiate the way their pastor's role needs to change when the congregation is either growing or declining.
4. Rifts deepen between those who support the pastor and those who think she should leave. In such a case, the strongest lay leaders will prevail, while others leave the congregation.
5. Younger or newer members have few opportunities to lead within the congregation, because older members refuse to relinquish their roles.
6. Over time, lay leaders begin a movement to fire the pastor or simply to force him out with passive-aggressive tactics. Clergy soon realize when they are being blocked at every turn and decide on their own to leave. The "flip" by lay leaders from being passive to being aggressive may indicate that they took the abuse involved in the downside of strong clergy leadership until they could take it no more—and then became the abusers.

Managing the Polarity Well: Action Steps

Just reading about the Early Warnings of this polarity is a downer! Clearly we need to minimize these two downsides and maximize the two upsides if our congregation is to thrive. Let's look at the Action Steps to maximize each upside. Map 5.2 on pages 110–111 illustrates this polarity.

Action Steps for the Upside of Strong Clergy Leadership

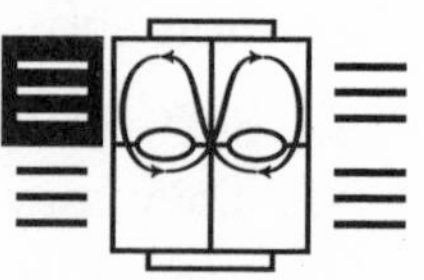

Action Steps Left

How do we maximize both upsides? What Action Steps can we take that will create a virtuous circle between *Strong Clergy Leadership AND Strong Laity Leadership*?

1. At least annually clergy and laity engage in mutual evaluation of their investment in executing their differing roles with energy and commitment. (Note that this is another High-leverage Action Step that shows up again as the first Action Step for Strong Lay Leadership.)

2. A pastor-parish relations committee is formed to understand what it is like to be a pastor in this congregation.
3. Clergy and laity together decide what aspects of the congregation's day-to-day operations are to be reported to the governing board. The board does not insist that the pastor make a monthly report on all her activities. At the same time, the board is informed about the challenges the pastor faces in managing the congregation. The board then sets policies that allow paid staff to address these challenges.
4. Clergy and lay leaders have frequent discussions about whether laity or clergy are to take the initiative to address certain challenges. Each group comes to understand its roles well. (This is another High-leverage Action Step. See step 4 of the Strong Lay Leadership Action Steps.)
5. The congregation generously supports with both money and time the pastor's participation in continuing-education seminars that promise to increase the pastor's competence.
6. The governing board supports the pastor's request to find a coach to assist him in guiding the congregation through complex issues.
7. The congregation offers the pastor a three-month sabbatical every four years, freeing up the pastor to visit other congregations and to interview other clergy and laity on how they managed tough challenges within their congregations.

Action Steps for the Upside of Strong Lay Leadership

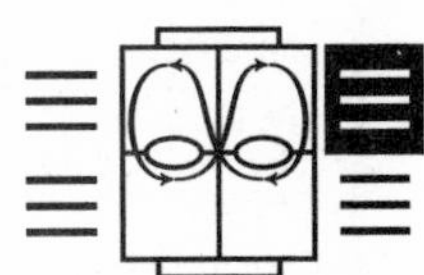
Action Steps Right

With the possibilities above to support Strong Clergy Leadership, what might be done to support Strong Lay Leadership?

1. At least annually clergy and laity engage in mutual evaluation of their investment in executing their differing roles with energy and commitment.
2. Care is given to placing lay leaders in roles that both challenge them and give them satisfaction. This effort may include offering a "gifts discernment" seminar that encourages lay leaders to reflect on their

Polarity Management®

Action Steps

How will we gain or maintain the positive results from focusing on this left pole? What? Who? By when? Measures?

1. At least annually clergy and laity engage in mutual evaluation of their roles within the congregation.
2. A pastor-parish relations committee is formed to understand what it is like to be a pastor in this congregation.
3. Clergy and laity together decide what aspects of the congregation's day-to-day operations are to be reported to the governing board.
4. Clergy and lay leaders have frequent discussions about whether laity or clergy are to take initiative to address certain challenges.
5. The congregation generously supports with both money and time the pastor's participation in continuing education events.

Early Warnings

Measurable indicators (things you can count) that will let you know you are getting into the downside of this left pole.

1. The pastor stops engaging congregational leaders on tough parish issues.
2. The pastor feels lay leaders are not capable of understanding congregational challenges.
3. The pastor exploits lay leaders, assuming they are too weak to challenge the time they take off.
4. Clergy are underpaid and underappreciated; some becoming cynical and disillusioned.
5. The congregation is always in a financial crisis, due largely to the lack of involvement of lay people in congregational decisions and actions.

Greater Purpose Statement (GPS)

Thriving

Values = positive results from focusing on the left pole

1. Clergy possess theological and biblical depth and draw on these gifts to lead the congregation well.
2. Clergy possess enough emotional intelligence to develop strong, trusting relationships with others.
3. Congregations are served well by clergy who know how to maintain balance in their lives.
4. Excellent pastoral care is offered either by clergy or by trained laity.
5. Strong, prophetic messages are delivered when necessary.

Strong Clergy Leadership

and

1. Laity feel inferior to clergy knowledge of Scripture and theology.
2. Clergy may try to micromanage other staff members and lay leaders.
3. Overfunctioning clergy may burn out and fall into exhaustion, cynicism, and disillusionment.
4. Energy of laity declines as they lack ownership of important decisions.
5. Clergy get "stoned" like the prophets of old.

Fears = negative results from overfocusing on the left pole to the neglect of the right pole

Declining

Deeper Fear from

Map

Why balance this polarity?

Congregation

Values = positive results from focusing on the right pole

1. Clergy and laity share a common scripturally and theologically based logic that can result in strong mission and vision.
2. Some laity understand the complexity of the clergy's role and support and guide their pastor's work in the congregation.
3. Gifted and called laity also offer pastoral care.
4. Positive change takes place when strong laity are involved.
5. Dedicated lay leaders participate with their pastor in challenging the congregation.

and **Strong Lay Leadership**

1. Conflict can result when strong lay leaders butt heads with strong clergy and one side wins.
2. Some laity try to micromanage their clergy.
3. Change is not possible because strong lay leaders insist that things be done the old way.
4. Energy of clergy declines as they lack ownership of important decisions.
5. Clergy are unwilling to deliver strong prophetic messages when needed.

Fears = negative results from overfocusing on the right pole to the neglect of the left pole

Congregation

lack of balance

Action Steps

How will we gain or maintain the positive results from focusing on this right pole? What? Who? By when? Measures?

1. At least annually clergy and laity engage in mutual evaluation of their roles within the congregation.
2. Care is given to place lay leaders in roles that both challenge them and give them satisfaction.
3. The congregation has a deliberate strategy to challenge members who have leadership potential to take on roles that will give them experience and increased competence.
4. Clergy and lay leaders have frequent discussions about whether laity or clergy are to take initiative to address certain challenges.
5. The congregation is accustomed to using outside experts when the need for them is evident.

Early Warnings

Measurable indicators (things you can count) that will let you know that you are getting into the downside of this right pole.

1. Lay leaders rarely set aside time to come to some mutual understanding with their clergy about goals and mission.
2. Lay Leaders increase demands that clergy account for how they spend the hours of each day.
3. Lay leaders are unwilling to negotiate the way their pastor's role needs to change when the congregation either grows or declines.
4. Rifts deepen between those who support the pastor and those who think she should leave.
5. Younger or newer members have few opportunities to lead within the congregation because older members refuse to relinquish their roles.

Map 5.2

personal gifts whose use would bring them the greatest joy and satisfaction within the congregation.

3. The congregation has a deliberate strategy to challenge congregational members who have leadership potential to take on roles that will give them experience and increase their competence.
4. Clergy and lay leaders frequently discuss when laity are to take the initiative to address certain challenges and when clergy are to take the initiative. Both come to understand their roles well.
5. The congregation is accustomed to using outside experts as resources. For example, the congregation is willing to hire a consultant to assist members in dealing with major conflicts in the congregation. In addition, the congregation contracts with outside resource people to train lay leaders in managing certain congregational challenges.
6. Special attention is given to lay leaders who have exerted extra effort to complete important roles within the congregation. The ministry of these lay leaders is celebrated in a creative way.
7. The congregation regularly honors those who carry out certain ministries, even though they are not viewed as "special." For example, leaders may honor all the Sunday school teachers or choir members by taking them and their spouses out to dinner. Committees involved in overseeing the ministries of members annually think up new ways to honor their service.

Thriving congregations have found ways to empower their clergy and to empower their laity. It is important to do both. One way is to reproduce this polarity on a single sheet of paper and ask for an hour's discussion at the next board meeting. The question that needs to be asked at such a time is this: "Are we managing this polarity well or managing it poorly?" If there is consensus that the congregation is managing it poorly, the board can ask for suggestions of Action Steps that might bring the two poles into better balance. If the suggestions are not particularly robust, a task force can be appointed to study the polarity and bring recommendations. Managing this polarity is worth that expenditure of energy.

CHAPTER 6

Inreach AND Outreach

In St. Francis's day, lepers were viewed as they had been in Jesus's day—with fear and hatred. Francis himself would ride three miles out of his way to avoid a leprosarium in a town near Assisi, so strong was his revulsion. A decisive moment in his conversion came when he felt compelled to get off his horse to embrace a leper. He later described it as the sweetest experience of his life. When Mother Teresa discovered a sick, starving person lying on the street, she would put her arms around him and gently rock him. She was always able to see Christ in the unfortunate ones, and when she coached others in this ministry, she would say, "Don't count the cost." She taught: do this for the love of Christ, rather than to sacrifice something of yourself for this other person. Both these saints had an extraordinary spiritual foundation for their outreach ministries. We might say they had experienced the joy and power of inreach through the witness of other faithful Christians and the work of the Holy Spirit. But when this polarity is well managed, individuals and congregations are most faithful to the callings we have received from God.

Meeting Members' Needs or Reaching Out?

Pastor Don was exhausted. It was Saturday afternoon. He and eight members of his congregation had just returned from a mission trip to New Orleans. The group had spent a week working with Habitat for Humanity to get a single small house built for a poor family that had lost everything in Hurricane Katrina. His volunteers thought the experience was great. They had begun each morning with a forty-five-minute Bible study followed by fifteen minutes of prayer. After working on the building site all day, the group sat around in the evenings drinking iced tea, singing, and chatting. Most felt strongly that they were making their faith active in love. Two of the group would offer a testimony of their faith at worship services the next morning.

As tired as he was, Pastor Don marveled at how much his little congregation of 180 members was doing in outreach. Every Wednesday night six members spent two hours tutoring kids in an inner-city school. The church operated a large food pantry in conjunction with other congregations, giving out several hundred pounds of food a day to people in need. Last year ten members had gone with Don to Uganda to help build a boarding school for kids who had lost their parents to AIDS.

Pastor Don decided to make a quick stop at the church to pick up a Sunday bulletin before heading home to his family. He glanced at the six pink message slips on his desk. Six people wanted a call from him. Laura, the Sunday school superintendent, couldn't find a teacher for the sixth-grade class for tomorrow morning. Tillie, a strong supportive member, had left word that Agnes, confined to her home for the past five years, was declining rapidly and had requested a visit from Pastor Don. A note from Jane, Don's part-time secretary, said the Commerfords were upset that their son James was going to have to wait a year to be confirmed because there were not enough teenagers to make up a confirmation class this year. George Saunders was dismayed that Pastor Don had not been present to lead the Saturday-morning Bible study. After reading his messages, Don scanned the Sunday bulletin. He found several significant errors—he had not been in the office to proofread Jane's work. He left feeling even more tired.

Arriving home, Pastor Don was greeted warmly by his wife, Ingrid, and son, Jared. Ingrid told him the Rogers family had called to say they were not happy that their aged grandmother had been in the hospital all week and no one from the church had gone to visit her. Pastor Don just shook his head.

Excusing himself, he went to call the congregational president. He told Judith that the mission project in New Orleans had been a great success. Some significant bonding had taken place between members on the project. Some wanted to sign up for another mission trip in six months. He also told her that some people were nipping at his heels because he had spent time away from the church again and that she should be prepared to hear complaints at church Sunday. He also asked her to do him the favor of teaching the sixth-grade class in the morning. "Sure, no problem—I'll do it," said Judith.

Pastor Don returned to Ingrid and Jared, who were eating popcorn in the kitchen. He felt tired, but it was a good tiredness. He was grateful for the way ministry at the church was unfolding. Fewer than a quarter of the members were involved in a social-justice outreach project, but almost none of this activity had been going on when he arrived some five years ago. A few long-time members continued to grumble about his frequent absence from the church, but the core leadership of the congregation was behind the mission outreach efforts. It would be great to hear what some of those who had gone to New Orleans would say in the worship services the next morning.

The Polarity to Be Managed

Map 6.1 on page 116 shows how the polarity Pastor Don has been struggling with would look on a polarity map.

This map appears in a sequence different from those in previous chapters to illustrate the two points of view that make up all polarity maps. First, walk in the shoes of Pastor Don and those in the congregation who value the upside of Outreach and have a legitimate fear of the downside of Inreach. Then walk in the shoes of those with the other point of view—who place an equally strong value on the upside of Inreach and have a legitimate fear of the downside of outreach. Then we will describe the process of "getting unstuck" to show how Pastor Don might effectively approach those resisting his promotion of outreach efforts. We begin with the pro-Outreach point of view, composed of fear of the downside of Inreach *and* value for the upside of Outreach.

The Downside of Inreach

When promoting outreach, Pastor Don and those who agree with him are likely to identify a legitimate set of concerns about what will happen in the congregation if it spends too much time and energy on inreach.

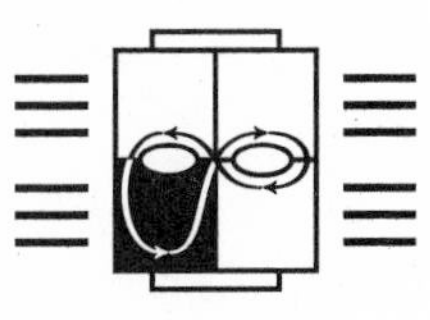

Downside Left

1. *The downside of Inreach encourages narcissism, codependence, and stagnation.* In our efforts to communicate to members that the congregation's role is to nurture them spiritually, we can overdo

Polarity Management® Map

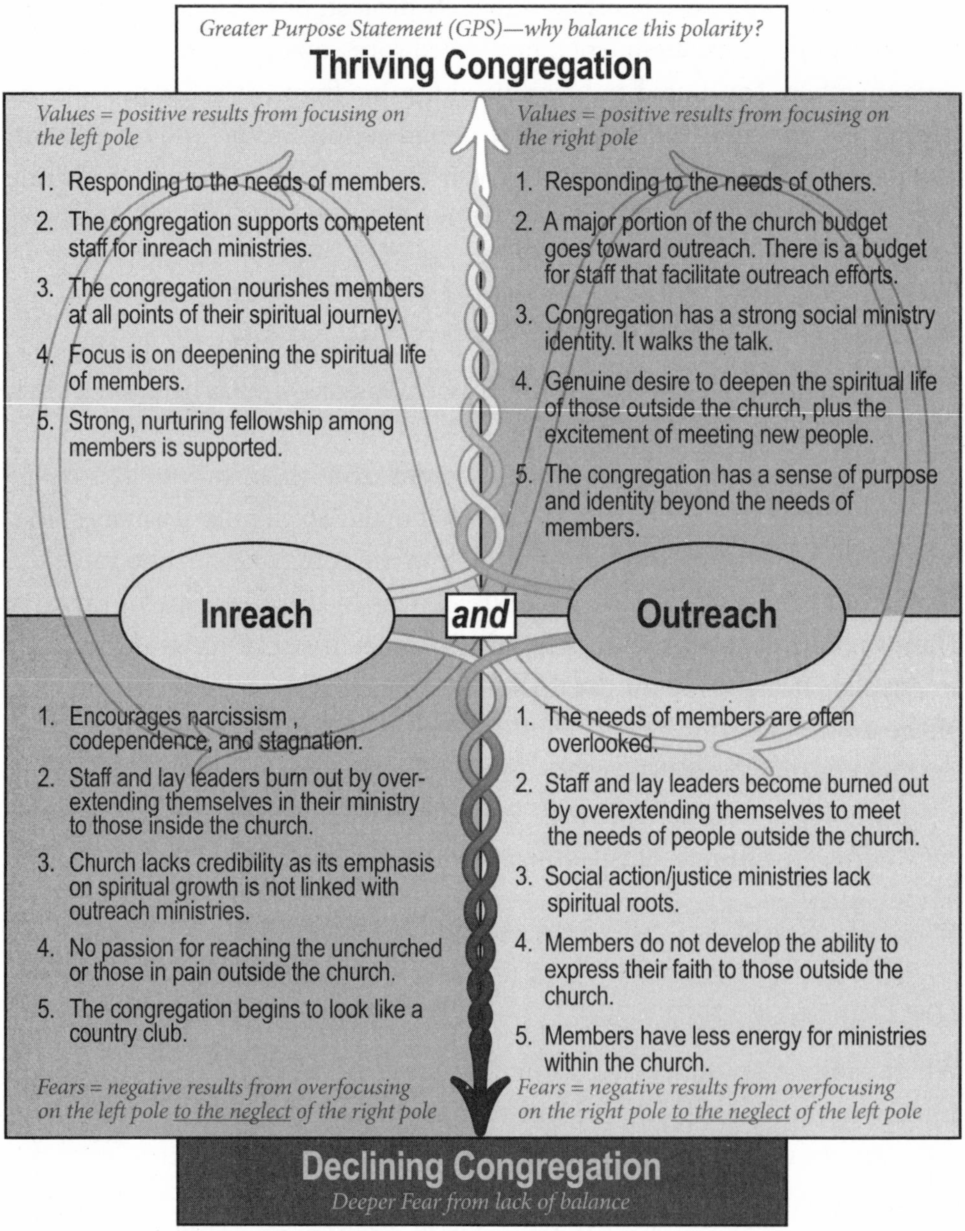

Greater Purpose Statement (GPS)—why balance this polarity?

Thriving Congregation

Values = positive results from focusing on the left pole

1. Responding to the needs of members.
2. The congregation supports competent staff for inreach ministries.
3. The congregation nourishes members at all points of their spiritual journey.
4. Focus is on deepening the spiritual life of members.
5. Strong, nurturing fellowship among members is supported.

Values = positive results from focusing on the right pole

1. Responding to the needs of others.
2. A major portion of the church budget goes toward outreach. There is a budget for staff that facilitate outreach efforts.
3. Congregation has a strong social ministry identity. It walks the talk.
4. Genuine desire to deepen the spiritual life of those outside the church, plus the excitement of meeting new people.
5. The congregation has a sense of purpose and identity beyond the needs of members.

Inreach *and* **Outreach**

1. Encourages narcissism , codependence, and stagnation.
2. Staff and lay leaders burn out by over-extending themselves in their ministry to those inside the church.
3. Church lacks credibility as its emphasis on spiritual growth is not linked with outreach ministries.
4. No passion for reaching the unchurched or those in pain outside the church.
5. The congregation begins to look like a country club.

Fears = negative results from overfocusing on the left pole to the neglect of the right pole

1. The needs of members are often overlooked.
2. Staff and lay leaders become burned out by overextending themselves to meet the needs of people outside the church.
3. Social action/justice ministries lack spiritual roots.
4. Members do not develop the ability to express their faith to those outside the church.
5. Members have less energy for ministries within the church.

Fears = negative results from overfocusing on the right pole to the neglect of the left pole

Declining Congregation

Deeper Fear from lack of balance

Map 6.1

the point, so that they come to assume that the congregation exists mainly to serve them. They may begin to ask, "If the church is supposed to serve my needs, why isn't it doing a better job?" and "What has the church done for me lately?" Without realizing it, we may create a codependence in which members miss the other part of the message—that deep faith results in works of mercy and charity. We may also be encouraging a spiritual narcissism, so that members believe that the congregation's work is all about them and how well they are served.

2. *In the downside of Inreach, staff and lay leaders burn out by overextending themselves in their ministry to those within the church.* Staff people know how demanding members can be. When members are unhappy about something in the congregation, they expect someone on the staff to fix the problem. When something goes wrong in their personal lives, they turn to the staff to help them through the crisis. In an effort to take care of congregants, staff members may burn themselves out. By far the greatest burnout of staff has to do with a congregation's demands that members be served well.

Congregations that experience high staff turnover may upon reflection realize that parishioners are extremely demanding. Such congregations view staff from the perspective of the "chaplaincy model." When staff members become more prophetic or challenge members to grow spiritually or to get more involved in mission, people hear the challenge from an either/or perspective, as staff members' betrayal of them. Staff members' employment is supported only so long as they make members feel good. If the staff continually pushes people to show their faith by their works or to mature spiritually, members either lobby to get rid of the offending staff members or look for a congregation that makes them feel good all the time. It is not uncommon for a pastor to have a heart attack or experience a marital breakup and for the members then to say to one another, "Why didn't someone tell us we were placing too many demands on the pastor?"

3. *In the downside of Inreach, the congregation lacks credibility, because its emphasis on spiritual growth is not linked with outreach ministries.* Excessive attention to the Inreach side can result in outsiders' having a negative view of the congregation. Church shoppers may be looking for clues to how genuine members' faith is. Do people just talk about doing works of charity for those in need, or do they follow up their words with actions? We read in

the letter of James that faith without works is dead. If we believe in a gracious God and are grateful for the benevolent universe God has created for us, we will want to be generous and benevolent ourselves. This attitude will manifest itself concretely, and visitors will witness for themselves the ways that members put their faith to work as a congregation.

4. *In the downside of Inreach, members do not feel passion for reaching nonchurchgoers or those in pain outside the church.* A congregation's overextensions in inreach will likely show up in a lack of passion for outreach to those in physical, emotional, or spiritual need. For a congregation to foster a passion for outreach, leaders need to ask congregants, "Who are the people for whom you weep?" Asking this question may take some effort, because members may not have an immediate answer. But when asked, they may get in touch with their own compassion for some group of people, whether those discriminated against because of religion, nationality, or ethnicity, or those in poverty who struggle with the increasing gap between rich and poor. Yet when we are stuck on the Inreach side of this polarity, we will focus, despite our compassion, on our desire that people minister to us, rather than on our call to minister to others in the name of Christ.

5. *In the downside of Inreach, the congregation begins to look like a country club rather than a mission outpost.* When we focus exclusively on building a warm, accepting environment for our members, we can become a virtual religious country club, whose mission is to ensure that members are happy and satisfied. We lose sight of the fact that one of a congregation's primary missions is to serve those less fortunate than its own members. To avoid sinking into this downside of the Inreach pole, we need to ensure that our warm, accepting church culture results in members' being equipped to minister to a broken and hurting world.

The Upside of Outreach

Part of the Outreach point of view is seen in the preceding list of concerns that arise when outreach is neglected. Even more of it is seen in the list below of positive outcomes for congregations that invest in Outreach.

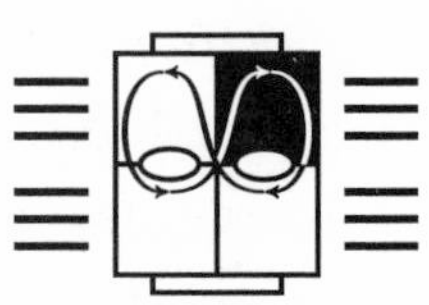

Upside Right

1. *In the upside of Outreach, the congregation responds to the needs of others.* In the Sermon on the Mount, Jesus warned the crowds to beware of false prophets. "[You] will know them by their fruits," he admonished (Matt. 7:16). The quality of a person's "fruits" is the standard by which we measure the authenticity of anyone's claim to be a person of deep faith. Has the person's relationship with God and God's people made a difference in the way she treats other people? Can we trust that she has experienced a compassionate relationship with God when she does not treat others with a similar compassion? One of the ways we can measure our growth in grace and faith is by observing the difference that comes over us when we experience joy and gratitude after engaging in outreach that addresses some need or pain around us.

2. *In the upside of Outreach, a large portion of the congregation's budget goes toward outreach, including staff people who manage outreach efforts.* A large United Methodist congregation which Roy led through a strategic-planning process exemplifies this type of commitment to outreach. The congregation employed a full-time worker to seek out and coordinate short-term mission projects for congregation members in their own neighborhood, in their city, in another part of the country, or in a Third World country. This congregation was known for its service orientation, and members would regularly spend a week of their vacation time participating in a project. Almost every two weeks in a worship service, the congregation would call forward a group of people who had signed up for a project and commission them to be ambassadors for Christ in the week ahead. This congregation attracted people who had a passion for outreach. Even when the congregation had financial difficulties, members would not dream of cutting the budget for the mission project coordinator.

A small number of congregations claim as part of their identity being a "fifty-fifty" congregation. That is, for every dollar they spend on themselves, they spend a dollar to serve people outside the congregation. Many other congregations that do not reach so high a percentage continually strive to increase their outreach dollars.

3. *In the upside of Outreach, the congregation has a strong social ministry identity. It walks the talk.* Although mainline Christians often are not skilled or comfortable talking about a personal relationship with Jesus, they can

bear witness to their faith by the way they treat people at work, and by volunteering to help those in pain, need, or distress. As St. Francis is quoted as saying, "Preach the gospel always, and when necessary use words."

Some congregations have a mission mentality built into their identity. It's virtually part of their DNA. This identity was forged over many years of Bible study and small-group discussions that laid a solid theological foundation for their becoming a mission-minded congregation. Governing boards spend much time in discernment about financing a program that serves others. The board is aware that it is accountable to the members, who will question whether the congregation is too focused on inreach and not doing enough in outreach.

4. *In the upside of Outreach, the congregation expresses a genuine desire to develop relationships with and deepen the spiritual life of those outside the church.* When a congregation begins to address seriously the struggles of people outside its membership, old, simplistic views of others begin to be challenged. Significant engagement with people outside the congregation can result in church growth and in the increasing heterogeneity of the congregation. Every urban setting has stories of inner-city congregations made up of well-to-do, educated white people who are unable to relate to the African American or Hispanic people living next door or across the street. Such congregations are often declining in membership and morale. If they had been more effective with their outreach, they might have experienced the rich texture of an ethnically and economically diverse congregation.

Outreach efforts tend to spice up the life of members, who may feel a sense of excitement and adventure in certain outreach efforts—engaging in what some call "Third World poverty tourism" or "disaster tourism." Getting to know new people, whether next door or across the globe, can have a transforming effect on church members as they discover that some of their generalizations about "them" do not hold water. Inevitably these members become more generous in their financial support of programs and projects that can have a positive impact on the new people they have met. They are also likely to push for designating a greater percentage of the church budget for mission outreach projects.

An example of this unfolding generosity is seen in the work of a colleague of Roy's, Antti Lepisto, a leader in the Finnish Lutheran church in both the United States and Finland, including the part of Finland that was taken over after World War II by the communists, whose influence ended only with the breakup of the Soviet Union. This part of Finland is much like America's Appalachia. Homes do not have running water or indoor plumbing. Many people are living on an income equivalent to one U.S. dollar a day. Yet these people are open to hearing about the gospel of Jesus Christ and to forming congregations. One year, Antti and his wife, Jane, took twenty people from the United States on a pilgrimage to Finland. The twenty became immersed in the lives of the people living in the impoverished region. On their return, the group decided to fund the construction of a church in one of the villages they had visited—an example of how people's generosity increases dramatically when they have had a firsthand experience with poor people.

5. *In the upside of Outreach, the congregation has a sense of purpose and identity beyond the needs of its members.* Particularly when coupled with thoughtful inreach, the challenge of effective outreach integrates faith and action. It creates a healthy discomfort with the realities of the real but sometimes hidden world. When inreach and outreach are taken together, it is much harder for members to become complacent about their faith. As the world around us changes at an increasing rate, members need continually to wrestle with issues of faith. In his book *Everything Must Change,* emergent church leader Brian McLaren tells how his views of Christianity changed as he traveled around the world witnessing the pain of Third World and Fourth World countries.[1] He concluded that large numbers of Christians do not perceive that it is Christ's desire that all of us serve the poor, the homeless, and the marginalized. These Christians' belief in Jesus seems to be focused mainly on ensuring their ticket to an eternal life in glory. Some Christians also see the degradation of our environment as positive—as a sign that we are living in the end time and that the reign of Jesus will soon begin. Hence, no effort should be expended on saving the environment. Participating in outreach can help Christians think deeply about what Jesus meant when he instructed his followers to love their neighbors.

Another byproduct of serious outreach efforts is a deeper connection with congregations of other denominations that are serious about addressing the social issues of their neighborhoods. When cooperating with other

Christian churches, we come to see ourselves as part of the larger body of Christ tackling the issues that were important to Jesus. This cooperation results in ecumenism at its best: joint efforts to put into concrete form a ministry that reflects the care and compassion of Christ.

Jesus said to his disciples, "If you try to hang onto your life, you will lose it, but if you lose your life for my sake you will find it" (Matt. 10:39, paraphrase). The congregation, as an expression of the body of Christ, is also called to lose its life and thereby discover a whole new life. How might a congregation "lose its life"? If it engages in a social-ministry project that brings outsiders into the church buildings for programs or activities, the wear and tear on its facilities will be noticeable. For example, a congregation might begin a day-care program for neighborhood children so that their parents are free to hold down a full-time job. Of course, some members will say, "These neighborhood children are going to come in here, spill stuff on our rugs, break our windows, mess up our washrooms, and tie up rooms so that we can't use them most of the time." Taking on such a venture is going to require strong leadership from the pastor and lay officers. Whether a congregation develops a preschool program or a soup kitchen or a shelter for the homeless, it will need to sacrifice having a pristine church building to find a ministry that brings new life to the congregation. It can be thrilling to serve those outside the church. Members can claim an identity as people who express their faith in action, finding a purpose in life beyond themselves. This discovery can be deeply satisfying. The pro-Outreach viewpoint contains a strong set of values described as the upside of Outreach and an equally strong set of fears described as the downside of Inreach. These two combine to constitute a strong argument for emphasizing outreach.

The Downside of Outreach

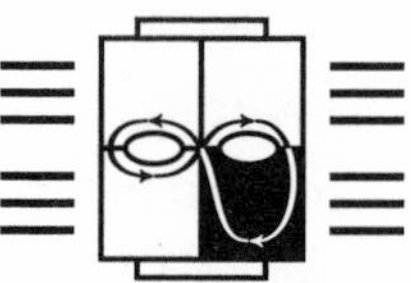
Downside Right

Now let's shift our perspective and examine the fears and values of those made anxious by Pastor Don's enthusiasm for outreach. What follows is the other point of view within the polarity map: the fears of the downside of Outreach and the values associated with the upside of Inreach. We will start with the downside of Outreach.

1. *In the downside of Outreach, the needs of members are often overlooked.* A congregation may get so caught up in ministry to those outside the church that members forget about the spiritual hunger of their own people. Roy spent an evening with a small Anglican congregation in Canada whose minister saw Christianity almost totally in terms of feeding the poor and homeless. The priest refused to take a salary, because his wife's job could support them both. The congregation sponsored a food pantry operated by volunteers seven days a week, an amazing effort, given that the congregation's weekly worship attendance rarely reached fifty. The priest spent most of his time collecting food from fast-food chains and grocery stores and was continually out trying to raise money to buy staples for the pantry.

When Roy talked with members, however, it was obvious that they were hungry for something more substantial for their own spiritual nourishment. The priest's sermons reflected a lack of preparation. The worship liturgy was conducted in a careless, perfunctory manner. The congregation did not have a choir or a Sunday school. Here was a congregation overextended on the Outreach pole to the neglect of any Inreach to its members. Very few congregations have this clergyman's passion for the hungry of the world, and one could not help admiring his devotion to this ministry, but he was neglecting the spiritual hunger of his own flock.

Outreach ministries can also be costly. One congregation in St. Louis adopted a class in an inner-city school and promised to pay for the college education of any child in the class who graduated from high school and could not afford college. Such a commitment is impressive, but did members realize how great their financial outlay could turn out to be as college tuition costs rise? To make good on its promise to these children, the congregation may in future years find itself financially strapped. This generous commitment is a concern for members who fear that their church might someday lack the funds to survive.

2. *In the downside of Outreach, staff and lay leaders become burned out by overextending themselves to meet the needs of people outside the church.* An overfocus on outreach can drain staff and lay leaders spiritually. They need the support and prayers of members of the congregation. As is seen on this polarity map, burnout can be found on both sides of this polarity. On the Inreach side, pastors, staff, and lay leaders burn out trying to minister to the

needs of members. On the Outreach side, they burn out trying to tackle too many critical social issues.

In his best-selling book *The Road Less Traveled,*[2] psychotherapist and writer Scott Peck asserts that love is giving your full attention to someone else. We do not have an unlimited capacity to give our full attention to others, however. Eventually, we need a time and place where we do not have to focus our energy but can allow our minds to roam. We also need to pay attention to the effect our efforts have on our bodies. In this polarity, we can burn out by giving our full attention to members, or by giving our full attention to prison inmates, inner-city children, or mothers on welfare.

3. *In the downside of Outreach, social action or justice ministries may lack spiritual roots.* We should be on the lookout for a paternalistic attitude that members can adopt when engaging in significant outreach. For example, we may assist a homeless person not because we see her as Christ in disguise, but so we can boost our self-image, seeing ourselves as superior to those we serve as well as to those who don't get involved. Self-righteousness is an ever-present temptation when we extend ourselves to those less fortunate than ourselves.

From a theological perspective, a kind of Pelagianism can infect some who engage in social-justice work. The Pelagian heresy is the belief that we need to—and can—earn our way into the grace of God. Pelagius acknowledged that everyone needs to be saved by grace, but he also believed that Christians could contribute to their salvation by good works. He was eventually labeled a heretic, but only after years of controversy. Of course, no heresy sticks around for long if there is not some truth in the perspective. When James says that faith without works is dead, he is pointing to the kernel of truth for which Pelagius was fighting.

Some members believe that the good deeds they do for others must certainly bring them closer to God, or that God favors them for their good works. Some loyal and dutiful church people think that their loyal service to the church must count for something in the eyes of God. From a theological perspective, the authors of this book believe that there is nothing we can do, either good or evil, that is going to change by one iota the way God sees us. We can live a pain-imposing life like an Adolf Hitler, or we can live a pain-responsive life like a Mother Teresa. In either case, we are incredibly loved by

God. This is a hard message for those who have a strong need to be dutiful and who believe that their service earns them credits with God.

It takes a mature spirituality to understand these concepts. To be sure, we should not wait until members have reached spiritual maturity before we ask them to get involved in a congregational outreach project, but we need to find ways to help members move in this direction. It is here that we move from the downside of this pole to the upside of Inreach. It is the task of inreach to build a spiritual and theological foundation for social-justice work.

4. *In the downside of Outreach, members do not develop the ability to express their faith to those outside the church.* Mainline Christians are not noted for their ability to articulate their faith to others. We are better at acts of mercy and justice. A Lutheran congregation in Florida has T-shirts printed for its confirmands carrying brief spiritual messages. For example, the front of one T-shirt says, "One man can make a difference." In large print on the back is one word: "JESUS." The confirmands were given the T-shirts once they felt comfortable wearing them and talking to schoolmates who asked about the message. This gift helped them become more articulate about their faith.

5. *In the downside of Outreach, members will have less energy for ministries within the church.* Outreach ministry can detract from the warm fellowship members experience in the congregation. If members put significant energy into reaching out to others in social ministry, they will have less energy to address the social and spiritual needs of other members. Some will not agree to serve on a committee, because they feel a greater call to minister to the poor, hungry, or disenfranchised people in their community. Congregational life and fellowship could be diminished by this stance.

The Upside of Inreach

Each point of view in a polarity includes both people's fear of the downside of one pole and the value they place on the upside of the opposite pole. The fear is based on legitimate concern about the potential loss of what is valued. Both aspects are respected when a polarity is well managed. In this polarity, the second point of view is completed by the upside of Inreach.

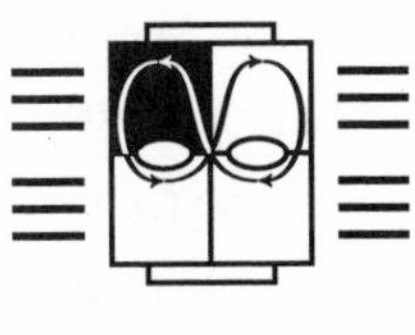

Upside Left

1. *In the upside of Inreach, congregations respond to the needs of members.* There is no doubt that a deep spiritual hunger pervades our society, and congregations that have the personnel and programs to address that hunger grow numerically as they continually focus on the spiritual nurture of members. Thriving congregations find ways to have their programs for spiritual nurture evaluated by members as a continual check on whether the programs are indeed addressing the spiritual hunger of members. In addition, when some do strategic planning, they have members reflect on ways the congregation could better address members' spiritual needs.

2. *In the upside of Inreach, healthy congregations support competent staff for inreach ministries.* A healthy congregation is well staffed. The role of this staff is not to engage in ministries that are the responsibility of laity, but to offer structure, guidance, and support. The majority of congregational staff members we meet find deep meaning in their ministries. Aspects of their work that they particularly value include:

- being the vehicle of God's love to others.
- serving as an ambassador of Christ.
- ministering to the pain of another person.
- offering a liberating word to someone awash in guilt.
- being present to ease the departure of a loved one.
- helping someone through a life transition.

Congregations are privileged to have staff members who bring great skill and dedication to this ministry.

3. *In the upside of Inreach, congregations nourish members at all points in their spiritual journey.* Deciding what programs to offer members to nurture them spiritually can be challenging but satisfying. The challenge is to determine how to address people's spiritual needs, whatever their point of spiritual growth. For those new to the faith, foundational courses are needed. These focus on the basics of the faith and offer members a spiritual grounding upon which they can build. At the other end of the faith-journey continuum are those who are part of the apostolic core of the congregation, who also need to be challenged to move ever deeper into surrender, gratitude, generosity, joy, and service. Inreach-oriented congregations continually stay one step ahead of people who want and need spiritual meat and potatoes,

not the spiritual milk offered to those less developed spiritually. Congregations may need to import specialists in theology or Bible to support these spiritual leaders, who are often called upon to lead a Bible study or theological course for other congregation members.

Walking with others on their spiritual journeys may be what nourishes some. We teach what we ourselves need to learn, and when we are asked to teach a course we ourselves have taken, we master the material at an ever-deeper level. Nonetheless, a congregation that is tending to inreach offers special support to its apostolic core. This attention may come in the form of weekend retreats, where these people can focus for a time on themselves and their own spiritual hunger. When a congregation attends to spiritually nurturing its apostolic core, the whole congregation becomes spiritually revitalized as the ministry of these people permeates the congregation.

Between newcomers to the faith and veterans of the faith are people who expect the congregation to help them strengthen their spiritual muscles. They will be put off by the repetition of material they already have learned and accepted, but they may not yet be ready for too much of a stretch. It is here that small-group ministries can be most useful. Once people are in a small group that is a match for their spiritual development, group members can decide upon a course of study or action that most would agree will nourish them in their next stage of spiritual growth.

4. *In the upside of Inreach, the focus of the congregation is on deepening the spiritual life of members.* Being fed and nurtured spiritually remains a legitimate expectation of members, and congregations that focus on inreach will likely meet that expectation. Often the chief reason people choose to join a particular congregation is for spiritual nurture. Visitors affiliate with a congregation believing that it will regularly give them spiritual nourishment. Large-membership congregations may have a greater chance of growing numerically than small-membership churches because they can offer a much greater variety of programs to address members' spiritual needs. The inreach a smaller congregation can offer is a personal touch where one is known by all, or almost all members, as well as a personal relationship with the pastor, the spiritual leader of the congregation. In congregations with an average Sunday worship attendance below fifty, inreach may consist of being

welcomed as part of the family and forming close ties with family members. Spiritual nurture takes place in the informal ways these members relate to each other.

As part of this spiritual nourishment, members share their faith stories with one another. Congregations that do inreach well look for opportunities where such interchange can take place, whether in small groups, retreats, Bible studies, or corporate worship. Members usually appreciate, once a month or so, hearing a member of the congregation in a worship service share a five-minute outline of his or her spiritual journey. When people are challenged to articulate their faith story, those listening begin to wonder what they themselves might say if given the opportunity. This is a good way to begin encouraging members to talk about their faith to nonchurchgoing people at work or in the neighborhood.

5. *In the upside of Inreach, strong, nurturing fellowship among members is supported.* It is also a legitimate expectation that whenever members experience a crisis, someone from the congregation will come to see them and to pray for and with them. In small-membership congregations, this visiting is usually done by the pastor. The exception would be congregations so small that they do not have resources to hire even a part-time pastor, or that have a contract with a part-time pastor that does not include pastoral-care visits. In these cases members provide pastoral care for each other.

When the Sunday worship attendance of a congregation grows closer to two hundred, congregations usually train lay members who have a call to a care ministry and are trained to administer it. Newcomers often base their judgments about which congregation to join on whether they believe the members will care for them when they encounter a personal crisis.

It is often said that charity begins at home. That would hold true in this polarity as members minister in love to the outer world because they continue to experience great love from God and from the staff and other members of the congregation. When care and compassion are modeled within a congregation, members are educated on how to offer care and compassion to those outside the church.

Congregations need to consistently review their internal climate to ensure that the congregation remains a place of warmth and acceptance. Unless there is a deep level of acceptance, little spiritual growth can be expected.

At root, a congregation's culture needs to reflect the grace and goodness of God, to embody the gospel story.

When inreach is strong, members enjoy a stable and safe environment where they can explore troubling issues, either events in the world around them or personal struggles. When they feel beaten up by life, they know that they can come to their church and get a hug and a listening ear. They can also expect that others will accompany them as they explore the troubling questions that haunt them.

Congregational Change from a Polarity Perspective

As with all polarities, an inherent tension exists between the two poles, and the question is this: How do we tap this tension and create a virtuous circle between the two poles in service of our mission as a congregation?

First, we must appreciate that in a polarity both sides are correct. They are also interdependent. If the tension between the poles is seen as a problem to solve and each side sees its preferred pole as the "solution," the congregation is in for a rough ride. A power struggle will ensue, wasting huge amounts of energy. This fight is as ridiculous as the one about whether inhaling or exhaling is more important. In congregational life, to follow this analogy, it doesn't matter who wins; the congregation will be blue in the face soon after the victory.

In the case of *Inreach AND Outreach*, as mentioned earlier, a congregation will pay twice for misdiagnosing this issue as a problem to solve rather than a polarity to manage. It pays first during the fight, which results in spent energy, damaged relationships, and reduced attention to either inreach or outreach. It pays the second time when one side "wins." At that point, the congregation will first find itself in the downside of the winners' preferred pole. If the overfocus on the "winners'" pole persists, the congregation will experience the second downside as well.

Congregations that have been treating a polarity as a problem need to change as they come to a new understanding of the issue they have struggled with, learning to treat it as a polarity and to manage it well. To explore the nature of this change, let's revisit Pastor Don and the congregation.

The Value and Limits of "Gap Analysis"

Often clergy and lay leaders try to bring about a change in their congregation by pointing out the problems with the present situation as well as casting a vision of where the congregation needs to go in the future. The third piece of this change proposal is a strategy to bridge the gap between the present situation (a problem) and the preferred future (a solution). The strategy looks like figure 6.1 below.

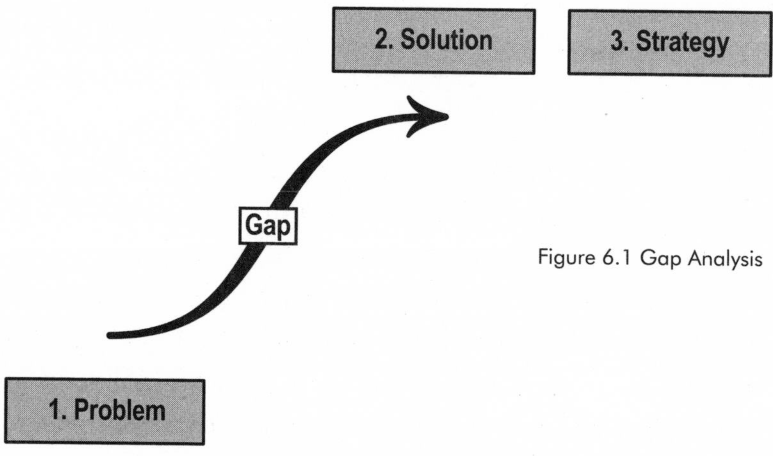

Figure 6.1 Gap Analysis

The value of gap analysis is that it calls attention to three important considerations in any change. The limitation of gap analysis is that it does not include other important considerations. When you put the gap-analysis elements on a polarity infinity loop, it quickly becomes clear what is missing. (See fig. 6.2 on page 131.) If Pastor Don and the other Outreach advocates define the downside of Inreach as the problem and the upside of Outreach as the solution, they will generate considerable resistance from members of the congregation who are legitimately fearful of losing what they value in the upside of Inreach and getting caught in the downside of Outreach. The clearer Pastor Don and the others are about their definition of the "problem" and the "solution," the greater the resistance they will encounter from those valuing Inreach. They will propose an alternate "solution," to fight for the upside of Inreach and to avoid the downside of Outreach. Both sides are trying to save the congregation from the other and they are both right!

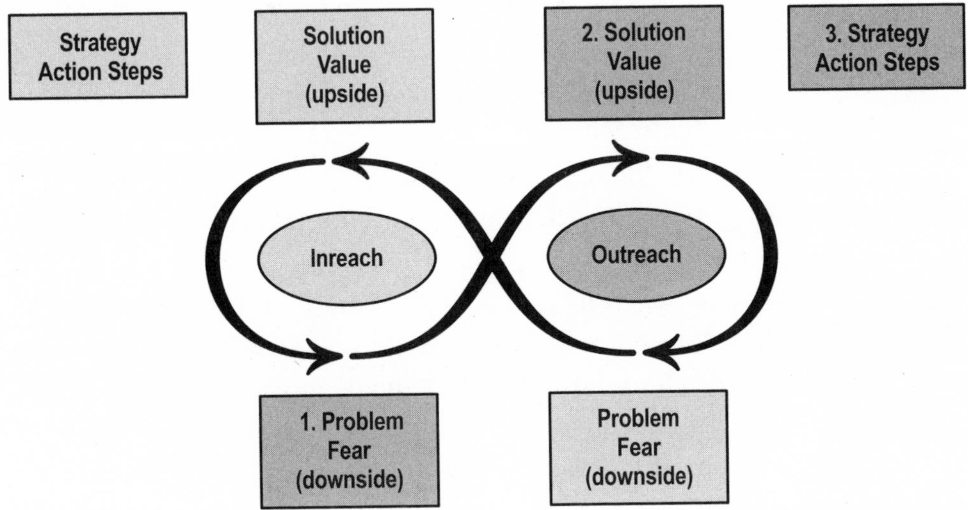

Figure 6.2 Gap Analysis

The Process of "Getting Unstuck"

So how should Pastor Don and the other Outreach advocates approach those trying to hold on to Inreach? When they experience resistance to their push for Outreach, they should first assume that there is wisdom in the resistance. Those resisting are holding on to their point of view. It contains values and fears that are important to recognize and support. If we do not listen to those holding on to the Inreach pole, and if they have sufficient power, it will be easy for the congregation to get stuck in the downside of the Inreach pole. The harder those advocating the upside of Outreach argue their point, the more those resisting will point to all the downsides of Outreach. At this point the congregation can get stuck.

From a polarity perspective, we get stuck when we are in the downside of one pole and seem unable to follow the normal flow of the infinity loop to the upside of the other pole. Instead of complaining more about the downside of Inreach and praising more strongly the virtues of Outreach, we suggest that Pastor Don try the following steps to get unstuck.

1. Start by recognizing the legitimate upsides for Inreach and commit to ensuring that action steps will not be lost.

2. Recognize the downsides of Outreach as an understandable source of concern, and commit to minimizing those downsides.
3. Ask Inreach advocates if they would help explore ways to get some of the upsides of Outreach . . .
4. . . . without losing the upsides of Inreach . . .
5. . . . in order to become a thriving congregation.

In figure 6.3 on page 133, notice that steps 1 and 2 affirm the values and fears of those supporting Inreach. It is their point of view. Also, after raising the question in step 3 about how to "supplement" inreach with outreach to add the upsides of Outreach, Pastor Don in step 4 reaffirms the upside of Inreach. This is important, because those favoring Inreach are likely to assume, from an either/or perspective, that to support the outreach effort will undermine the inreach effort. This process for getting unstuck involves saying at the beginning (step 1) and again almost at the end (step 4) that Pastor Don is not asking the inreach advocates to let go of their preferred pole. Indeed, he assures them they must hold on to it because a thriving congregation (step 5) needs both.

Another way to say it: The effort by Pastor Don and other advocates for more outreach needs to be seen as a segment of an ongoing infinity loop rather than as a problem (the downside of Inreach) with a solution (the upside of Outreach).

If Pastor Don and the other outreach supporters misdiagnose the situation and see it as a problem to solve rather than as a polarity to manage, their perspective will radically undermine the ability of the congregation to thrive for the following reasons:

1. The misdiagnosis will reduce the likelihood of the congregation's ever moving through the necessary self-correction from the downside of Inreach to the upside of Outreach, because of the resistance it will create among those fearing the loss of inreach.
2. If the resistance is overcome, the process of getting to the upside of Outreach will be slower and more painful than necessary.
3. If the congregation gets to the upside of Outreach, the ministry will be unsustainable and eventually move into the downside of Outreach.

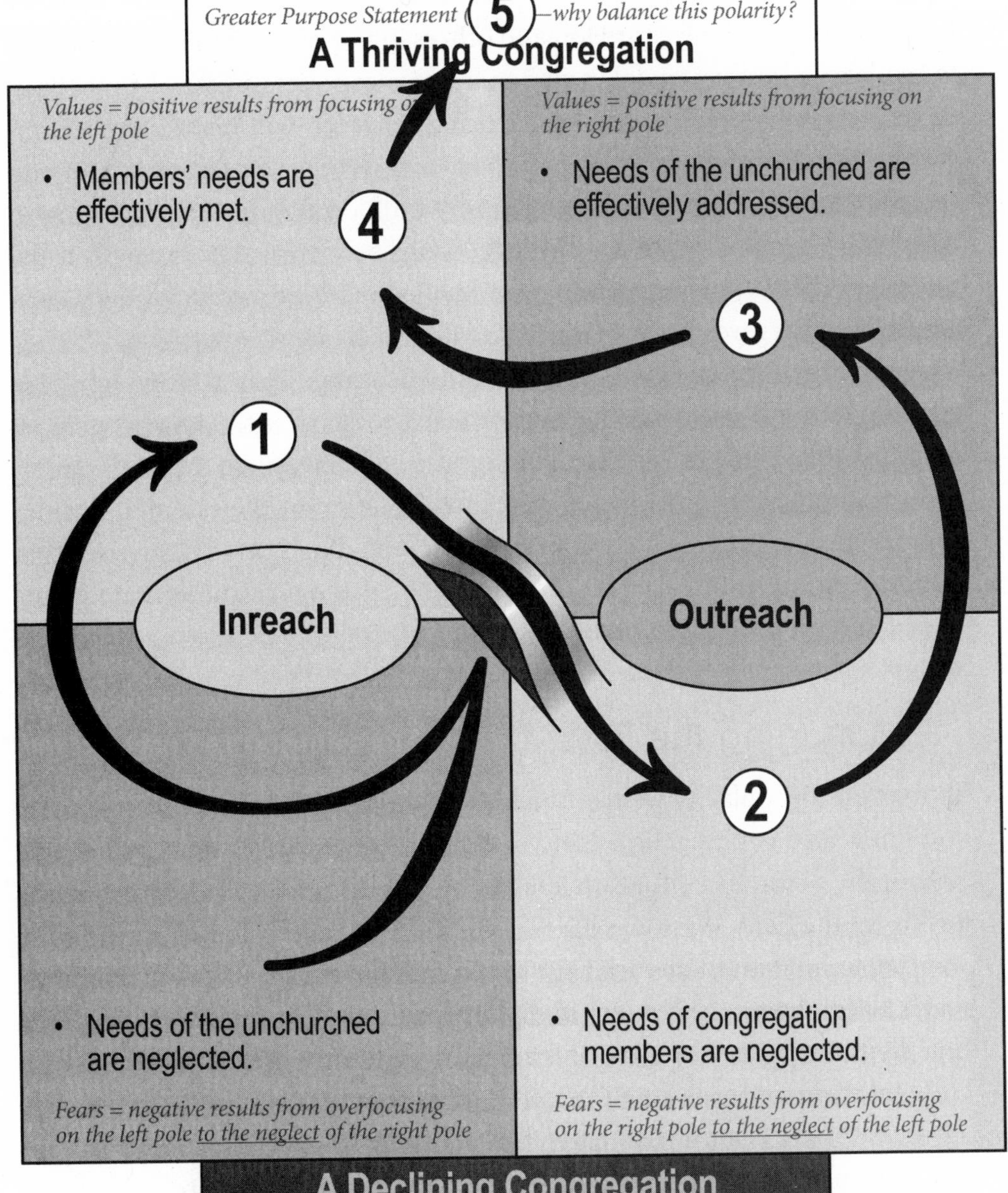
Getting Unstuck
Greater Purpose Statement (5)—why balance this polarity?
A Thriving Congregation
Values = positive results from focusing on the left pole
• Members' needs are effectively met.
Values = positive results from focusing on the right pole
• Needs of the unchurched are effectively addressed.
4
3
1
2
Inreach
Outreach
• Needs of the unchurched are neglected.
Fears = negative results from overfocusing on the left pole to the neglect of the right pole
• Needs of congregation members are neglected.
Fears = negative results from overfocusing on the right pole to the neglect of the left pole
A Declining Congregation
Deeper Fear from lack of balance

Figure 6.3

4. All of the above will happen in the midst of self-righteous indignation, frustration, the departure of disillusioned members, and a vicious circle leading to the Deeper Fear: a declining congregation.

If the issue is seen by Pastor Don and others in the congregation as a polarity to manage, a power struggle will be seen as a complete waste of time. Both those favoring inreach and those favoring outreach will realize the need to get the benefits of both upsides to have a thriving congregation. How do you maximize both upsides and minimize both downsides? Pay attention to Early Warnings and build on the suggestions below for Action Steps. If the suggested Early Warnings and Action Steps don't quite work for your congregation, disregard the ones that don't fit and create your own.

In identifying Action Steps, we would encourage Pastor Don and those creating or implementing the Action Steps to start with steps to gain or maintain the upside of Inreach. This approach will reaffirm that the congregation is not asking the Inreach advocates to let go of the essential upsides of Inreach. The congregation is willing to invest efforts on making clear that Action Steps must be taken to ensure that the upsides of Inreach are maintained and even strengthened.

Managing the Polarity Poorly: Early Warnings

To manage any polarity well, it is helpful to agree on Early Warnings that let you know as a congregation that you are getting into the downside of one pole or the other. In a situation like Pastor Don's, we would recommend focusing on the Early Warnings for the downside of Outreach first, since those wanting to hold on to inreach have a legitimate fear of the downside of Outreach. Recognizing the content in the downside quadrant of Outreach is the first step toward assuring the Inreach advocates that they have been heard and that their concerns are respected. The second step is to say, "We not only agree that there is a downside to Outreach, but we are willing to work with you to identify Early Warnings that will let us know when we are getting into that downside so that we can make corrections before it becomes a significant problem for our congregation."

As you examine these Early Warnings and combine them with your own, we encourage you to choose phenomena you can measure. The more easily measured they are, the more useful they will be. Think of something you can count that would either increase or decrease, or something that would start or stop happening. We have attempted to pay attention to this guideline in our suggestions.

Early Warnings for the Downside of Outreach

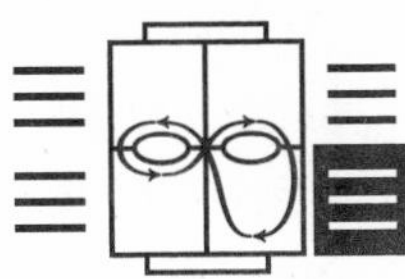
Early Warnings Right

1. The budget item for inreach ministries continues to decline.
2. The congregation has not had an adult baptism in years.
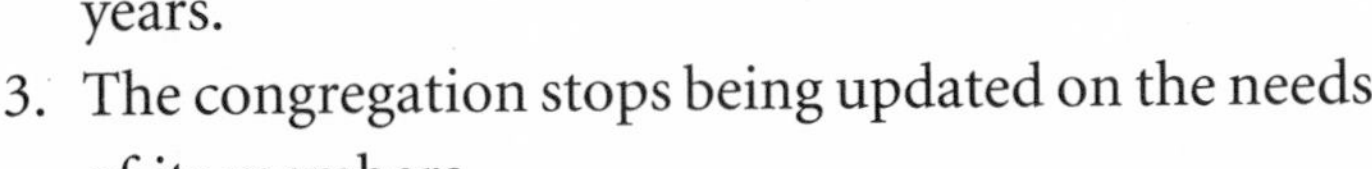
3. The congregation stops being updated on the needs of its members.
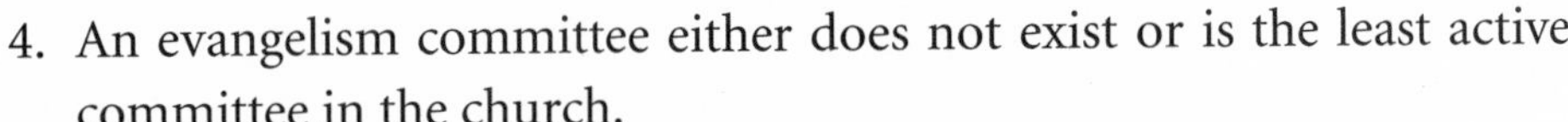
4. An evangelism committee either does not exist or is the least active committee in the church.
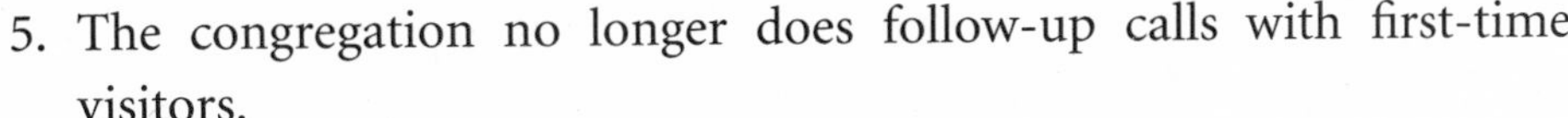
5. The congregation no longer does follow-up calls with first-time visitors.

Early Warnings for the Downside of Inreach

Early Warnings Left

1. The congregation rarely pays its full benevolence apportionment, because the emphasis is on paying its own bills first.
2. The congregation has made no provision for helping hungry people who knock on its doors.
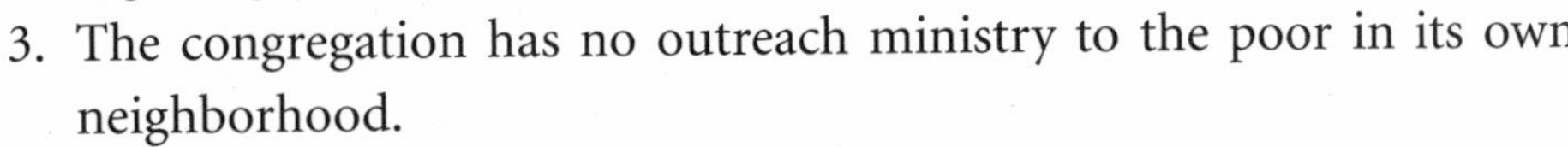
3. The congregation has no outreach ministry to the poor in its own neighborhood.
4. The average age of congregants continues to rise, because youth and young families are no longer attracted to this congregation.
5. The congregation feels more like a country club than a mission outpost for the unchurched and the broken, because it does little or nothing to address current social problems.

With a clear understanding by both Inreach and Outreach advocates that this is a polarity to manage, and with a shared commitment to maximize both upsides and minimize both downsides, Pastor Don and his congregation are much more likely to be a thriving congregation with an effective combination of inreach and outreach.

Managing the Polarity Well: Action Steps

Pick some Action Steps from the suggestions below for the upside of Inreach, or create your own. A consideration of Action Steps for Outreach follows. Map 6.2 on pages 140–141 illustrates Action Steps and Early Warnings for this polarity.

Action Steps for Inreach

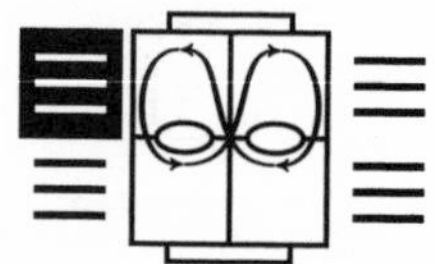
Action Steps Left

1. As church membership grows, competent staff members are hired to bring quality and variety to congregational programs and educational opportunities.
2. Whenever a member experiences a personal crisis, he or she receives immediate attention from either the clergy or trained lay ministers. This care of members is monitored closely by senior clergy and key lay leaders.
3. The congregation has periodic intergenerational meals and projects intended to promote deeper caring among members of all ages.
4. Conflicts are addressed head-on and brought to resolution, keeping the church climate warm and accepting. This is a High-leverage Action Step that applies to both upsides.
5. Opportunities for spiritual enrichment abound as planning and care go into learning and fellowship events to address the needs of congregants at various levels of spiritual maturity.

   Members are invited to sign up for a course on writing a spiritual autobiography. Contained in this spiritual autobiography are all the experiences that have drawn them into a deeper relationship with God. After a number of weekly sessions working on this task, participants are invited to give a three- to five-minute summary of the most important aspects of their spiritual journey. This, then, is their witness. Sharing these spiritual autobiographies is often a rich experience, both for those sharing and for those listening. Once a person shares within the safety of a small group of fellow pilgrims in the faith, she might be more open to sharing the same highlights with someone at her workplace who is experiencing tough times. Using this approach, members also gain spiritual sustenance by reaching into their own grace-filled experiences in life. This step benefits both inreach and outreach.

STAFFING FOR GROWTH

A congregation can ensure that it remains on the upside of this Inreach pole by seeing to it that it is staffed for growth. (This is a High-leverage Action Step that applies to both Inreach and Outreach.) Congregations that want to grow try their best to raise a budget large enough to meet the spiritual needs of their own members but also to attract nonmembers. Many spiritual needs are best met by hiring a full-time or part-time staff member who can take charge of a church's program offering and significantly raise its quality. A helpful formula for determining how many staff members a congregation might hire is the ratio between the number of people who participate in a program each week and the number of program staff people the congregation needs to support. The formula, a simple one, has gained virtually universal acceptance as a guide for adding program staff. For every one hundred people who show up for a program in a congregation each week, that congregation should have one program staff member. Do not count people twice. Let's assume that a congregation averages 250 people who show up weekly for a program or worship:

- Staffed for growth: three-plus program staff members
- Staffed to maintain: two and a half program staff members
- Staffed for decline: two and one-fourth program staff members

The pastor should be considered a program staff person. A congregation with an average attendance of 250 that is staffed for growth might have (1) a full-time pastor, (2) a full-time associate pastor, and (3) four quarter-time program people, who bring excellence to music, education, youth ministry, and outreach. Support staff, such as the parish administrator, receptionist, secretary, or custodian, are not counted in this formula.

It should be obvious that the more programs of high quality a congregation offers, the richer will be its spiritual life. Yet congregations may think that their financial resources are already stretched too thin, and that adding another half- or quarter-time staff member would be a burden. Such a congregation is likely to say, "Let's wait until we've added another twenty-five people to our average attendance, and then we'll hire the next quarter-time person." Another way to look at this challenge, however, is for the governing board to say, "Let's go out on a limb and hire the next quarter-time program specialist, and within two years, that person will have paid for herself, because she will improve the quality of a program that will attract some new members."

WORKING WITH ACTION STEPS

After exploring the possibilities above and creating your own set of Action Steps for the upside of Inreach, it will be much clearer to the Inreach supporters that you are not asking them or the congregation to let go of inreach. In coming up with Action Steps for Inreach, we encourage you to ask the Inreach advocates whether they think the Action Steps to gain or maintain the upside of inreach are sufficient to ensure that the congregation will not let go of the upside of Inreach. If they are still anxious, explore with them what else could be done to make sure the upside of Inreach is not lost. When the Inreach advocates believe that there is solid support within the Action Steps for Inreach, it is time to shift focus to the upside of the equally important Outreach pole.

Action Steps for Outreach

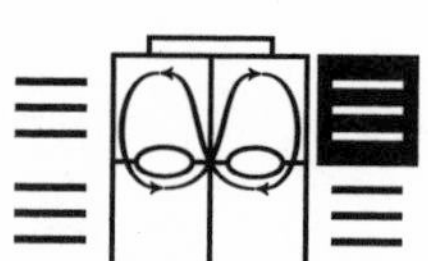
Action Steps Right

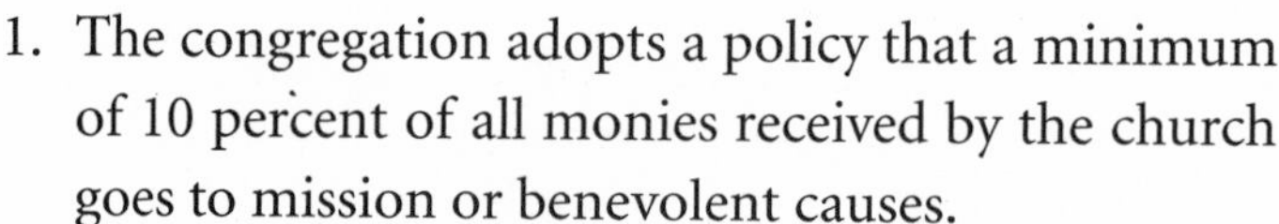

1. The congregation adopts a policy that a minimum of 10 percent of all monies received by the church goes to mission or benevolent causes.
2. Members are challenged to move toward giving a tithe of their income to church and charity.
3. Members are encouraged every year to select an outreach ministry in which they will participate.

4. The congregation has a specific plan for reaching a specific group of people who are moving into its neighborhood. Members may have identified these people by purchasing a demographic profile of their community from a church-related firm that gathers and organizes such data—for example, Percept or Visions/Decision.[3]
5. Each year the congregation plans at least one mission trip, which members take to a Third World country, where they complete a specific project.

TAKING ON CONTROVERSIAL OUTREACH MINISTRIES

The governing board of a congregation may want to discuss how many members it is prepared to lose to establish a controversial outreach project. There is no question that certain outreach efforts are going to create conflict within a congregation. Example of such ministries would be for a congregation to invite the African American teenagers in the neighborhood to use the church gymnasium for basketball, or to set up cots in the church basement in the cold months and invite homeless people to sleep in the warm building. Such a conversation can be helpful, because when governing boards are prepared to lose some members over a controversial social-ministry project, they can come to the defense of those who strongly advocate such a project.. If the governing board said it was willing to lose six families to establish such an outreach ministry and discovered that only two were lost, board members would think they were ahead. Without such a discussion, the loss of members could come as a surprise and cause hard feelings. This is a High-leverage Action Step that applies also to Inreach.

Summary

It is obvious that a thriving congregation needs to manage this polarity well. But this polarity is not easy to manage. In a way, the *Spiritual Health AND Institutional Health* polarity (chapter 3) ties in with this polarity. A key factor in that polarity is the way institutional survival nearly always trumps primary religious experience. Institutions unconsciously seek always to survive, and we can see that outreach ministries do not contribute to institutional

Polarity Management®

Action Steps

How will we gain or maintain the positive results from focusing on this left pole? What? Who? By when? Measures?

1. As church membership grows, competent staff is hired to bring quality and variety to congregational programs and educational opportunities.
2. Whenever a member experiences a personal crisis, he or she receives immediate attention from either the clergy or trained lay ministers. This care of members is monitored closely by senior clergy and key lay leaders.
3. The congregation has periodic intergenerational meals and projects intended to promote a deeper caring between members of all ages.
4. Conflicts are addressed head-on and brought to resolution, keeping the church climate warm and accepting.
5. Opportunities for spiritual enrichment abound as planning and care go into learning and fellowship events to address the needs of congregants at various levels of spiritual maturity.

Early Warnings

Measurable indicators (things you can count) that will let you know that you are getting into the downside of this left pole.

1. The congregation rarely pays its full benevolence apportionment, because the emphasis is on paying its own bills first.
2. The congregation has made no provision for helping hungry people who knock on its doors.
3. The congregation has no outreach ministry to the poor in its own neighborhood.
4. The average age of congregants continues to rise because young people and young families are no longer attracted to this congregation.
5. The congregation feels more like a country club than a mission outpost for the unchurched and the broken.

Greater Purpose Statement (GPS)

Thriving

Values = positive results from focusing on the left pole

1. Responding to the needs of members.
2. Congregations supports competent staff for inreach ministries.
3. Congregations nourish members at all points of their spiritual journey.
4. Focus is on deepening the spiritual life of members.
5. Strong nurturing fellowship among members is supported.

Inreach **and**

1. Encourages narcissism , codependence, and stagnation.
2. Staff and lay leaders burn out by over-extending themselves in their ministry to those inside the church.
3. Church lacks credibility as its emphasis on spiritual growth is not linked with outreach ministries.
4. There is no passion for reaching the unchurched or those in pain outside the church.
5. The congregation begins to look like a country club.

Fears = negative results from overfocusing on the left pole to the neglect of the right pole

Declining

Deeper Fear from

Map

Why balance this polarity?

Congregation

Values = positive results from focusing on the right pole

1. Responding to the needs of others.
2. A major portion of the church budget goes toward outreach. There is a budget for staff that facilitate outreach efforts.
3. The congregation has a strong social ministry identity. It walks the talk.
4. Genuine desire to deepen the spiritual life of those outside the church, plus the excitement of meeting new people.
5. The congregation has a sense of purpose and identity beyond the needs of members.

and **Outreach**

1. The needs of members are often overlooked.
2. Staff and lay leaders become burned out by overextending themselves to meet the needs of people outside the church.
3. Social action/justice ministries lack spiritual roots.
4. Members do not develop the ability to express their faith to those outside the church.
5. Members have less energy for ministries within the church.

Fears = negative results from overfocusing on the right pole to the neglect of the left pole

Congregation

lack of balance

Action Steps

How will we gain or maintain the positive results from focusing on this right pole? What? Who? By when? Measures?

1. The congregation has followed a norm that a minimum of 10% of all monies received by the church goes to mission or benevolent causes.
2. Members are challenged to move towards a 10% tithe of their income going to church and charity.
3. Members are encouraged every year to select an outreach ministry in which they will participate.
4. The congregation has a specific plan for reaching a specific group of people that are moving into its neighborhood. They may have identified these people by purchasing a demographic portrayal of their community from a church-related firm that can produce this kind of data, such as "Percept" or "Visions/Decision."
5. Each year the congregation plans at least one mission trip, which members take to a third world country to complete a specific project.

Early Warnings

Measurable indicators (things you can count) that will let you know that you are getting into the downside of this right pole.

1. The budget item for inreach ministries continues to decline.
2. The congregation has not had an adult baptism in years.
3. The congregation stops being updated on the needs of its members.
4. An evangelism committee either does not exist or is the least active committee in the church.
5. The congregation no longer does follow-up calls to first-time visitors.

Map 6.2

survival the way inreach does. Congregations need to remind themselves continually of their primary mission. Certainly one part of the mission is the spiritual nurture of members. Yet if a congregation overemphasizes nurture of members to the point that evangelism or social justice is not viewed as important, the congregation risks experiencing all the downside effects of hanging onto the Inreach pole too hard and too long.

Probably hundreds of church fights have been focused on this polarity. Thousands of people have left congregations because they disagreed with the way a congregation was either trying to manage this polarity more effectively or refusing to manage it better. Strong advocates of Inreach might say, "If we as a church involve ourselves in this particular outreach mission, I'm out of here," and advocates of Outreach might say, "Unless we try to do something to address this issue just outside our church doors, I'm out of here." Either way, this polarity must be managed effectively if a congregation is to thrive. It cannot be managed well as an either/or proposition.

CHAPTER 7

Nurture AND Transformation

Most members of faith communities would agree that the church is in the business of changing lives. We also know that human transformation works best when people feel loved and cared for. Together, these views establish the dilemma of this polarity. Within the church we need to love people as they are, warts and all, AND we need to help them become more devoted, generous, compassionate, faithful people. Some might genuinely ask, "If you love me just as I am, why do you want me to change into something else? Do you love me only for what you can make out of me?"

Two Faces of Ministry

Pastor Jo had two significant appointments on Monday afternoon. The first was with Mary Sue, whose husband, Herbert, had gone off with another woman, leaving her with three children under the age of ten. Mary Sue was devastated by Herbert's announcement that he was leaving her. She had had no idea that anything was amiss in their marriage. Pastor Jo was going to need to be an agent of God's care for Mary Sue and help her see that she was held in the arms of God even as she felt abandoned. She also needed to know that she had the good fortune of belonging to a congregation that embraced her and would stand by her. Here was a deeply wounded person who needed to be surrounded by love and protected in her pain.

Pastor Jo's second appointment was with Sam Jacobs, a talented and successful businessman who had allowed his pursuit of a career to take precedence over every other part of his life. His wife, Linda, had confided in Pastor Jo that Sam was putting in twelve-hour days, six and sometimes seven days a week. Overwork was ruining his health. He had put on thirty pounds over the past year—simply because he did not take time to exercise or eat well. He was getting half his meals at fast-food restaurants. He was neglecting his children, especially twelve-year-old Joey. He was also neglecting church responsibilities he had taken on six months ago. He had promised to head a capital-funds drive that would allow the congregation to add to its educational wing. He had yet to call the first meeting, though some committee members had jogged his memory about it. The campaign was scheduled to start in five months. Time was running short. Sam was attending worship services only sporadically, whereas a couple of years ago he was in church every Sunday. Jo wondered whether he even had a prayer life anymore. She planned to begin her conversation with Sam by asking when he had last taken time to pray. She would then challenge him on other responsibilities he was neglecting.

The Polarity to Be Managed

That Monday afternoon, Pastor Jo was challenged to manage this polarity well. With Mary Sue she would be attending primarily to the Nurture pole. With Sam she would be emphasizing Transformation. Over time, of course, she needed to make sure that both Mary Sue and Sam got the upsides of both poles. Let's look at how *Nurture AND Transformation* might appear on a polarity map. (See map 7.1 on page 145.)

The Upside of Nurture

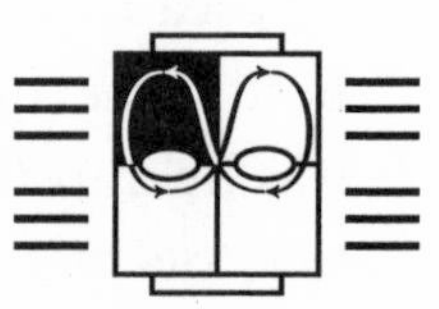
Upside Left

1. *In the upside of Nurture, the unconditional love of God is preached and lived.* When a congregation understands *Nurture AND Transformation* as a polarity, staff and members appreciate that it is possible, indeed necessary, to affirm both poles. In this context, sermons focused on nurture could be understood as half the message. At the heart of this message is a God who loves us unconditionally, regardless of our attitudes or actions. Unconditional love and forgiveness are seen as the heart of the gospel itself. When we look at Scripture as a whole, we see that all of it points to a God of great compassion. In New Testament congregations it was expected that

Polarity Management® Map

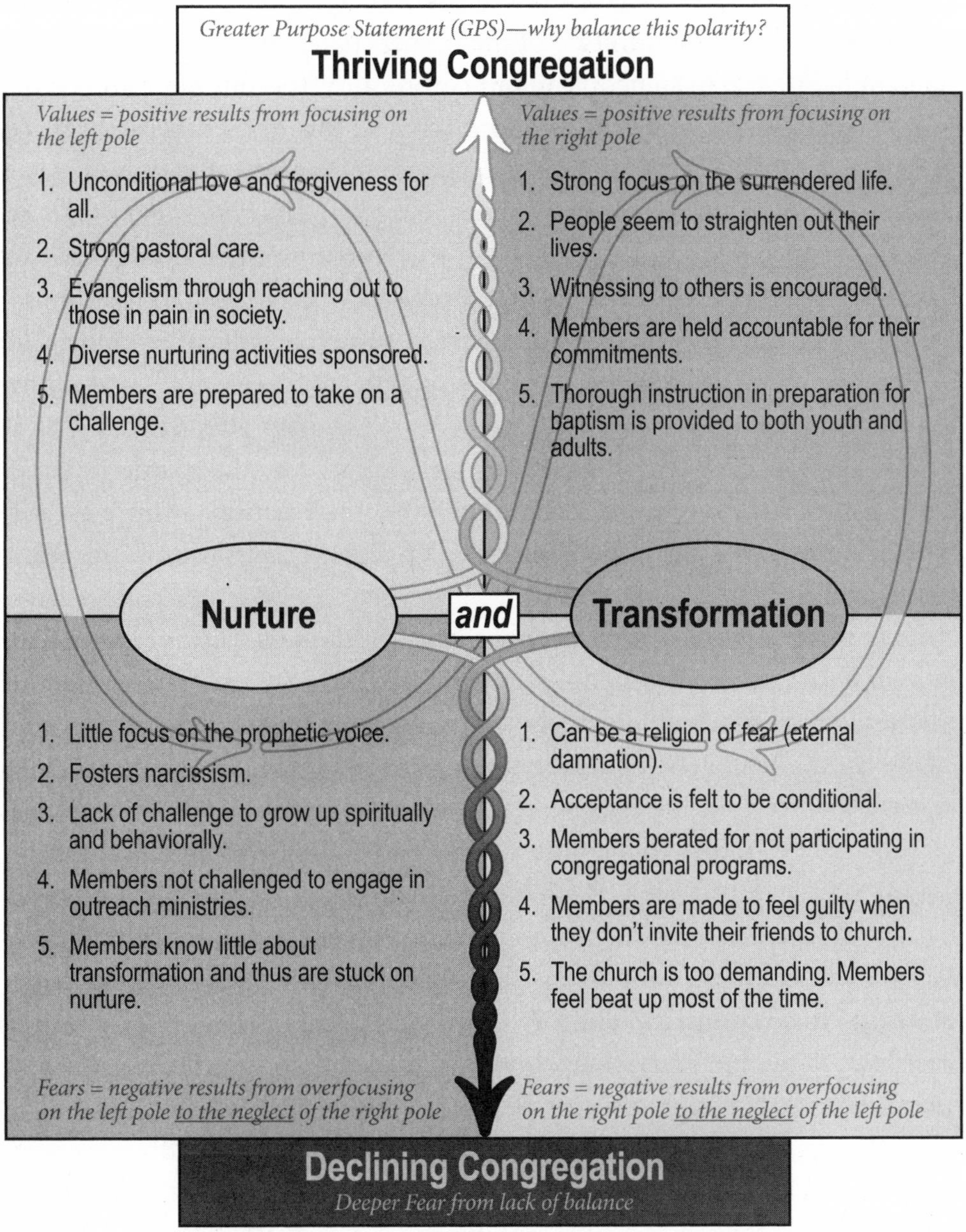

Greater Purpose Statement (GPS)—why balance this polarity?

Thriving Congregation

Values = positive results from focusing on the left pole

1. Unconditional love and forgiveness for all.
2. Strong pastoral care.
3. Evangelism through reaching out to those in pain in society.
4. Diverse nurturing activities sponsored.
5. Members are prepared to take on a challenge.

Values = positive results from focusing on the right pole

1. Strong focus on the surrendered life.
2. People seem to straighten out their lives.
3. Witnessing to others is encouraged.
4. Members are held accountable for their commitments.
5. Thorough instruction in preparation for baptism is provided to both youth and adults.

Nurture ***and*** **Transformation**

1. Little focus on the prophetic voice.
2. Fosters narcissism.
3. Lack of challenge to grow up spiritually and behaviorally.
4. Members not challenged to engage in outreach ministries.
5. Members know little about transformation and thus are stuck on nurture.

Fears = negative results from overfocusing on the left pole to the neglect of the right pole

1. Can be a religion of fear (eternal damnation).
2. Acceptance is felt to be conditional.
3. Members berated for not participating in congregational programs.
4. Members are made to feel guilty when they don't invite their friends to church.
5. The church is too demanding. Members feel beat up most of the time.

Fears = negative results from overfocusing on the right pole to the neglect of the left pole

Declining Congregation

Deeper Fear from lack of balance

Map 7.1

because Christians were loved by this compassionate God, they were to grow in their compassion for others.

This love is at the center of a nurturing congregation. It is here that we Christians transcend our likes and dislikes of people. The *koinonia* (from the Greek for "loving community") of the gospel challenges us to reach out the hand of fellowship to all people in our community. It is our hope and prayer that anyone visiting our congregations will feel this immediate acceptance. It is because of this caring that people choose to join our churches.

2. *In the upside of Nurture, pastoral care is offered by both clergy and laity.* The first thing that comes to mind on the Nurture pole is compassionate pastoral care. It is a legitimate expectation that when people in the congregation are hurting or in some kind of crisis, someone will come to their aid or just be present with them. In smaller congregations (family- and pastoral-size congregations, whose average Sunday worship attendance is below 150, including children), this care is usually offered by the pastor. In larger congregations (program- and corporate-size congregations, whose average worship attendance is above 150), this task is shifted to a pastoral-care team, made up mostly of lay volunteers.

3. *In the upside of Nurture, evangelism is done through reaching out to those in pain in society.* We should not be surprised that a congregation noted for its strength in nurturing members will extend that caring to all people, anywhere on the planet. Such caring takes seriously the admonition of Scripture that "since God loved us so much, we also ought to love one another" (1 John 4:11). Across this country we observe congregations that get involved in such ministries as rebuilding homes in communities devastated by natural disasters, sponsoring soup kitchens, running thrift shops that carry inexpensive clothing, supporting schools in Africa, and developing clinics in Third World countries. The love people have experienced in their church overflows to people everywhere. Some people who are touched by this love want to consider joining the congregation.

4. *In the upside of Nurture, a diversity of nurturing activities are underway.* Any congregational activity that brings people out to be with each other contributes to their being nurtured by the congregation. Nurturing congregations often plan intergenerational activities to get people of all ages invested in each other's lives. These can vary from potluck dinners to plays

produced by members to committee work. Some people who are nurtured by music join a choral group, finding a rich fellowship in the church choir.

As Loren Mead, founder of the Alban Institute, has declared repeatedly: If we didn't have congregations, we'd have to develop something that functioned like a congregation, where people could gather regularly and be accepted for who and what they are. When people face a crisis, they often look to the church for comfort. When church members are socked by a difficult or tragic event, they can at least come to church to find a listening ear and a warm embrace.

5. *The upside of Nurture prepares members for spiritual growth.* As we look at this polarity, we can see how each pole "needs" the other. Congregations that are in the business of changing people's lives know that people need to feel compassion and support before they are ready for the challenge to change and grow spiritually. When members don't feel loved and supported, there are limits to what we can do for them. Any challenge feels to them like simply one more putdown.

The Upside of Transformation

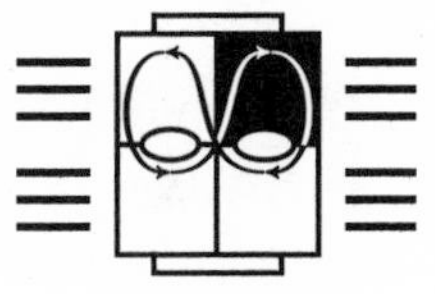

Upside Right

1. *In the upside of Transformation, there is a strong focus on the surrendered life.* To understand the thrust of this pole, we need to listen to the urgency some clergy bring to their calling. For them nothing is more important in this life than to surrender to the path Jesus taught. For conservative congregations, this means accepting Jesus Christ as one's personal savior (and for some, believing that those who do not have such a relationship with Jesus will spend eternity in hell). Denominations with a more liberal perspective may emphasize a broader view of Jesus's work, based on such passages as 2 Corinthians 5:19: "In Christ God was reconciling the world to himself."

Our observations tell us that many of us are longing for something we can't define. We can see that we are in bondage to our own false gods—our kids, our house and car, our pension plan, our family, our healthy body, our good looks, anything other than God. When we look at our relationship with God in this way, we see that nothing is more important than to surrender our lives to God. This surrender is the only thing that leads to true freedom.

When surrender to God is central, everything else begins to fall into place. We are graced with a new heart. We gain a new perspective on ourselves, our family, our job, and our possessions. Only then can we find true peace. When turning our life over to God is central, generosity and service to others become more important, and we are no longer anxious about our future. No wonder congregations that have a strong emphasis on transformation celebrate the conversion of another member.

Congregations that emphasize personal transformation generally have ways to celebrate conversion. A Roman Catholic friend of Roy's invited him to attend the Easter Vigil at her church, an African American charismatic congregation. The service started at 10:30 on Saturday night, yet to get a seat in the large church he had to arrive an hour early, as the place would be packed; and he did not leave the church until 1:00 AM.

The singing was breathtaking. At points portions of Scripture were acted out. A dance troupe offered its interpretation of resurrection. The bishop of the diocese preached for thirty minutes, and the audience was raucous in its appreciation.

Most noticeable were the catechumens (candidates for baptism), who had just completed two years of study. Clad in white robes, they were embraced by members expressing joy at their decision to be baptized. When it came time for a catechumen to be baptized, he or she walked down steps into the water of a baptismal pool at the back of the church, where a priest was waiting. Each came out dripping wet with a big smile. As each one emerged from the water, a shout that shook the rafters went up from the congregation. The celebration was glorious!

2. *In the upside of Transformation, members move toward a higher standard of moral and ethical behavior.* Once someone has surrendered her life to Christ, the clergy and congregation begin working with her to "get her life straightened out." This is especially true of people who have been living a tragic or unhealthy life, when a life problem has brought them to a place of surrender. They finally give up trying to manage on their own, and simply "turn this over to the Lord."

Breaking the addiction to alcohol is one example of the surrendered life. Because Alcoholics Anonymous is a deeply spiritual movement, the Twelve Steps of AA may stand out as a model for transformation. The first three steps are:

> 1. We admitted we were powerless over alcohol—that our lives had become unmanageable.
> 2. Came to believe that a Power greater than ourselves could restore us to sanity.
> 3. Made a decision to turn our will and our lives over to the care of God *as we understood Him.*[1]

Most AA meetings begin with a standard ritual. It goes like this: One person stands up and says, "Hi, I'm Brett, and I'm an alcoholic." The entire group responds, "Hi, Brett." Around the circle, for each person, this introduction and the acknowledgment are repeated. "Hi, I'm Janelle, and I'm an alcoholic." "Hi, Janelle!" This ritual is members' way of making confession and receiving absolution, and a deep bonding takes place when people disclose themselves and are welcomed in this way. They form partnerships that offer them a lifeline should they fall off the wagon or find themselves tempted. This partnership is available 24/7. Any time, night or day, they can be in touch with a buddy when the going gets rough. The miracle of this movement is that no paid staff people run these meetings. Each meeting has only loose ties with other AA groups. Yet this movement has continued to offer a way out for millions of alcoholics.

As we study forms of transformation, one thing that seems consistent is that people generally need a "push" to get them to commit. Alcoholics will deceive themselves into thinking that they have control of their disease, and often a confrontational meeting must be staged before an alcoholic will commit to getting treatment or other help. There is a double message to the person confronted that represents both upsides of the *Nurture AND Transformation* polarity: We love you *and* we are holding you accountable for your actions and your impact on yourself and others, including those of us who care about you. In general, transformation is not a painless process. People become aware of a loving God who has been waiting for them to surrender and to begin living a transformed life, a life that conforms to high moral and social values. Usually those who experience transformation, including alcoholics, find that they need to say "I'm sorry" to some significant people in their lives, and they learn to live in a new way.

One addiction we should not overlook is workaholism. This has been an issue for Barry and represents the *Work AND Home* polarity. Dana, his wife, along with two close friends, John and David, staged a powerful confrontation with Barry on this issue in 1994. From that point forward, the two of them have been more mindful of managing the *Work AND Home* polarity; their efforts have resulted in a more wholesome life, including better relationships with friends and family and more sustainable effectiveness in Barry's work.

Those who have committed their lives to Christ are expected to begin moving toward a higher standard of moral and ethical behavior. When we meet people we would describe as having a pure heart, we can only imagine the spiritual challenges they had to overcome to reach that state. The converted are challenged to become more generous with both their money and their service to others, and to become more forgiving of others. Graced with a new heart, they view life in a new way. God's love moves them to live in gratitude much of the time.

3. *In the upside of Transformation, witnessing to others is encouraged.* When members of a congregation have engaged in a life-transforming experience, they feel a strong need to witness to others, especially those they see living a destructive life. They would like these people to experience the joy and peace of a transformed life. Personal witnessing is something they don't tire of, as their transformation is the thing they most want to share with others.

For many compelling reasons we should talk to others about our faith in Jesus Christ. It is important that all congregations and all clergy identify those compelling reasons and make witnessing a part of the congregation's identity. This is a first step toward becoming more evangelistic and reaching out to people in the neighborhood.

4. *In the upside of Transformation, members are held accountable to their commitments.* Holding people accountable is often not a pleasant task. It requires clergy and lay leaders to make their members feel uncomfortable occasionally. Most church members have a psychological contract with their

pastor, a tacit understanding that it is his or her job to hold members accountable and even to make them feel uncomfortable from time to time. These members, after a sermon that makes them feel as though a sword has sliced them open, greet their pastor at the door and say, "Thank you very much. I needed that!" Other members, however, do not buy into this contract, and when the preacher's sermon makes them uncomfortable, they may seethe in anger and plot revenge. This reaction comes in part from an either/or mindset—they believe that the pastor has to be *either* caring *or* challenging, and of course they prefer a caring minister who does not challenge.

It's no wonder that clergy and lay leaders who remain true to the transformation side of this polarity sometimes find their lives or careers in danger. We have a multitude of examples in Scripture of occasions when the people of God stoned their prophets and crucified their leaders. Clergy need to have a solid core of congregational leaders who will come to their aid when some members begin to seek ways to have their pastor thrown out of the congregation or publicly humiliated.

In one of the first books published by the Alban Institute more than thirty years ago, *Stress, Power, and Ministry,*[2] John Harris, an Episcopal priest, talks directly to this issue. He declares that for clergy to remain true to a prophetic ministry, they need to know that there are other professions they can turn to should their pastoral ministry be taken from them. When clergy are dependent upon their role as pastor psychologically, and their profession economically, he says, they will have great difficulty embracing a prophetic ministry. Because of their dependence on the continued role of ordained minister, they continually hang out on the Nurture pole of this polarity and spend most of their time trying to make members feel good about themselves and their congregation.

Transformational congregations hold members accountable. We go back to Pastor Jo's visit with Sam Jacobs in our opening story. We believe the norms of most congregations do permit a pastor or lay leader to express concern about how a member is living his or her life. But we also believe that the transformational side of pastoral care says, "We care enough to confront." Love is caring and confronting. Caring without confronting is not love; it is cowardice. Confronting without caring is not love; it is cruelty.

5. *In the upside of Transformation, foundational courses in Christianity are offered in preparation for baptism.* A congregation that consistently works to transform people's lives offers foundational courses in Christianity for people new to the faith. Almost 50 percent of people in North America these days have had no experience with the Christian faith. What they know about Christianity they have picked up from casual comments by others or from television. Every congregation needs at least one course to introduce these people to the fundamental beliefs and rituals of the church. Some congregations rely on standard foundational courses, such as a Cursillo weekend, a Walk to Emmaus course, a Via de Christo weekend, or an Alpha course.[3] Most recently, an alternative to the Alpha Course, one more in sync with mainline theology, "Living the Questions,"[4] has been developed. When a congregation does not have at least one foundational course to offer people who know nothing about Christianity, it has in essence decided to ignore those who have never explored the Christian faith. For the most part, congregations are at a loss to know how to reach out to such people. When they take in new members, they usually do so by attracting parishioners of other Christian congregations. We will be considering this pole more directly in chapter 8, where we discuss the polarity of *Making Disciples: Easy Process AND Challenging Process.*

The Downside of Transformation

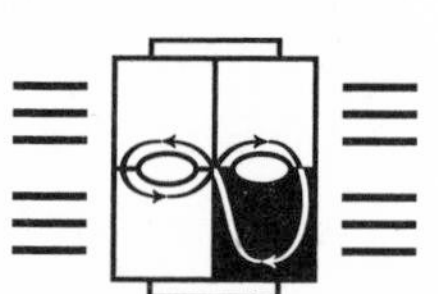

Downside Right

What negative outcomes result when a congregation overfocuses on Transformation to the neglect of Nurture?

1. *In the downside of Transformation, Christianity may become a fear-based religion.* Within liberal congregations, members are often chastised for not doing more to change the social order. They may be told, directly or indirectly, that it is their responsibility to right the injustices of the day and that unless they show up on the picket lines protesting war and violence, they are less than faithful. Members are constantly reminded of Jesus's ministry to the poor, the homeless, the marginalized, and the disenfranchised.

Conservative congregations may focus so intently on the goal of obtaining eternal salvation that members are driven by fear into a commitment to

Christ. Members hear frequent warnings from the pulpit that the devil is always trying to entice Christians to renounce their faith. They are repeatedly advised to be vigilant, lest they suffer dire consequences.

Before Vatican II, the Roman Catholic Church lacked balance with this polarity. It was caught in the downside of Transformation, with fear as a primary motivator. Members were continually reminded to fulfill their obligations as Catholics. If they ate meat on Fridays, failed to make confession before receiving communion, or did not say their "Hail Marys" each day, they would spend years in purgatory. The risk to one's faith was even more serious when one married a non-Catholic or did not have one's children baptized in the faith. Members of the Catholic Church were often left hanging, wondering whether they were doing enough to merit eternal salvation. Much of this emphasis changed with Vatican II, when the Catholic Church began to focus on the "being" of members along with their "doing." The church's teachings created a better equilibrium with this *Nurture AND Transformation* polarity by including more of the upside of Nurture.

2. *In the downside of Transformation, acceptance is felt to be conditional.* When transformation is viewed as a requirement and "necessary," people are never really sure they have done enough to be accepted by clergy and other church members. When there are clear standards about who is in and who is out, members can be quite protective about their private lives. They may believe that they would not measure up to group expectations if everything about them were revealed. They have the sense that "if people really knew me and my lifestyle, I might not be accepted anymore."

3. *In the downside of transformation, members are told they are "bad" or "wrong" when they don't respond positively to a challenge.* When a person does make a profession of faith, she is often watched carefully to see whether she responds favorably to invitations to witness or serve. When such emphasis is placed on one's personal response to transformation, those who look on passively rather than immediately accepting a challenge to serve others are not regarded favorably. They may even be viewed with suspicion as other members begin to guess why they are hanging back. At a minimum they are not regarded as highly within the congregation as those who respond enthusiastically to the congregation's program.

4. *In the downside of Transformation, members feel inadequate and guilty for not inviting their friends to church.* It is assumed that once a new Christian has experienced living the surrendered life, he or she will want to share this joy with others and will want to invite friends and family members to a similar transformation. Those who fail to invite others to share their experience are looked upon with suspicion. Members begin to question whether a new convert's transformation was for real.

5. *In the downside of Transformation, the church is viewed as too demanding.* There is such a thing as preaching too many prophetic sermons. People come to church to feel good about themselves but go home knowing that they have failed again at living the Christian life. People who haven't made a profession of faith may believe that they have failed if they do not come forward in response to the altar call.

From another perspective, a church that propounds many rules and warns of harsh consequences creates a legalistic and cruel culture. It becomes increasingly difficult for members to own up to their shortcomings, even to themselves. When we can't acknowledge our failings, we find someone else to project them on, becoming judgmental and intolerant of others.

The Downside of Nurture

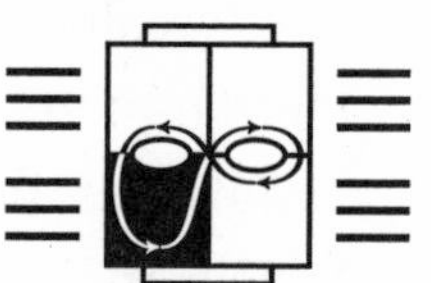
Downside Left

Now let's look at what happens when we overfocus on Nurture to the neglect of Transformation.

1. *In the downside of Nurture, the congregation lacks a prophetic voice.* The prophetic voice is lost in the pursuit of the caring voice. Leaders do not confront tough issues within the congregation or in the larger community. It becomes more difficult to distinguish the values of the congregation from those of the country club. Members resent being made to feel uncomfortable; they organize against sermons that demand something of them.

2. *In the downside of Nurture members become narcissistic.* Caring congregations can fall into the trap of allowing people to think that the sole purpose of the congregation is to take care of the parishioners. Members' narcissism becomes an issue as people become accustomed to expecting that everything will go their way or that other members will drop everything and come to their aid in a crisis. People who are not church members go church

shopping and compare congregations, trying to assess which one will offer them the best of what they are looking for. In an effort to attract new members, congregations may fall into the trap of communicating to newcomers that theirs is the most caring fellowship to be found in the area. The spiritual challenge then becomes diverting new members from focusing on what the congregation can offer them to asking, "What can I do now to best serve my Lord?" Many people stay stuck in the belief that the congregation exists mainly to support the congregants.

3. *In the downside of Nurture, members are not challenged to grow up spiritually and behaviorally.* A congregation that does a good job of caring for its members and for newcomers may have a hard time challenging them. Without a challenge, members can get stuck in an immature spiritual state. No congregation will thrive if it is not a caring community for its members, but we can overplay that strong suit. Our job is to help people grow up spiritually, rarely a painless process.

Challenging a congregation is no easy task. It requires a strategic vision that is widely accepted by congregants. But a strategic plan whose goals are "a stretch" for members will not be embraced automatically. The vision should inspire congregants to become more accepting of less attractive people, to give more generously, to wrestle with controversial issues, to receive training to become effective leaders, and to witness about their faith to nonchurchgoing friends and family members. Without such a challenge, the caring can become soft and mushy. The caring extended to fellow members should also communicate the message that we are called to grow in grace and faith—and to take risks.

Sometimes a commitment to "nurture" can mistakenly foster a reluctance to hold people accountable or to confront irresponsible behavior. In "Christianity Lite," members can take on certain responsibilities and then relinquish those obligations, thinking, "It's only the church." No one holds them accountable, because we want to be "nice" to everyone. The church as a whole loses when such behavior is not addressed. In a thriving congregation, people are asked to commit to a challenge and are held accountable to that commitment.

A strong, nurturing congregation may also fall into the trap of accepting everything a member does or believes, rather than drawing the line and affirming the basic tenets of the faith. Members are in effect told, "It doesn't matter what you believe as long as you are sincere." Irresponsible or immoral behavior is not confronted. For example, a member is allowed to show up drunk to committee meetings. Members just try to work around him. Even though members talk to each other about the irresponsibility of such behavior, no one confronts the offender directly.

4. *In the downside of Nurture, congregational leaders know little about human transformation and are thus stuck on nurture.* Often mainline clergy and church leaders know a lot about nurture but little about conversion. Many mainline clergy were born into the church and did not have a life-transforming experience in adulthood. Mainline seminaries do not have a lot to say about conversion and rarely offer courses on conversion. It is expected that seminarians, once ordained, will be managers of a congregation, offering compelling sermons and excellent pastoral care. Yet the process of shepherding an unbeliever into a faith relationship with Christ remains a mystery to many Protestant clergy.

In an exercise with clergy, we ask, "Those who were born into a Christian family, go to this side of the room. Those who came to faith through an adult conversion experience, go to the other side of the room." Inevitably, 95 percent of the clergy were born into a Christian environment. We then ask, "How many of you had a course in seminary on conversion?" Out of a group of thirty-five to fifty, three or four clergy—generally people who did not go to a mainline seminary but were trained at a fundamentalist or evangelical seminary—will raise their hands. Often this question elicits snickers. Yet when we ask the follow-up question, "How many of you believe it is your congregation's job to transform people's lives?" all the hands go up. It is then easy to point out the contradiction. Clergy believe it is their job to transform people's lives, yet they have not had a conversion experience themselves, nor did they receive any training about conversion. We think a polarity perspective can shed light on why this appears to be the case.

Map 7.2 on page 157 is a small, simplified map of the *Nurture AND Transformation* polarity containing only item 5 from each of the four quadrants of the larger map.

As we learned in chapter 2, the more we value the upside of one pole (nine on a ten scale), the more we will fear the downside of the opposite

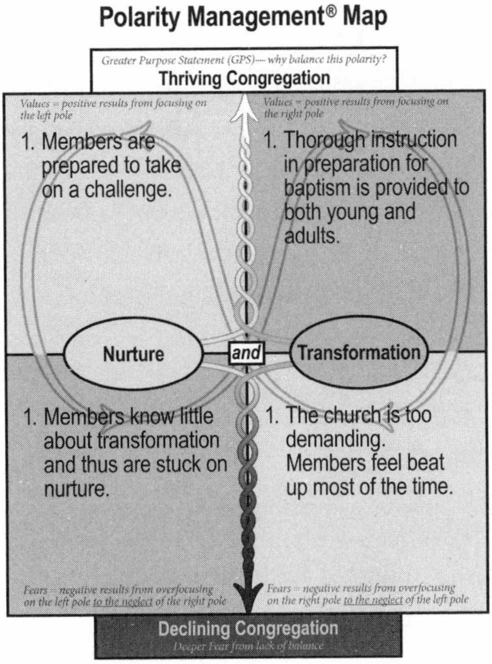

Polarity Management® Map

Greater Purpose Statement (GPS)—why balance this polarity?
Thriving Congregation

Values = positive results from focusing on the left pole
1. Members are prepared to take on a challenge.

Values = positive results from focusing on the right pole
1. Thorough instruction in preparation for baptism is provided to both young and adults.

Nurture **and** Transformation

1. Members know little about transformation and thus are stuck on nurture.
Fears = negative results from overfocusing on the left pole to the neglect of the right pole

1. The church is too demanding. Members feel beat up most of the time.
Fears = negative results from overfocusing on the right pole to the neglect of the left pole

Declining Congregation
Deeper Fear from lack of balance

Map 7.2

pole (nine on a ten scale). The more a congregation values the upside of Nurture (people are prepared to take on a challenge), the more they will fear the downside of Transformation (being seen as too demanding, where people feel beat up a lot). When you combine these values and fears with the assumption that you must choose *either* Nurture *or* Transformation, your congregation (or denomination) is likely to overfocus on Nurture.

The result of this overfocus is a drop into the downside of Nurture. When the upside of Nurture is highly valued and the downside of Transformation highly feared, the congregation is likely to be insensitive to the downside of Nurture. Congregants are also likely to overtolerate this downside, even when they are aware of it. From an either/or perspective, the assumption is that one must choose either one downside or the other. Given this false choice, people will choose the "lesser of the two evils"—for them, the downside of their professed pole rather than the downside of the pole they reject.

A typical comment reflects the congregation's overtolerance: "We have our problems, sure. But at least we aren't self-righteous and judgmental like *them*." The reference, of course, is to those church groups that prefer the Transformation pole. Overtolerating the downside of Transformation increases a congregation's fear of "them." Of course, congregations and denominations that highly value the upside of Transformation (strong advocacy for members to surrender their lives to God) will, if caught in an either/or mindset, be equally fearful of those who seem caught in the downside of Nurture (lack of support for and interest in conversion). Both sides have values essential to a thriving congregation. Both sides have legitimate fears of the downside of "them." What is needed is a polarity perspective to support both *Nurture AND Transformation.*

POLARITY PRINCIPLE 14

The more individuals or groups value the upside of one pole and fear the downside of the other pole, the more difficult it will be for them to gain access to the upside of the other pole.

As we see in Polarity Principle 14, the more strongly congregations value the upside of Nurture and fear the downside of Transformation, the more difficult it is for them to tap into the power of the upside of Transformation. This inability to tap the upside of Transformation significantly undermines the congregation's ability to thrive.

POLARITY PRINCIPLE 15

When a power struggle erupts between advocates of the two poles of a polarity, the smaller a group or the less powerful its advocates, the more it needs to be listened to.

Polarity Principle 15 points to another problem that can appear when a group adopts an either/or mindset and is unable to support both poles. If a fight breaks out in a congregation between those who favor Transformation and those who favor Nurture, people are likely to start counting heads. Whose position has the greatest support? If one side has a significantly larger number of supporters than the other, the larger group will try to use the power of numbers to ensure a stronger emphasis on its preferred pole. This reaction is understandable, especially when a group has an either/or mindset. "Let's be democratic about this. We clearly have the most votes, so it is obvious that we need to focus on Transformation [Nurture]." We know from the way polarities work that this dilemma is a setup for significant future problems, no matter which pole is supported by the majority.

If the Nurture advocates constitute a significant majority, the congregation is vulnerable to getting into the downside of Nurture. If members of this group see they are dealing with a polarity and apply principle 15, however, they will recognize that they need to pay special attention to those advocating Transformation and tap their wisdom to empower both poles. This step will allow the creation of a virtuous circle between the poles for the sake of the overall health of the congregation. If a congregation wants to thrive, it empowers the weaker pole.

Preparing for Transformation

I (Roy) have personal experience with this inability to gain access to the upside of Transformation, and I identify with much of mainline Protestantism's lack of insight into or experience of conversion. Before I relate my experiences, let me make a confession. Given my four years of training in a Lutheran seminary, I empathize with the clergy in these stories. Suppose, upon my graduation from seminary, someone had asked me, "Roy, what is your plan for transforming people's lives? What is your plan for making non-Christians into Christians? What is your plan for drawing peripheral members into becoming committed Christians? What is your plan for moving committed Christians ever deeper into compassion, love, and generosity?" To all these questions my answer would have been the same: Preach well-crafted sermons within inspiring worship experiences. Make sure there are classes for children, youth, and adults that teach the Christian faith. Finally, give people excellent pastoral care. I believed that if a pastor did these things well, lives would be transformed. All this took place in the 1960s, when I assumed that everybody believed in God and that I was there to help them understand more fully who this God was. So as I relate the following stories, I wince to recall that once I would have done exactly what these clergy did.

At one of the seminars I conducted for the Alban Institute, a clergywoman came to me after a training session and said, "A college student made an appointment to see me. He said he had had absolutely no upbringing in a church and knew little or nothing about Christianity. He thought he would like to become a Christian, and could I help him do that?" She did not even know where to begin.

What is wrong with this picture? Here is a person who had received three years of seminary training yet didn't have a clue about how to introduce Christianity to someone new to the faith. I responded: "Well, do you think you could teach him some basic ways to pray and then ask him if he would take some time to pray every day?" Yes, she thought she could do that. "Could you also ask him to read a chapter of one of the Gospels each day and write down his questions about those readings? And could you ask three people of mature faith in your congregation to meet with this student every Sunday morning to reflect with him on what he was experiencing when he prayed, and discuss some of the questions he had about his Bible readings?" Yes, she thought she could do that. "Do you think you could meet with him once a month to introduce him to some of the basic tenets of the faith?" Yes, she could do that. She appreciated my help and became excited about engaging this student in such a process. She certainly would be more prepared the next time she faced such a situation.

A second story: Through the Alban Institute, I offered a four-day seminar called "Transformational Spirituality." One afternoon I decided to scrap the agenda and simply ask the eighteen people present to share stories of how they had been a catalyst in bringing an adult to faith in God and Christ. The group sat in silence for about five minutes. No one had a story to tell about bringing an adult to faith in Jesus Christ.

Finally one participant spoke up. "This isn't a story about how I brought anyone to faith, but it is a story of a strange experience I had several months ago." She had been asked to visit a man in the hospital, someone she did not know. Much to her surprise, as she visited with the man, he quickly began to lay out his life to her. He had been through a number of traumatic experiences in the preceding months, and now his heart had given out on him.

"Well," I said, "that was a perfect opening for you to talk to him about turning his life over to God and experiencing a whole new way of living—one filled with compassion, joy, and peace. You could have said, 'If you think you would be ready to do that, I would be willing to pray with you as you surrender you life to God.'"

"Well," said the pastor, "I wouldn't know how to do that." Soon the rest of the group began to chime in. "Maybe you could get him and his wife into some marital therapy." Others began to build on that idea. I could not believe it. Here were eighteen clergy who, given an opening to talk about a living faith in Christ, turned to psychology as an answer to this man's problems. These pastors' responses can be explained partly by their lack of training in seminary, and partly by our strong preference for the upside of Nurture and our fear of the downside of Transformation.

Managing the Polarity Poorly: Early Warnings

There is a downside to Nurture and to the exclusion of Transformation, and it isn't pretty. Congregations get there when they combine either/or thinking with valuing the upside of Nurture and fearing the downside of Transformation. This mindset results in a lack of awareness that the congregation is in the downside of Nurture and an overtolerance of this downside when it is acknowledged. It is overtolerated because it is contrasted with the downside of Transformation, which is considered worse. As a result, many congregations have trouble getting into the upside of transformation. Of course, all of these dynamics are equally true for those congregations that value the upside of Transformation and fear the downside of Nurture.

Seeing this issue as *either* Nurture *or* Transformation will lead to power struggles, hurt feelings, and each side's chronic frustration with the other. This impasse contributes to the congregation's declining rather than thriving. Congregations that want to thrive need to appreciate this issue as a polarity to manage and address it from a both/and (polarity) mindset. Then they will have to be mindful about getting to the upsides of both poles. Let's look at Early Warnings for each downside that will help alert us that we are overfocusing on either pole.

Early Warnings Left

Early Warnings for the Downside of Nurture

1. The congregation continually capitulates to parents who insist that their children cannot possibly attend confirmation classes, because the schedule or the time required conflicts with extracurricular sports or other school activities. Maintaining well-designed spiritual-formation experiences is often difficult in a congregation that overvalues nurture, as leaders are continually asked to compromise their requirements for participation.
2. The congregation has no foundational course in place for people new to Christianity, such as Cursillo, Walk to Emmaus, Via de Christo, Alpha, Living the Questions, or an adult catechumenate program.
3. When certain members make newcomers feel unwelcome because of their race, ethnicity, sexual orientation, lifestyle, or economic status, the offenders are not confronted about their behavior.
4. When the pastor suggests to the board that the congregation adopt a nine- to twelve-month catechumenate to prepare newcomers for membership, the board strongly objects.
5. The clergy and staff spend an inordinate amount of time coddling congregants who seem upset much of the time. There is little backing by the board for confronting these congregants on their lack of spiritual maturity.

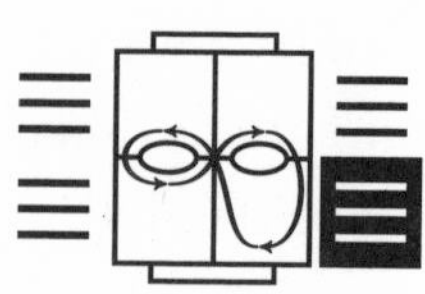
Early Warnings Right

Early Warnings for the Downside of Transformation

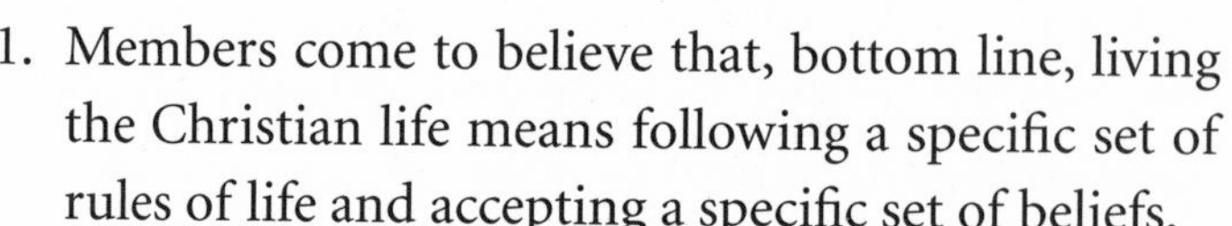

1. Members come to believe that, bottom line, living the Christian life means following a specific set of rules of life and accepting a specific set of beliefs.
2. Members rarely find a "peace that passes understanding" and are continually off balance, not knowing if they have done enough, believed strongly enough, given enough.

3. Members remain secretive about their personal lives. They fear that if church leaders really knew the way they lived their daily lives, they would not be accepted in the church.
4. Members are expected to conform to specific cultural and political values.
5. People who question some basic tenet of the faith are ridiculed or ostracized.

Managing the Polarity Well: Action Steps

Now let's revisit this polarity and look at some Action Steps congregations have taken to manage it well. Thriving congregations are effective at getting to the upsides of both poles. Some of these Action Steps might work in your congregation, along with others. What's important is to see the Action Steps in the context of a polarity to manage, and to do what works best for your congregation to get to the upside of both poles. Map 7.3 on pages 166–167 illustrates this polarity.

Action Steps to Maintain the Upside of Nurture

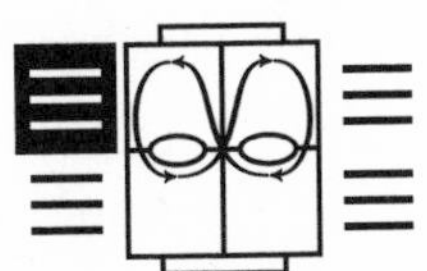

Action Steps Left

1. Hire a coordinator of pastoral care or recruit a lay volunteer coordinator who has a heart for pastoral ministry and who knows the congregation well. The coordinator does not make a lot of pastoral calls. Instead he or she trains, coordinates, and supports lay visitors who do the day-to-day ministry. He or she also regularly assesses who needs pastoral attention, and both clergy and laity are assigned to conduct these calls.
2. Annually sponsor a banquet to honor all congregants involved in pastoral-care ministries. Facilitators of small-group ministries should be included in this celebration.
3. Appoint a pastor-parish relations committee that will meet regularly with the pastor, attempting to understand the pastoral load he or she is carrying.

4. Create a training program for small-group ministry facilitators. (See appendix A for four key small-group polarities.)
5. As a congregation, ask members to sign a behavioral covenant committing themselves to:
   a. Introduce themselves after worship to someone they have never met or don't know well, before going to talk with their usual circle of friends.
   b. Refuse to participate in any conversation when someone begins to speak negatively about another member or member of the staff. Members would be instructed to say to that individual, "I'm sorry. We have agreed we would not participate in negative conversations about others in the congregation. You will need to talk with that person directly. I'll go with you if it is too much of a challenge for you to go alone."
6. Plan diverse activities that allow members to get to know each other better. Activities that bring members of all ages together include:
   - gathering for a church picnic
   - producing a musical
   - holding a strawberry festival or other celebration after church, outdoors if weather permits
   - taking a trip to see a musical or play
   - assembling a pictorial directory of the congregation
7. Produce CDs members can use for their prayer time, perhaps during a long commute to work. A CD might include centering prayer, chants, and Scripture readings. Another segment might guide members in debriefing their day and putting it into perspective, given the grace God showers on them.[5]
8. Provide healing opportunities for members. For example, an increasing number of congregations designate "healing stations" in the sanctuary during the distribution of Holy Communion. After members have received the communion elements, they may go to a corner of the sanctuary or kneel at a certain section of the communion rail, where hands are laid upon them and prayers of healing are offered. Still other congregations hold special healing services.

Action Steps for Transformation

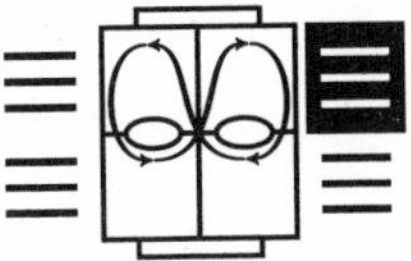

Action Steps Right

1. Regularly invite outside speakers to address significant issues such as racism, the need for affordable health care, or the exploitation of immigrants or undocumented workers.
2. Sponsor a pilgrimage every year, taking people to the Holy Land or to a Third World country. Pilgrimages, when planned carefully, can be powerful transformational experiences. One example is a pilgrimage to trek the Himalayas. The mountains are beautiful and awesome, yet Nepal is the world's fifth-poorest country.
3. Plan a series of presentations for your community on Scripture and theology, promoting your congregation as a place where the Christian faith is treated with spiritual depth and intellectual integrity.
4. Sponsor a four-week series of workshops for your community on the basics of prayer, including three separate segments in each workshop: lecture, experience, and group sharing.
5. Confirm teenagers when they have made a personal profession of faith, rather than because they have attended a series of confirmation classes.
6. Regularly set aside five minutes in the worship service for a layperson to talk about what moved him or her to become a committed Christian.
7. Develop a variety of service projects that will have a transformative effect on people. Going to a Third World country and living in the homes of poor people can have a significant impact on participants. To be sure, something similar can happen closer to home, especially if there is direct and sustained contact with poor people, but more stories are told about how people's lives are changed when they live for a short time among the poor.
8. Develop small-group ministries. Supporting such ministries can be an Action Step for both Nurture and Transformation. Within small groups, members often feel accepted and nurtured by others, but they can also challenge each other, sometimes serving as the catalyst for profound change.

Polarity Management®

Action Steps

How will we gain or maintain the positive results from focusing on this left pole? What? Who? By When? Measures?

1. Appoint oversight taskforce for pastoral care.
2. Create training program for small group ministry facilitators.
3. Promote a congregational norm that members are to introduce themselves to someone they don't know before going to talk with friends.
4. Sponsor a variety of intergenerational social events.
5. Develop a CD for commuters that remind them of the grace that surrounds them.
6. Develop a healing ministry utilizing both clergy and laity.

Early Warnings

Measurable indicators (things you can count) that will let you know that you are getting into the downside of this left pole.

1. Confirmation instruction is sacrificed when school sports have priority.
2. No foundational course for new Christians.
3. Unwelcoming members are not confronted about their behavior.
4. Board rejects catachumenate for newcomers.
5. Continually upset members are coddled.

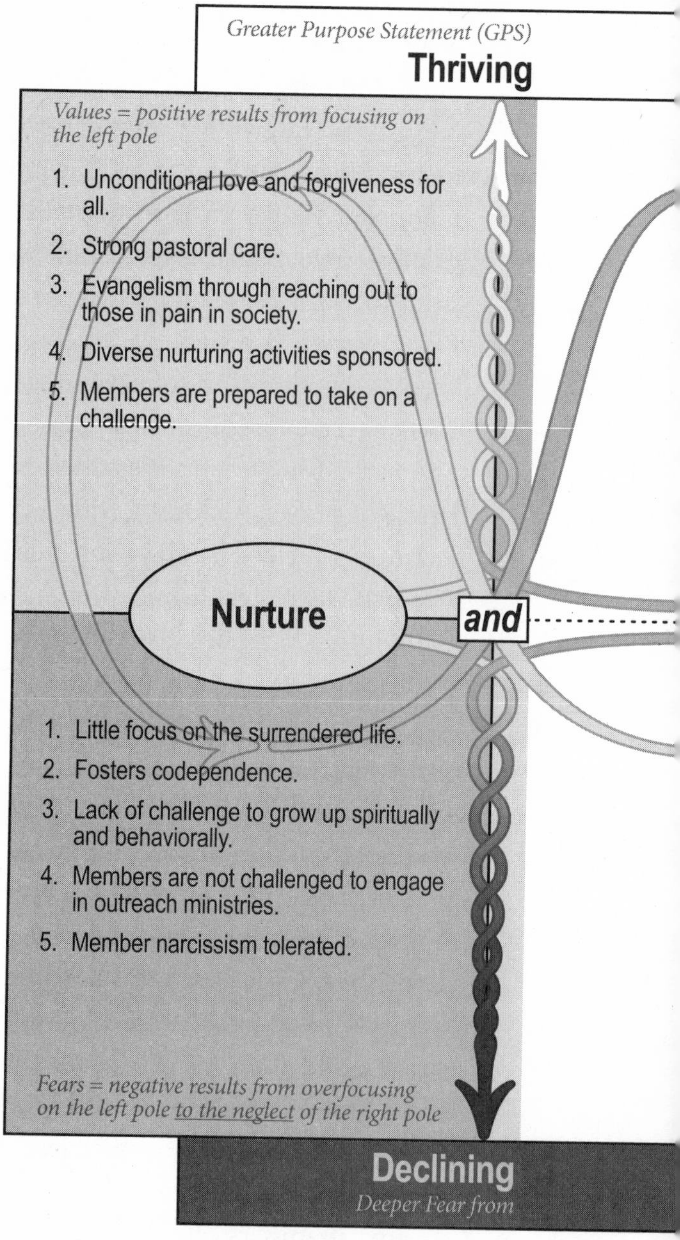

Greater Purpose Statement (GPS)

Thriving

Values = positive results from focusing on the left pole

1. Unconditional love and forgiveness for all.
2. Strong pastoral care.
3. Evangelism through reaching out to those in pain in society.
4. Diverse nurturing activities sponsored.
5. Members are prepared to take on a challenge.

Nurture **and**

1. Little focus on the surrendered life.
2. Fosters codependence.
3. Lack of challenge to grow up spiritually and behaviorally.
4. Members are not challenged to engage in outreach ministries.
5. Member narcissism tolerated.

Fears = negative results from overfocusing on the left pole to the neglect of the right pole

Declining

Deeper Fear from

Map

Why balance this polarity?

Congregation

Values = positive results from focusing on the right pole

1. There is a strong focus on the surrendered life.
2. Conversion is celebrated.
3. Witnessing to others is encouraged.
4. Members are challenged to engage in outreach ministries.
5. Thorough instruction in preparation for baptism is provided to both youth and adults.

and **Transformation**

1. Can be a religion of fear (eternal damnation).
2. Minimal pastoral care.
3. Members are berated for not participating in congregational programs.
4. Members made to feel guilty when they don't respond positively to a challenge.
5. The church is too demanding. Members feel beat up most of the time.

Fears = negative results from overfocusing on the right pole to the neglect of the left pole

Congregation

lack of balance

Action Steps

How will we gain or maintain the positive results from focusing on this right pole? What? Who? By when? Measures?

1. Support for clergy "back-up" plan.
2. Sponsor service based pilgrimages each year.
3. Establish one fundamental course in Christianity.
4. Establish a group to teach prayer life to unchurched.
5. Create Nurture & Transformation-focused sermon series.

Early Warnings

Measurable indicators (things you can count) that will let you know that you are getting into the downside of this right pole.

1. Members feel that Christianity is following a set of rules.
2. Members cannot really feel at peace.
3. Members are secretive about their personal lives.
4. Members are expected to conform to specific cultural and political values.
5. People who question some basic tenet of the faith are ridiculed or ostracized.

Map 7.3

Summary

Thriving congregations manage to be good at both *Nurture AND Transformation.* As we have mentioned before, you may have different names for the poles and may want to edit the content in the map. You may also want to come up with additional Early Warnings and Action Steps if some or most of ours are not on the mark for your congregation. We encourage you to change the map to fit your congregation, although we strongly recommend that the whole congregation or a representative group participate in crafting the changes.

CHAPTER 8

Making Disciples: Easy Process AND Challenging Process

The polarity we will consider in this chapter is about the way we help people develop into mature Christians. This polarity applies to both children and adults, although we will focus primarily on adults who have had no meaningful experience in a church and are new to Christianity. For some denominations, accepting people into the Christian faith involves preparation for adult baptism. This polarity asks how deep and wide that preparation should be. The polarity also applies to those who were raised in a church but have drifted away and now want to reestablish a relationship with a congregation, perhaps one affiliated with a denomination other than the one they were part of as youth.

Making Disciples

Pastor Arthur had two calls to make on Monday evening. He was following up with two couples who were newcomers to St. Mark's. Both couples had indicated that they were interested in joining the church. Margaret and Paul were the parents of two children who had recently started coming to Sunday school at St. Mark's. As a couple they had decided to attend worship services rather than just dropping off their children at the church. After formalities and coffee, Pastor Arthur indicated to Margaret and Paul that St. Mark's had two ways for newcomers to become members of the church—a short process and an extended process. The short process involved prospective members' coming to three new-member classes in the evening. The extended process involved a nine-month catechumenate. They could become full members of the church by either process. Pastor Arthur hoped they would choose the extended process, as he wanted the couple to be grounded in the basics of the faith, but if that was too much of a challenge, they could opt for the shorter process. As Margaret and Paul reflected on what was going on in their lives, both concluded that they simply would not have time for the extended sessions. They chose the three new-member classes.

Pastor Arthur's next visit was with Naomi and Stellar Gunderson. He had performed the couple's wedding ceremony eighteen months earlier, and now Naomi was in her sixth month of pregnancy. Naomi, although born into a Jewish family, had never been active in a synagogue. Stellar had been raised as a Lutheran and, despite some years of drifting, had stayed active in his church. When Pastor Arthur gave them the choice of joining through a short process or an extended process, the couple asked for time to think about it. They said they would call in a few days to let him know of their choice.

When Naomi called back, she told Pastor Arthur that they both would like to become part of the adult catechumenate. Naomi was still struggling with whether to convert and had decided she needed to make an informed decision; hence she wanted to delve deeply into Christian faith and practice. Stellar wanted to join her in that exploration. This choice seemed to suit them both in their quest for an authentic expression of the faith, one they could embrace fully.

The Polarity to Be Managed

At the heart of this polarity is a question: Should our congregation make it easy for people to join and have strategies in place to help them mature in the faith as they participate in congregational life, or should we offer people a challenging membership process that grounds them in the basics of the faith from the outset? As with all polarities, the answer is yes. We can easily see that both poles have something positive to offer.

This polarity addresses two methods of orienting newcomers to the Christian faith and helping them move into deeper discipleship as followers of Christ. We are assuming that congregational leaders agree that the chief task of any Christian congregation is making disciples of newcomers and members. Our task is not to be "successful" or to become a famous congregation, or to increase our budget every year. Our task is to foster and sustain lives of discipleship. This polarity follows on the heels of the *Nurture AND Transformation* polarity and offers several ways to begin the transformation process with new members. The primary question is, how do we go about this task?

The goal of making disciples and sustaining them is always the same—surrendered lives committed to Christ's way of living, loving, and dying. This task is particularly challenging in North America, where individual interests and needs are highly valued. When people search for a congregation, they focus on what a congregation has to offer them. "Yes, the Episcopal congregation in our area has a great organ and choir, but we hear that the local Lutheran church has an outstanding preacher. And our kids heard wonderful things about the youth group at the United Methodist church." Denominational loyalty not being what it used to be, people look for a church that will meet their needs.

Every congregation knows this process and tries to put on its best face when greeting visitors. Members would like to impress visitors with all the good things the congregation has to offer. Yet once people have joined a church, it is the congregation's job to help them focus less on what the congregation can do for them and more on the transformation to discipleship, so that eventually these new disciples will ask, "What can I do to serve my Lord?" Is that transformation an easy process? Is it painless? Hardly!

Congregational leaders need to think carefully about how that transformation will take place. Sometimes we find ourselves proclaiming a surrenderless Christianity. We invite people just to come and hang out with us—attend our worship services and social gatherings, and maybe even put something in the offering plate. We do not expect people to surrender their lives to Christ, to make a commitment to a life of discipleship. Yet some of the greatest difficulties we have in Christian congregations are rooted in this lack of commitment. Reluctant stewardship, lack of volunteers, and indifferent social ministry can all be traced to this core issue.

Given that deep faith commitment is an essential ingredient in congregational life, what will our stance be when people ask to become members? Do we start right at the entry point to develop strong, committed Christians, or do we make it easy for them at this fragile point in their faith development and devise other methods to invite them to move deeper into surrender and commitment?

To see this issue on a polarity map, refer to map 8.1 on page 173. In the context of this map, let's look at each of the quadrants in more detail.

The Upside of the Easy Process

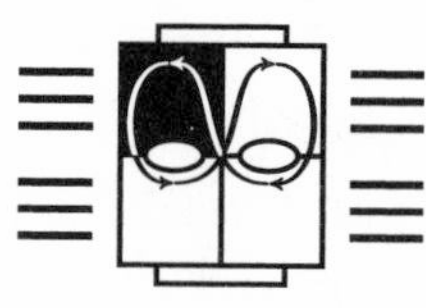

Upside Left

1. *On the upside, the Easy Process is nonthreatening.* It does not require a whole lot of commitment to say yes to three new-member classes. We can also go easy within this short orientation and allow members to join even if they miss a session or two—or don't attend any. The easy process fits a mobile society in which people are heavily committed to other aspects of their lives.

2. *On the upside, the Easy Process is quick and easy for staff and lay leaders.* It is far less demanding on clergy, other staff members, and volunteers. Some clergy like it because it leaves parishioners with the immediate impression that the congregation is growing numerically. When newcomers join quickly, the membership increase looks good on the record and costs the congregation less in staff time.

3. *On the upside, the Easy Process is grace-centered.* It assumes an open-ended approach to spiritual maturity. Once people have joined or become members through adult baptism, it is assumed that they will take advantage of opportunities offered by the congregation to move more intentionally into surrender and service. In this way, the process is grace-oriented. Newcomers don't need to work their way into the congregation by submitting to an extended process. We minimize the hoops people have to jump through to become full-fledged members.

Some biblical passages support speedy acceptance into the Christian faith. In the book of Acts we read of the Ethiopian eunuch who asked, after Philip had given him a quick orientation to the Christian faith, "What is to prevent me from being baptized in this river now?" Philip saw no obstacle, and the two of them immediately waded into the river, where the eunuch was baptized.

Polarity Management® Map

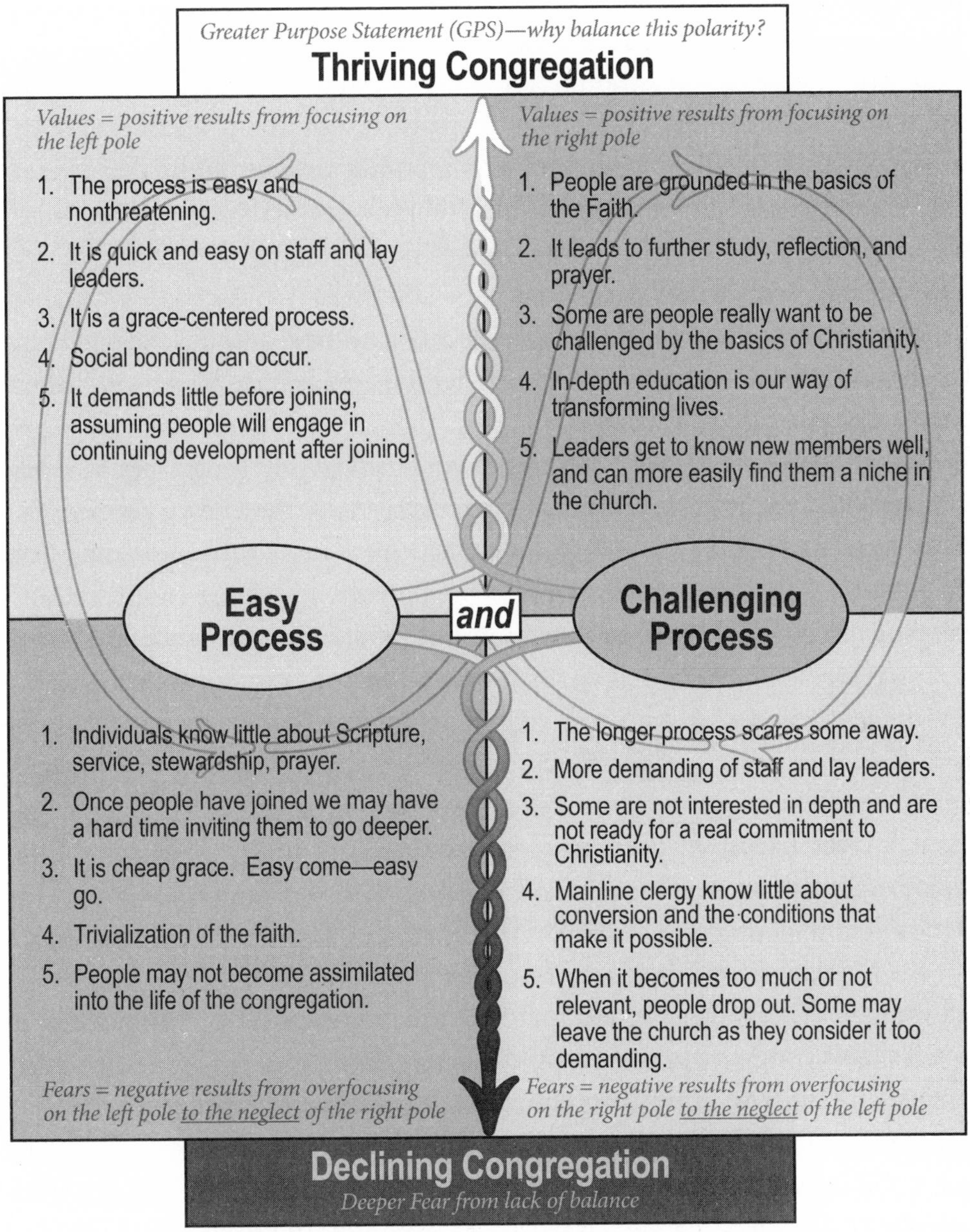

Greater Purpose Statement (GPS)—why balance this polarity?

Thriving Congregation

Values = positive results from focusing on the left pole

1. The process is easy and nonthreatening.
2. It is quick and easy on staff and lay leaders.
3. It is a grace-centered process.
4. Social bonding can occur.
5. It demands little before joining, assuming people will engage in continuing development after joining.

Values = positive results from focusing on the right pole

1. People are grounded in the basics of the Faith.
2. It leads to further study, reflection, and prayer.
3. Some are people really want to be challenged by the basics of Christianity.
4. In-depth education is our way of transforming lives.
5. Leaders get to know new members well, and can more easily find them a niche in the church.

Easy Process *and* **Challenging Process**

1. Individuals know little about Scripture, service, stewardship, prayer.
2. Once people have joined we may have a hard time inviting them to go deeper.
3. It is cheap grace. Easy come—easy go.
4. Trivialization of the faith.
5. People may not become assimilated into the life of the congregation.

Fears = negative results from overfocusing on the left pole to the neglect of the right pole

1. The longer process scares some away.
2. More demanding of staff and lay leaders.
3. Some are not interested in depth and are not ready for a real commitment to Christianity.
4. Mainline clergy know little about conversion and the conditions that make it possible.
5. When it becomes too much or not relevant, people drop out. Some may leave the church as they consider it too demanding.

Fears = negative results from overfocusing on the right pole to the neglect of the left pole

Declining Congregation

Deeper Fear from lack of balance

Map 8.1

4. *In the upside of the Easy Process, social bonding can occur.* These shorter processes are usually led by clergy. The new-member class offers an opportunity for newcomers and their pastor to have some time together and get to know each other. Clergy are busy people, and many members do not get to spend extended time with their pastor.

These shorter sessions should not, however, consist mainly of lectures by the pastor pushing church doctrine but rather should engage participants in dialogue. In this way, clergy get to know much more about these newcomers and can recommend to them further involvement in both study and service. Such a process also allows newcomers to begin developing closer relationships with fellow class members. Longtime members are probably deeply involved already with other longtime members and have less energy for getting to know newer members, so helping newcomers bond with other newcomers is a good thing.

5. *On the upside, the Easy Process demands little before people join, assuming that they will take the initiative to go deeper once they become members.* The hoped-for result when newcomers participate in a simple new-member orientation is that they will quickly become involved with the congregation, participating fully and being drawn into the lives of other members.

The Upside of a Challenging Process

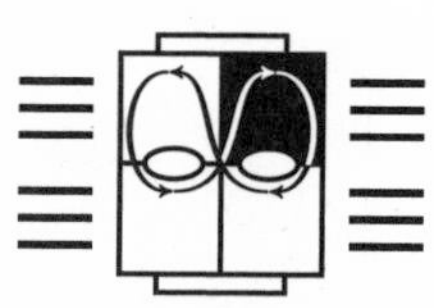

Upside Right

Programs in the adult catechumenate (a course of instruction in basic Christian teachings leading to full church membership) have become a major offering of national denominational offices. The North American Association for the Catechumenate has been formed to link denominations so that they can share material and review ways of promoting it within their congregations. Several denominations have produced liturgies for use in public worship throughout the process so that catechumens receive the support and blessing of the entire faith community.

In these programs, congregations are sometimes invited to pair each catechumen with a more seasoned Christian from the congregation's apostolic core. Each mentor is invited to walk with a newcomer throughout the entire course, relating to him or her individually on matters of faith and practice. The mentor continues to pray for and with the catechumen throughout the course.

Those entering this course are asked to practice certain home rituals daily. Instruction is given in the basics of prayer, and options for prayers before a meal are offered. The newcomers are also asked to read from one of the Gospels every day. They are asked to consider becoming more generous in their contributions to church and charity.

With this basic overview of what a longer process could offer seekers in the faith, we begin with the upside of such a course.

1. *In the upside of a Challenging Process, people are grounded in the basics of the faith.* When people take part in a yearlong study process, they will probably come away with a more profound sense of the Bible as a guide to life. They will also gain some familiarity with the theology of the denomination and ways of practicing the faith. Generosity and service are the likely byproducts of the extended study period.

With a grounding in the basics of the faith, these people are more likely to want to go deeper following the yearlong course. They are less likely to feel embarrassed to start attending a Bible study if they know enough about the Bible not to fear that they look foolish in the eyes of fellow members.

Our basic expectation of those entering the faith is that these catechumens will more fully experience the reality of being part of a community, part of the body of Christ. We can expect that lifelong relationships with other members in the course will begin to take shape. They will come to know that within a congregation, members come to care for one another and learn to walk with fellow Christians when they are in need.

These catechumens will also be taught the connection between faith and action, that faith without works is dead. They will be encouraged to keep in their prayers the people for whom they weep. This activity might lead to their joining in social-action or social-justice work during or after the course.

2. *On the upside, a Challenging Process leads to further study, reflection, and prayer.* The normal practice within a catechumenate class is that participants are asked to pray and to read a portion of Scripture daily. As they meet with their mentors in a class setting, participants are asked about their prayer life—what they find meaningful and what they find challenging. Often catechumens are taught two forms of prayer, *kataphatic* prayer (talking

to God) and *apophatic* prayer (moving into silence and listening to God). They can be asked about the things they seem to be hearing from God. In relation to their daily reading in a Gospel, they can be asked what questions they bring to the class about their readings. Once the course is over, there is a greater chance that these people will continue the practice of daily prayer and Bible reading. In this way, the catechumenate grounds people in the praxis of Christianity. They become practicing Christians.

3. *In the upside of a Challenging Process, newcomers who desire an in-depth process will enjoy the challenge.* While many people would be put off by such a prerequisite for joining the church, others have been wrestling with faith issues for a lifetime and want to test whether Christianity has answers to issues that have long troubled them. A colleague of Roy's, Charles Kiblinger, former dean of the Episcopal cathedral in Denver, instituted a six-month catechumenate for new members. Every month he would put an ad in the *Denver Post* that said: "If you want a faith that has spiritual depth and intellectual integrity, we are the people to come and see." What he found were well-educated individuals who wanted to know if "this Christianity thing" had any intellectual integrity. Some had developed the notion that they would have to sacrifice their brains to become Christians. Kiblinger's ads drew people to one of the primary strengths of mainline denominations: namely a theology that has intellectual integrity. Kiblinger reported that from twenty to thirty people joined the congregation every year because of this ad and that his congregation was for a time the fastest-growing Episcopal parish in the city. Although we tend to think that people would never commit to a longer process to explore the Christian faith, we need to know that this is exactly what some people are looking for. They would clearly be disappointed if offered a quick summary of the faith in a three-session new-member class.

4. *In the upside of a Challenging Process, in-depth education is our way of transforming lives.* Most mainline denominations do not offer altar calls at the end of worship, inviting those ready to commit their lives to Christ to come forward. We do not teach "four steps to Jesus," with an invitation to follow those steps and to commit to a life of discipleship. We do not try to shoehorn simplistic answers into such a complex life issue as when life begins or the mystery of death. Our process is to invite people on a journey

that will lead them to wrestle with difficult life issues and to become familiar with the complexities of a life of faith.

Martin Luther wrote the small and large catechisms to orient people to the Christian faith. He believed in an educated laity. He believed that study is the way people are brought to a faith relationship with God and Christ. Education in matters of the faith is mainline Christians' way of instilling faith. When we look at what most congregations offer their members, study and worship are offered most. It is our way of developing faithful Christians.

5. *In the upside of the Challenging Process, leaders get to know new members well and can more easily find them a niche in the church.*

We have looked at both upsides and at the positive results from tapping the best of the Easy Process and the best of the Challenging Process. Now let's look at the negative results of overfocusing on one to the neglect of the other.

The Downside of an Easy Process

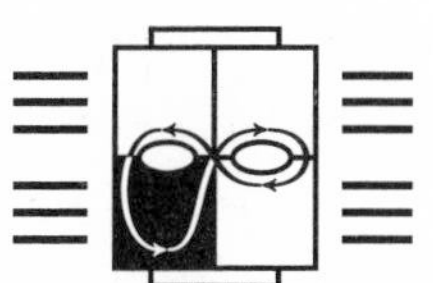

Downside Left

1. *In the downside of the Easy Process, individuals will know little about Scripture, service, stewardship, and prayer.* When people receive only a quick orientation to the Christian faith, we end up with new Christians who know little about the basic tenets of the faith. A large majority of church members are biblically illiterate, and we can point to this practice as a reason. Many members do not attend Bible study classes at least partly because they fear looking stupid in knowing so little about Scripture—contrary to the perception that new Christians, after joining a faith community, will continue to explore the deeper dimensions of Christianity. Once they join, people often pick up the bad habits of other members, who rarely engage in any study. Another bad habit they may adopt is attending worship infrequently. A congregation's low expectations of its new members may also explain why their stewardship is often poor. They may wonder, "Why engage in sacrificial giving when we don't really get why Christianity is important in the first place?"

2. *In the downside of the Easy Process, once people have joined, it may become difficult to encourage them to go deeper.* Another negative is the short period of time for the pastor and congregants to get to know these new join-

ers. They miss the bonding that could take place between them and other new members in a yearlong process. A shorter process also makes it more difficult for congregation leaders to help newcomers find a volunteer role within the church that suits their talents and their motivation to serve. Congregants who don't find a meaningful role in the church generally become less active and less invested in congregational life.

3. *In the downside of the Easy Process, it is grace-filled, but the grace is cheap.* It is true that allowing people to join quickly without much preparation for membership emphasizes grace, but it is cheap grace. Grace may not have great significance for these new Christians if they did not come to comprehend the *two* gifts of God, namely law and grace. Not having been grounded in the law of God, they may come to view grace as meaning, "Anything we do is OK." In short, grace becomes meaningless. They may have missed the point that even though God forgives us all our sins and shortcomings, we are continually invited to become more godlike—or to become true disciples of Jesus by patterning our lives after his healing, his compassion, his wisdom, and his mission. Moreover, church membership, when acquired so easily, will likely have less meaning for them. Easy come, easy go!

4. *In the downside of the Easy Process, the faith can be trivialized.* We risk trivializing Christianity by communicating to people that we can explain most of it in three easy sessions. "This Christianity stuff is really no big deal. All you have to do is love God and love your neighbor a bit." This oversimplification may explain why members are reluctant to bear witness to their faith to friends and family members, and hesitate to invite them to church. The Christian faith had very little time to take root and become firmly ensconced in their lives. What would these new members have to say to others about their faith when they never really "got it" in the first place themselves?

5. *In the downside of Easy Process, people may not become assimilated into the life of the congregation.* Another negative has to do with there being such a short period of time to really get to know these new joiners, and their missing the bonding that could take place between them and other new members. This shorter process also makes it much more difficult for the congregation to find them a volunteer role within the church that suits their

talents and their motivation to serve. The congregation won't have enough information about these newcomers to make such a recommendation.

The Downside of a Challenging Process

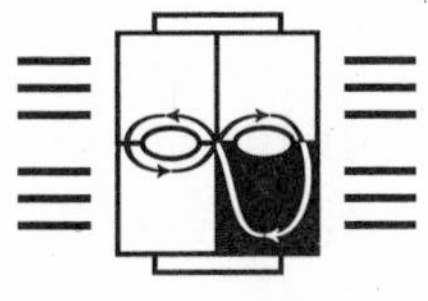
Downside Right

The majority of mainline congregations on this continent would not think of asking potential members to make a commitment to a yearlong process such as the catechumenate. We need to face squarely the downside of this pole and be aware that we will meet resistance from some potential congregants. If there were no downside to this pole, the majority of congregations on this continent would offer a yearlong process—but few do.

1. *In the downside of a Challenging Process, the longer course of study drives some away.* Some visitors who would like to join the church will be discouraged from doing so by a yearlong process. They may only want to put their toe in the water rather than diving in. These people may know that if they go to the church across the street, they can join without attending any classes. It is for this reason that congregations should have two ways to join, an easy way and a challenging way. People who are intimidated or put off by the request that they engage in a nine- to twelve-month process have another way of joining the congregation.

In a society known for quick fixes, we need to understand that our asking prospective members to engage in an extended process may simply be beyond their comprehension. The complaint of clergy that they often have difficulty getting newcomers to attend even three new-member sessions says something about the expectations of some newcomers.

2. *In the downside of a Challenging Process, it puts greater demands on clergy and lay leaders.* Should those who organize a long process do it poorly, some people may realize partway through that they are not getting much out of the experience and quit coming, making them, their sponsors, and the course leaders feel uncomfortable. Then, feeling embarrassed about having dropped out, the newcomers may decide to leave the church before even joining it. It is for this reason that the longer process needs to be in capable hands. The planning and execution of a theologically sound course demand

much of church leaders. Smaller congregations may not have lay leaders who can put before newcomers a well-crafted product. To ask the pastor to be the sole presenter would claim a huge block of time in his or her schedule. Some clergy would say that they don't have the time. In some cases, lay leaders would resent the pastor's spending so much time on a few newcomers.

3. *In the downside of a Challenging Process, some newcomers are not ready for an in-depth study or a deep commitment to Christianity.* Newcomers have many reasons for joining a church—and some folk are not on a quest for a deeper spiritual faith. Some may want to join because they have friends who belong to the church. Some congregations that operate a highly regarded day-care center may offer a reduced fee to congregation members, and people may join only for that reason. Such congregations may see this offering as an evangelical outreach. When these people join, the congregation has a chance to get to know them better and see if they can be drawn deeper into community and service. These people would never join if they were asked to become part of a yearlong catechumenate.

4. *In the downside of a Challenging Process, many mainline clergy know little about conversion and the conditions that make it a possibility.* Mainline clergy who received little training in seminary about the Christian conversion experience may not know how to develop a process to make such a life-changing event possible. If this is true, a longer course results only in newcomers' accumulating more facts about the Christian life, without experiencing a real shift in the way they view themselves and the world. Transformed human lives are not the outcome of such a process. These seekers are not graced with a new heart.

5. *In the downside of a Challenging Process, if the course is too demanding or not relevant to the needs of participants, they may drop out, creating tension between them and the congregation.* If people enter a nine- to twelve-month process in good faith and then discover that it does not meet their needs, they are likely to quit. What do you do with people who have quit the course? How can you repair the relationship so that they still feel welcome in the congregation? Who will deal with the tension that possibly resulted in their refusal to continue? If church leaders fear losing potential members by requiring a longer membership process, they may decide not to proceed with it. They may believe that it is too risky.

Church leaders may hesitate to engage in a longer process out of fear that it creates two categories of church members. Those who chose the longer process may feel self-righteous because they "did it right" while others "copped out" by taking the shorter route. Other people may feel that the longer process is the one that they really *should* take, yet they don't want to and resent being asked to jump through hoops to become a well-received member.

Managing the Polarity Poorly: Early Warnings

With a better understanding of the content of this map, let's look at possible Early Warnings to help us recognize when we are getting into the downside of each pole.

Early Warnings for an Easy Process

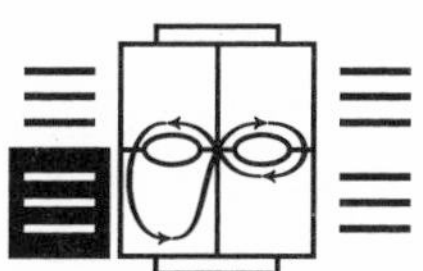

Early Warnings Left

1. The congregation does not reach out as fervently to members joining through this process. Newcomers are not consistently invited to participate in additional study processes and activities that keep them growing in the Christian faith.
2. New members become acquainted primarily with the pastor, and little effort is made to help newcomers become acquainted with other congregational leaders.
3. The staff that conducts these few sessions does not portray the depth of the Christian faith that would draw newcomers to do further reading and study.
4. Those joining in the shorter process are not invited into leadership roles within the congregation, while those participating in the longer process are.
5. Those conducting the orientation sessions come to view them as perfunctory and cease searching for ways to bring new life to them.

Early Warnings for a Challenging Process

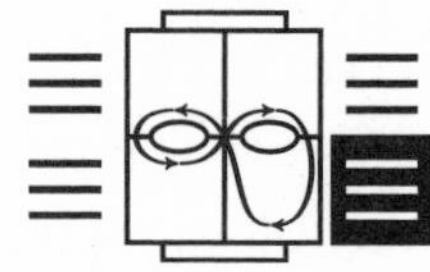
Early Warnings Right

1. The congregation gets the reputation of being too demanding of newcomers, and word gets around town.
2. Other aspects of church programming suffer as the congregation's best leaders are tied up with the adult catechumenate. Members come to resent their key leaders' unavailability for their classes.
3. This extended process adds days of extra work on already overloaded clergy.
4. Complaints are increasingly heard that people going through the longer process feel "superior to" or "better than" those going through the short course. Cutting remarks are made to newcomers engaged in the shorter process.
5. Newcomers believe that they have not been given a choice of two ways to join; the message they think they hear is "If you want to be taken seriously in this congregation, you will go through the longer process."

Managing the Polarity Well: Action Steps

We know that thriving congregations are able to tap both upsides of this polarity. The following are Action Steps that might be taken to ensure that both poles are embraced and valued. Map 8.2 on pages 186–187 provides a picture of this polarity.

Action Steps for the Easy Process

Action Steps Left

How do you gain or maintain the upside of the Easy Process?

1. The coordinator of lay ministries or the task force managing this dimension of the congregation's ministry tells new members about opportunities to volunteer in the congregation so that they get to know other members and begin to feel that they are indeed full-fledged members.

2. Since the bonding of newcomers to other newcomers is seen as important, the congregation waits until a substantial number of people are ready to take the three sessions so that these new relationships have an opportunity to form.
3. Leaders and members put as much energy into making these new members an integral part of the congregation as they do for those who participated in the longer process. Their joining is celebrated with a social event at which they and those joining through the longer process meet and become acquainted with other members of the congregation.
4. Every few months clergy or key lay leaders check in with those who have participated, to see if they are continuing the practice of daily prayer and Bible study.
5. The shorter sessions are not only intended to pass on the basics of the Christian faith, but are also designed to be highly interactive. For example, participants are invited to share their spiritual autobiographies at one of the sessions. In addition to providing a way for newcomers to become more engaged with one another, this activity allows the pastor and lay leaders to see where these newcomers can engage in a volunteer role that fits their skills and interests.

Action Steps for a Challenging Process

How do we gain or maintain the upside of a Challenging Process?

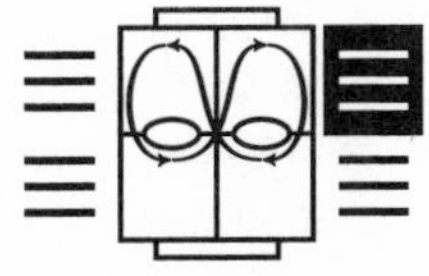
Action Steps Right

1. The congregation chooses its apostolic core (faithful members who have made prayer and Scripture reading part of their daily life) to become mentors to those going through this longer process.
2. High energy is put into the variety of experiences offered newcomers in this longer new-member orientation process. That is, the course involves not only lectures and discussions but also distinctive experiences such as engaging in a Via de Christo weekend, watching a movie and discerning the theology of its major characters, or spending a day in contemplative prayer.

Polarity Management®

Action Steps

How will we gain or maintain the positive results from focusing on this left pole? What? Who? By when? Measures?

1. Opportunities for service are offered quickly to these newcomers.
2. The congregation waits until the class is large enough so that social bonding can take place.
3. Energy is put into making these people feel as welcome as those going through the longer process.
4. Occasional calls are made to these people inquiring if they are continuing the practice of daily prayer and Scripture reading.
5. This shorter course is highly interactive so group members become bonded to the pastor and to one another.

Early Warnings

Measurable indicators (things you can count) that will let you know that you are getting into the downside of this left pole.

1. The congregation is less accepting of people joining through an easy process.
2. Little effort is made to acquaint these newcomers to other congregational leaders.
3. Those teaching this course may not portray the depth of Christianity that would draw people into further reading and study.
4. Those joining in through the shorter course are not invited into leadership roles in the congregation.
5. People teaching this course cease to find ways to bring new life to the sessions.

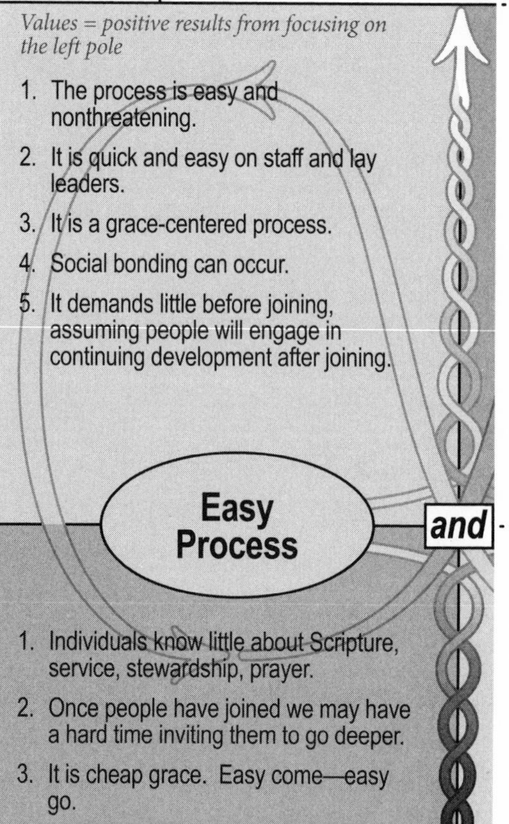

Map

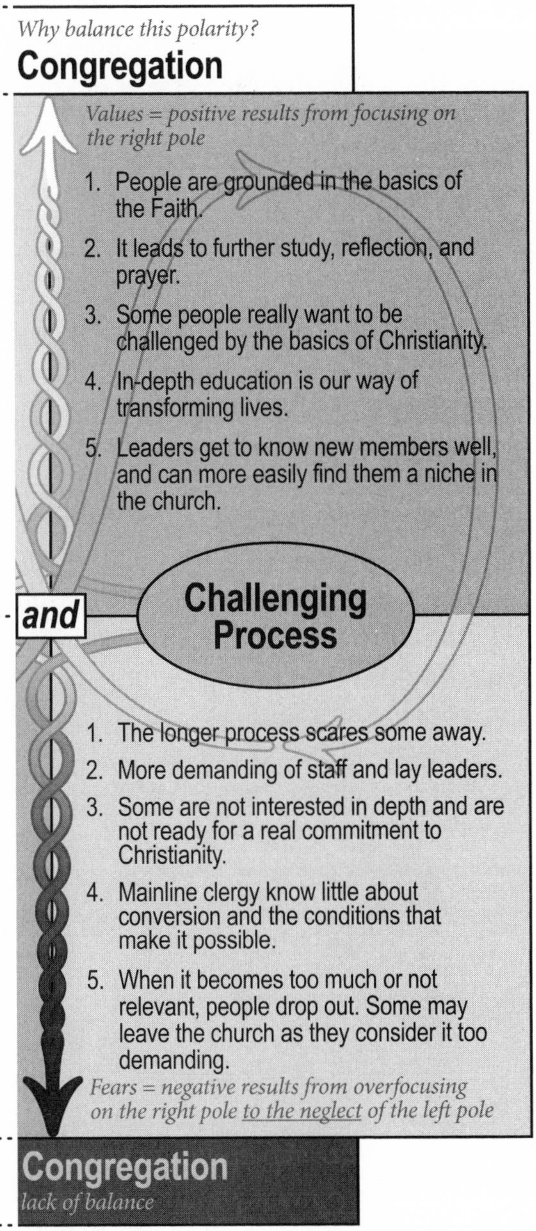

Why balance this polarity?

Congregation

Values = positive results from focusing on the right pole

1. People are grounded in the basics of the Faith.
2. It leads to further study, reflection, and prayer.
3. Some people really want to be challenged by the basics of Christianity.
4. In-depth education is our way of transforming lives.
5. Leaders get to know new members well, and can more easily find them a niche in the church.

and

Challenging Process

1. The longer process scares some away.
2. More demanding of staff and lay leaders.
3. Some are not interested in depth and are not ready for a real commitment to Christianity.
4. Mainline clergy know little about conversion and the conditions that make it possible.
5. When it becomes too much or not relevant, people drop out. Some may leave the church as they consider it too demanding.

Fears = negative results from overfocusing on the right pole to the neglect of the left pole

Congregation

lack of balance

Action Steps

How will we gain or maintain the positive results from focusing on this right pole? What? Who? By when? Measures?

1. The congregation calls upon their "apostolic core" to become mentors to these newcomers.
2. High energy is put into the variety of experiences offered these newcomers.
3. The course is evaluated yearly to see that quality remains high.
4. People are challenged to develop a statement of faith near course end.
5. Once the course is over these newcomers are invited to become part of the outreach efforts of the congregation.

Early Warnings

Measurable indicators (things you can count) that will let you know that you are getting into the downside of this right pole.

1. The congregation gets the reputation of being too demanding of newcomers.
2. The course occupies the congregation's best leaders, making them unavailable for other congregational roles.
3. This extended process adds days of extra work to already overloaded clergy.
4. Complaints are heard that people going through the longer process feel "superior" to those going through the shorter process.
5. When offered two choices, newcomers get the message that "if you want to be taken seriously in this congregation you will go through the longer process."

Map 8.2

3. Each year the challenging process is evaluated to ensure that the quality remains high.
4. Toward the end of the course, participants are challenged to develop a statement of faith, focusing especially on how this process has made an impact on their lives. Some of these may be published, and some new members may be invited to offer a five-minute version of their statement of faith in a worship service.
5. Because new converts are usually more enthusiastic about the Christian faith than longtime adherents, those graduating from this longer process are invited to become part of the congregation's outreach efforts.

Summary

In concluding this chapter, let us note that three polarities have some similarity. In the *Spiritual Health AND Institutional Health* polarity, we observed that every congregation needs to wrestle with providing spiritual nourishment to its members in addition to maintaining a healthy congregation organizationally. In the *Nurture AND Transformation* polarity we explored the importance not only of supporting and caring for members, but also of challenging them to move more deeply into discipleship. In this polarity on making disciples, we explored two ways to go about transforming people's lives. All three polarities are integrally involved in the spiritual vitality of a congregation.

Every congregation is already managing every polarity in this book. Whether it is managing them well or poorly is a judgment left to each congregation. In this sense, every congregation is using its experience, intuition, and collective wisdom to address these polarities. They are an integral part of congregational life, just as activity and rest are an integral part of our personal lives.

Thriving congregations have managed, without a formal lesson on Polarity Management, to recognize the upside of both poles of many of these key polarities. What Polarity Management does is to create a context in which to understand these polarities better. Learning about this process allows tacit wisdom to become explicit and increases the possibility that clergy and laity alike can be more effective in managing these polarities and others. This effort will support them in becoming and remaining a thriving congregation.

Thriving congregations, when managing this polarity well, will continue to oscillate between the two upper quadrants of these two poles. In short, we recommend that every congregation have in place two ways a person can become a baptized member of the congregation. We might first talk about our preference that newcomers engage in the yearlong process, but if that is clearly more of a commitment than they are willing to make, we can explain to them the option of becoming full-fledged members by attending three new-member classes. The point must be made that the congregation does not consider those taking the shorter route to be second-class members. Those taking the shorter course should be given the opportunity to take the yearlong catechumenate at some later point, or they can choose not to do so but move deeper into the Christian faith by other means

CHAPTER 9

Call AND Duty

One way we serve God is by volunteering for tasks related to our church, either inreach or outreach. We serve best when our motivation is high and less well when it is low. This polarity offers guidance about how best to keep our own and our members' motivation high.

At the macro level we serve best when we believe that what we are doing is a call that grows intrinsically out of our basic values and our sense of what God would have our lives to be about. At the micro level are those smaller duties that may or may not relate to this larger sense of what we want our lives to be about. There may have been a time when a particular call was clear, but we change, and so do the opportunities for ministry. From time to time, we need to stop and reassess our lives and consider how a call may have changed for us. Whatever the work we carry out, however, both *Call AND Duty* enter in.

What Motivates Us to Serve

Trinity Church decided in its strategic plan to spend a year focusing on God's call to all Christians. Each quarter the congregation zeroed in on one of four themes: God's call to a life of faith, God's call to a life of obedience, God's call to a life of generosity, and God's call to a life of service. Once a month during worship, a member of the congregation shared his or her story in a five-minute witness. The series had gone well, and the congregation was now in the fourth quarter. Pastor Joe had the task of asking two members to talk about their call to service. Two lay members noted for their service came quickly to mind as he reflected on this theme.

The first member he thought of was Adrian Springer, a county social worker. Adrian worked with delinquent young people assigned to him by the county court. He had a way with these youth, and most of those assigned to him stayed out of trouble. In the summer he would take a few kids fishing at the lake. During the winter, he would take them skiing. He had not been at this job long when he began noticing the county's homeless people. He discovered that some were former patients at the county psychiatric hospital. At some point the county had concluded that, given its necessary funding cuts, the care of these people was costing too much, so the patients had been released and no longer received care. Adrian obtained permission from the county to work with some of the homeless to ensure that they would continue to receive needed medication. Adrian attended worship every Sunday at Trinity. He was occasionally asked to volunteer for tasks or roles at the church, but he always turned down the invitation. He strongly believed that God wanted him to put his time and energy into the social work he did for the county. He often worked overtime taking care of the people he believed God had given to him.

The second speaker would be Mary Saunders. Mary was often seen at the church carrying out a variety of tasks. She claimed to be mediocre at many things and exceptional at none. She often joked that though her name was Mary, it should have been Martha—an allusion to the qualities of the two sisters of Lazarus whom Jesus visited. Mary had a part-time job to help pay for her children's education, but she believed that her call was to serve her church. Trinity meant a lot to Mary, and she insisted that it had saved her life. As a child she had been severely abused by her father, but she had somehow found her way to Trinity. A previous pastor had gotten to know her and her situation, and he had worked to have her removed from her parents' custody and placed in the home of foster parents who were members of the congregation. It seemed as though the whole congregation had adopted her, and she stayed with her foster family through high school and college. She had even met her husband at Trinity. Mary could be counted on to volunteer for any task that seemed important to the church. It was her way of giving something back to Trinity since the congregation had given her so much. No job was too menial for her. The kids at Trinity called her the "church lady."

The Polarity to Be Managed

As we look at this polarity, we encounter the concept of lay ministry in a broad sense. This term usually refers to the work of the people of God, those who are called first to a life of faith. It involves both what people do to earn a living and what they volunteer to do, in the church or some other nonprofit organization, as well as other forms of service. Some people say that their call comes from a deep sense of conviction. Some Christians speak of their call from God to do certain things or to be a certain kind of person. Many of us talk about doing something that grows out of our core values or our beliefs. Some people have disciplined themselves to come up with a mission statement—what they want their life to be about.

Within our call to faith and our call to "be about" some mission, we are called to more specific vocations, roles, or tasks. For example, someone may be called to be a spiritual leader. As an outgrowth of that call, he may find that he is called to the role of Sunday school teacher at one point in his life and then later called to serve as director of a church day school, eventually to become a faculty member at a seminary and perhaps later to coach newly ordained clergy. Our call involves a variety of factors, including the call to be a disciple of Jesus, as well as our age, experience, need for an income, family situation, and the opportunities that are open to us.

Duties, on the other hand, are obligatory tasks we perform. Many duties grow out of our sense of what we want our life to be about. In fact, any call we accept will involve obligatory tasks. Someone who feels called to be a parish pastor will need to attend many meetings, conduct funerals and weddings, visit people in crisis, and lead an exemplary life. These obligatory tasks are a way of fulfilling that call. A person may enjoy some tasks more than others. When, however, a parish pastor loses his or her sense of call, fulfilling these duties becomes a real burden. It may be in the course of doing these duties that he concludes he no longer feels called to be a parish pastor.

As another example, someone who feels a deep sense of call to preserve our natural environment may find herself dutifully attending the meetings of a local nature conservatory, heading a task force in the church to make it more environmentally friendly, or mobilizing a write-in campaign to urge local politicians to change environmental policies. These self-imposed duties may not be satisfying at times. In fact, they may be boring and require hard work. But she continues to do them because of the call she feels to help save our planet.

This polarity, *Call AND Duty*, is a reminder that all of us need to keep these two poles in alignment—that is, to stay in touch with our sense of call, which will change over time, and to see that the duties we perform are congruent with what we want our life to be about.

Our sense of call can be an ever-moving feast. What we feel called to do at age twenty will likely change before we reach age thirty. At age fifty we may find ourselves hearing a radically different call. It is for this reason that congregations need to continually provide opportunities for members to engage in conversations that ground them in their core values and beliefs. They can then more intentionally align themselves with tasks that fit their sense of call. Ultimately, of course, people need to take responsibility for this sense of call themselves. Congregational leaders can hold up the importance of paying attention to our callings, give people tools for discerning their call, support them in their discernment, and point out to members that they can always say no to a task that does not fit their sense of call. But in the end, leaders cannot babysit perhaps hundreds of members who need to change some aspect of their involvement or maybe even just say no.

When striving to manage this polarity effectively, congregational leaders need to keep in mind that members are also called to tasks or jobs outside the church. A teacher, for example, may feel called to an inner-city school as the venue where she can best offer her teaching gifts to a broken and hurting world. Such a ministry can be exceptionally challenging and draining, and she may not be the person her congregation should ask to take on a major volunteer role. By the time the weekend arrives, she may be so exhausted that she needs to join a group of people who will listen to her struggles with this vocation, pray for her, and thank her for her courage and fortitude. Such a group would include others who believe that their call involves their daily work and who also need a listening ear and prayers.

Because our sense of call is an ever-moving feast, churches increasingly need to find ways to assist people in determining where and to what they are called. Larger congregations often employ, either full time or part time, a coordinator of lay ministries who helps members find meaningful roles within or outside the church. Such coordinators try to get to know congregation members' interests and abilities and help them find a committee or role that helps them feel they are part of the church. When a committee or community organization needs a new volunteer, it will contact the lay-ministries coordinator for a recommendation.

A coordinator of lay ministries may spend most of her time with newer members and inactive members. When church members are engaged in congregational tasks that align with their core values, they are more likely to become and remain active participants. The coordinator also stays in touch with the congregation's core volunteers, to make sure the role or tasks they have taken on continue to have meaning for them.

Occasionally a coordinator will sponsor a discernment process that helps people see more clearly where and to what God is calling them. Busy people often don't take the time to discern where they are being called. Congregations should realize that when they ask people to volunteer for roles or activities in the church, they are serving up a banquet. These volunteers are doing the church a favor, but the church is also doing them a favor by allowing them to serve in a meaningful way. Knowing this, a coordinator of lay ministries will often work with members to discern their "growing edge."

Sometimes, however, there are tasks in the church that no one feels called to take on, yet getting these jobs done is essential for a healthy, vibrant congregation. In such cases we need to rely on members' sense of duty to the congregation.

The way we see this tension on a polarity map is illustrated on page 194. In the context of this map, let's look at each of the quadrants in more detail.

The Upside of Call

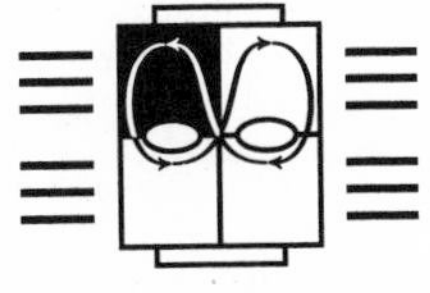
Upside Left

1. *In the upside of Call, people feel a sense of fulfillment in serving as an instrument of God.* Any congregation will be well served if it develops a process whereby every member is guided to reflect on his or her sense of God's calls. Calls are ever changing as people grow spiritually and as they feel challenged to stretch by assuming a role or activity new to them. People are more motivated to take on a new respon-

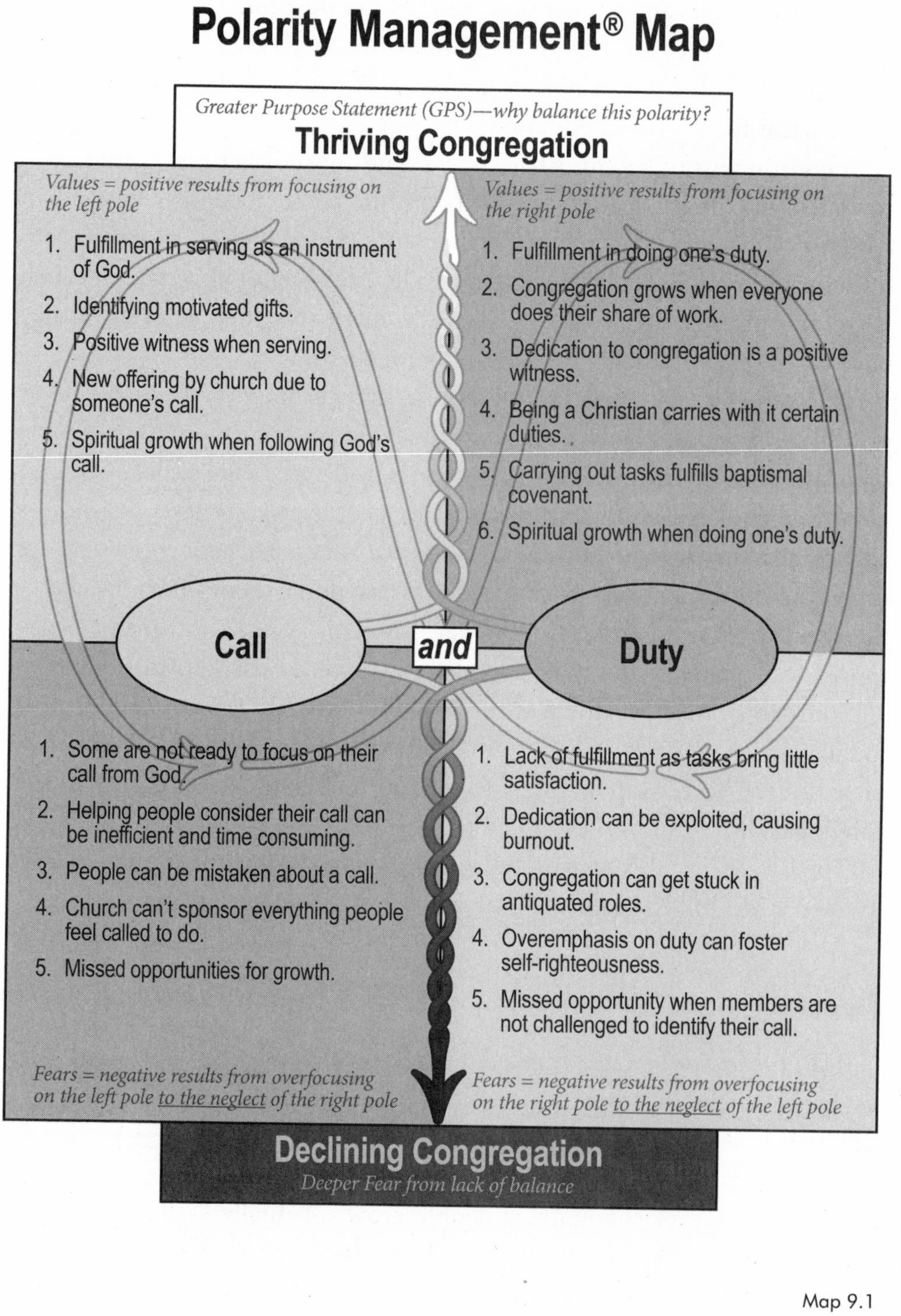

Polarity Management® Map

Greater Purpose Statement (GPS)—why balance this polarity?

Thriving Congregation

Values = positive results from focusing on the left pole

1. Fulfillment in serving as an instrument of God.
2. Identifying motivated gifts.
3. Positive witness when serving.
4. New offering by church due to someone's call.
5. Spiritual growth when following God's call.

Values = positive results from focusing on the right pole

1. Fulfillment in doing one's duty.
2. Congregation grows when everyone does their share of work.
3. Dedication to congregation is a positive witness.
4. Being a Christian carries with it certain duties.
5. Carrying out tasks fulfills baptismal covenant.
6. Spiritual growth when doing one's duty.

Call *and* **Duty**

1. Some are not ready to focus on their call from God.
2. Helping people consider their call can be inefficient and time consuming.
3. People can be mistaken about a call.
4. Church can't sponsor everything people feel called to do.
5. Missed opportunities for growth.

Fears = negative results from overfocusing on the left pole to the neglect of the right pole

1. Lack of fulfillment as tasks bring little satisfaction.
2. Dedication can be exploited, causing burnout.
3. Congregation can get stuck in antiquated roles.
4. Overemphasis on duty can foster self-righteousness.
5. Missed opportunity when members are not challenged to identify their call.

Fears = negative results from overfocusing on the right pole to the neglect of the left pole

Declining Congregation

Deeper Fear from lack of balance

Map 9.1

sibility when they believe that it is what God wants them to do at this point in life. If it is seen as a call, the task is likely to be more satisfying. This sense of being called by God has the potential to bring excitement and passion to an activity. People are much less likely to experience burnout in fulfilling a role to which they feel called. The congregation also has the opportunity to watch people become more self-actualized as they develop new talents and skills, and the congregation gains as people acquire new abilities. People are much more likely to be positive witnesses to their faith when they bring a sense of joy and commitment to their new calling. The discernment process itself will encourage people to wrestle with the Spirit, and spiritual growth will result.

2. *In the upside of Call, part of our call involves identifying our motivated gifts.* For some, the notion that we receive direction from God to a particular vocation or task is too much of a stretch. In such cases, we can talk about "motivated gifts." An individual may be motivated to explore whether he has a particular gift. For example, someone who has never taught a class may wonder whether he has any talent for teaching. He may feel motivated to teach a sixth-grade Sunday school class or to lead a group of adults through a study course. His situation is very different from that of a professional teacher who knows she can do a good job teaching a class. Is she motivated to apply that gift to a Sunday school class? Probably not, given that she is already teaching five days a week. If she is skilled in music, however, her motivated gift may be to direct a choir, something she has never done but has always wanted to try. She would value that opportunity. Of course, we are making a leap if we say that someone who is motivated to try something new is necessarily receiving a call from God. Still, exploring a potential talent may be integral to a person's spiritual formation, because God talks to us in many ways. When we attend to people's motivated gifts, we tap into a natural curiosity and energy for growth.

3. *In the upside of Call, members will be more positive witnesses when serving out of a sense of call.* When members serve out of a belief that God has called them to a task or that they are using a motivated gift, they are more likely to be positive witnesses to others. The energy they bring to the task will be impressive. For the most part, they will be admired for the way they exercise their care for other people, especially people in pain. In this way

they will be seen as committed disciples of Jesus, who always seemed to take the side of the poor, the oppressed, and the marginalized.

4. *In the upside of Call, a congregation will be able to serve members and nonmembers in new ways because of someone's call to ministry.* Marlene Wilson, author of the classic book *How to Mobilize Church Volunteers,*[1] told a story in a workshop Roy and she led together years ago about members of the church she attended. Some of them came to her saying, "We can't get people to volunteer for things here." She responded in disbelief. "With all the talent in this church, I can't believe that you have problems finding volunteers. Allow me to set a challenge before you. Just identify fifty members, a cross-section of the congregation, and each one of you on the committee interview a portion of this group. Ask them this: if they could offer anything to the church that would be in keeping with our mission, what would it be?" The committee did that. After interviewing only half of the group, they had to stop the process. They were already overwhelmed with the new things people wanted to offer the church. Here are some of the gifts they offered:

- "Well, I love to paint with watercolors. I would be delighted to offer an afternoon a month to anyone in the congregation who would like to try their hand at watercolor painting."
- "I love backpacking. Some spring or summer, I'd love to take some of our youth on a backpacking trip."
- "Every morning before breakfast I do thirty minutes of hatha yoga stretching, followed by fifteen minutes of contemplative prayer. I'd be willing to lead a group at the church, once a week for six weeks, at 7:00 on Wednesday mornings."

This congregation was energized by these many new offerings from its members.

5. *In the upside of Call, people who believe they are responding to God's call to ministry grow spiritually.* People who take seriously the belief that they have received a call from God to a specific ministry will experience greater spiritual growth than those who don't. Sometimes what they believe God is calling them to be and do is such a challenge that they suffer frequent setbacks. When this happens, these people generally take their struggle to God and fuss with God about their call, much as the prophet Jeremiah did. Some

curse God for what they think God has gotten them into. They probably spend more time on their knees praying than they did before accepting the challenge. In the end, their quarrel with God usually leads them to surrender to the givens of a role or situation, accepting it as a call to greater humility and greater dependence on God to see them through. Their call to a specific ministry can be like the refiner's fire that changes their lives. We have to grow into this concept and mature into listening more carefully to what we sense God is calling us to do and be.

Former president Jimmy Carter, in an interview with journalist Bill Moyers many years ago, recalled talking to his pastor about following God's call to ministry. His pastor had advised him to forsake his political career and attend seminary to become an ordained minister. Carter talked about the anger he had felt toward his pastor, who could only see God calling people to serve the church as clergy. Most of us would bear witness to the fact that Jimmy Carter's call to a life in politics has had a profound impact on his spiritual life. His continued service to humanity after his presidency is an inspiration to many of us, regardless of how we view his presidency.

The Upside of Duty

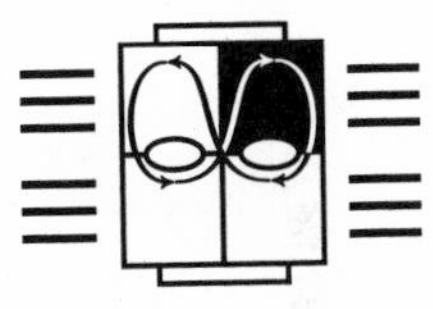

Upside Right

1. *In the upside of Duty, taking on tasks out of a sense of duty has its own rewards.* For some people, doing a congregational task as a duty may leave them feeling that they are needed and are contributing to the overall mission of the congregation. Duty and belonging are and always have been a way of life for them. Those familiar with the Myers-Briggs Type Indicator (MBTI)[2] may recall that out of the four basic temperaments, people of one temperament, the Sensing/Judging type, feel most fulfilled when they are doing things from a sense of duty. It is the way they are wired, and we need to affirm and appreciate them for it. These super-responsible people will probably say yes to anything congregational leaders ask them to do. They are often confused that other people don't share their commitment to duty and responsibility. In fact, people in none of the other three temperaments in the MBTI will ever be as responsible as those who score high on Sensing and Judging.

Doing one's duty is far less complicated than wrestling with issues of call. It requires far less introspection by those asked to complete a task, and for some people, introspection is not valued. They might comment, "What is all this navel gazing about? Let's just get on with what it takes to make this congregation thrive." These people like to keep things simple: "Ask me specifically what you want me to do, and then I can give you a simple yes or no."

2. *In the upside of Duty, congregations and secular organizations grow when everyone does a fair share of the work.* It has often been said that we need to be faithful in big undertakings, and that we also need to be faithful in the little tasks. Many congregations would not have become thriving communities of faith without the teamwork of dedicated lay leaders. Some of these laity feel called to specific roles within the church, and others feel called to something broader—to do whatever it takes to create a thriving, caring, spiritual community. This teamwork makes for a hearty, compassionate congregation. The reality that things get done when everyone accepts a share of the load applies to any organization that relies on volunteers. The ministries of the United Way, the Red Cross, or the Peace Corps would soon grind to a halt without individuals who respond to requests for help out of a sense of duty.

There will always be tasks to which no one feels called—taking down the Christmas decorations and putting them in storage, cleaning the church kitchen, shoveling snow from church sidewalks, and washing the windows. Still, people will do them because of their larger call to be responsible members of the congregation. They may feel a commitment to help the group live within its budget, rather than hiring people to do some of these tasks. In this regard, all members need to pitch in to get the grunt work done. The fact that someone feels called to some other ministry, whether in the congregation or elsewhere, doesn't mean that he or she can simply leave when there are dishes to be washed, rooms to be put back in order, and floors to be swept.

Finally, however, a congregation thrives and grows when a sense of teamwork unites those who serve out of a sense of duty and those who serve out of a broader sense of call. A congregation falters when one of these poles is stronger than the other. The best of all worlds is for everyone in the congregation to do some tasks out of a sense of call and others out of a sense of duty.

3. *In the upside of Duty, people offer a positive witness to life with Jesus when serving out of a sense of duty.* Some members make a positive witness to others about their life as disciples of Jesus by serving out of a sense of call, while others make that witness from a sense of duty. We need both kinds of witnesses, as each will appeal to a different group of people. Some are impressed by the volunteer who mobilizes a congregation to set up a soup kitchen for the community's homeless people, while others admire people who are always ready to pitch in, regardless of the task. As in every polarity, both sides have positive features; one is not better than the other.

As we reflect on what it means to be a disciple of Christ, we see that the terms *duty* and *obedience* are closely aligned. In Philippians 2:5–11 we read that Jesus responded out of a sense of obedience to the Father by humbling himself, taking on the form of a servant, and becoming obedient unto death, even death on a cross. In like manner, we are obedient to God as we respond out of a sense of duty to accomplish important things, whether in a congregation and or another service organization.

4. *In the upside of Duty, we carry out certain tasks that being a Christian entails.* These are some things that most Christians would say is part of their duty as followers of Christ. We try not to exploit others, especially the poor. We try to reduce violence in the world. We accept the dignity of all people regardless of race, creed, or lifestyle. We seek to become more generous.

Each of us would emphasize some of these duties more than others, and we will disagree with others about what our common duties ought to be, but we hope to stay in dialogue with fellow Christians about these things. The more deeply we come to love and honor Jesus, the more we will want our lives to remain dutiful to his teachings.

Sometime we are challenged to address enormous problems, such as the degradation of our environment, the plight of millions of refugees throughout the world, global hunger, and human injustice. We are taught to be more generous, yet even if we tithe our income to the church and charity, we are also called to be responsible in the way we spend the remaining 90 percent of our income. In this way we can see that as Christians we are called to be dutiful in the way we live our lives. This is what obedience to Christ means. Our broader call to be disciples of Christ involves being dutiful in a variety of ways.

5. *In the upside of Duty, as we carry out tasks, we fulfill the call of our baptismal covenant.* Part of our understanding of baptism has to do with being initiated into a community of faith. That carries with it some duties connected to our relationship with the body of Christ, his church. The Great Commission is part of our baptismal covenant. We may carry significant guilt about not being better evangelists in our daily lives, but the responsibility to talk about our faith when others inquire and to live a life that bears witness to our faith remains.

6. *In the upside of Duty, all of us grow spiritually when doing our duty.* We may be surprised by what God has in store for us when we serve out of a sense of duty. For example, at the end of a church meeting, the group may begin to rearrange the chairs for a class that will meet the next morning. Everyone pitches in, and in the process two members strike up a conversation of significance—a conversation that would likely not have happened while they were doing the work of the committee. Attending a parent-teacher association meeting, we may meet people who have a concern like ours for the education of our children and for the way our school systems are run. In the workplace, as we exercise concern for fellow workers beyond their job performance, we may be enriched spiritually by listening more carefully to the struggles and courage of a colleague. As the reformer Martin Luther once observed, a person might find being dutiful to his sense of responsibility as a Christian so challenging that he needs to turn to God for strength, guidance, humility, and courage.

The Downside of Call

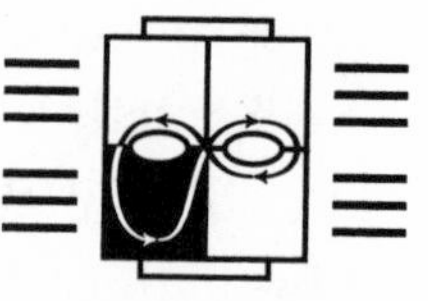
Downside Left

1. *In the downside of Call, some are not ready to focus on their call from God.* At some people's level of faith development, trying to discern a call may not make sense to them. They may feel so overwhelmed by other issues that they can't focus on this dimension of Christian living. Those who write about vocation suggest that many people do have a sense of what God wants them to do with their lives, but they will often choose to avoid getting in touch with this call, because they find their lives too complicated already and believe responding to God's call will put them over the

edge. Others may simply be nuts-and-bolts people who don't find it helpful to try to focus on the broader picture of what God is calling them to do.

2. *In the downside of Call, helping members consider their call can be inefficient and time-consuming.* Waiting for people to discern their call takes time. As a congregation starts up in the fall after a summer letdown, the congregation has to work hard to get programs up and running. What leaders need are some warm bodies to complete a few tasks. They don't have the luxury of waiting for someone to feel called to volunteer for some of those tasks. Taking members' varied calls seriously, however, might mean that a congregation is at least temporarily shorthanded.

3. *In the downside of Call, when we ask members to discern their call to ministry, some can be mistaken about it and try to serve in a ministry that does not match their gifts.* A person may mistakenly feel called to a certain role in a congregation. She may lack the skills to do it well. He may need lots of support and training. His misunderstanding can be time consuming for leaders. When it becomes clear that the person will not work out in a particular role, someone needs to work with her, either to help her reflect on whether she is called to this role or to inform her that the congregation needs to give the role to someone else. Someone else who feels called to a ministry within the congregation may hold onto the job for far too long, resisting the need to relinquish it to a successor. In such a case the member may be mistaken about the duration of his call.

4. *In the downside of Call, churches can't support everything people feel called to do.* As noted above, in Marlene Wilson's congregation, leaders were overwhelmed with the many gifts members wanted to offer the church, so overwhelmed that they stopped asking people how they would serve if they could. The congregation couldn't receive all its members' gifts.

An individual may feel called to pursue a controversial activity that will cause conflict within the congregation, such as making the congregation more open to all people, including gays or lesbians. That kind of call might require a multiyear effort and still not result in any change of attitude on the part of some members. In certain congregations, church leaders may refrain from giving an individual a formal role to pursue such a controversial issue. They may conclude that the congregation is not ready and that it would lose too many members in the process. On the other hand, leaders may nonetheless encourage the individual to pursue that call, with the understanding that it may take years for the congregation to respond.

A member may feel a call to some ministry for which the congregation does not have an outlet. For example, someone may feel called to begin a day-care center for working parents who need a safe, clean, well-managed place for their child to stay while the parents are at their jobs. Operating a day-care facility involves meeting state and local requirements, and the congregation may not have the capital to bring its building up to code or to meet other laws and ordinances governing such a ministry. In that case, should the individual continue to feel called to establish a day-care center, the task would need to include finding a way to finance the ministry. If one does not feel called to raise money for the effort, one may need to re-examine the call. On the other hand, other members who are good at fundraising might be sought out to work on financing a day-care center.

5. *In the downside of Call, opportunities for spiritual growth are missed when a congregation does not challenge people to be dutiful.* Being disciples of Jesus Christ involves doing our duty as his followers. Some duties may simply be unpleasant. They may require us to do things we would never dream of doing if we had not committed our lives to being Christ's disciples. Sacrificial giving is one example. We may be struggling to make ends meet financially, but even when we are cutting costs, we do not cut our pledge to our congregation, the United Way, or the Nature Conservancy.

When we meet a beggar on the street, all our good sense may tell us that he will spend any money we give him on alcohol or drugs. Yet some Christians have the sense that this panhandler may be Christ in disguise and will, out of a sense of duty, give money anyway, thereby contributing to his addiction.

In one of the more confrontational moments of Jesus's ministry, he told his followers, "Pick up your cross and follow me." One common interpretation of this command is that we are to pick up the very thing that drags us down and makes us want to stop and feel sorry for ourselves. This weight could be a physical disability or an ailment, a troubled relationship, an addiction, a socioeconomic circumstance, an emotional or mental-health issue, or a political situation. When we accept discipleship, we pick up this personal affliction or challenge and continue to be Christ's body in the world. This is the spiritual challenge we consciously take on, and it comes to us as duty. In these cases, we miss opportunities for spiritual growth by not taking seriously what our faith instructs us to do out of a sense of duty.

The Downside of Duty

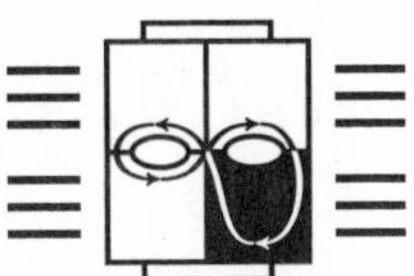
Downside Right

1. *In the downside of Duty, carrying out tasks may bring little satisfaction.* When a congregational member finds herself cleaning up the mess in the church kitchen for the umpteenth time and no one ever thanks her for doing so, the task begins to be less satisfying. Not surprisingly, most people lack a sense of ownership for such tasks. The sense of obligation can create real dilemmas for a congregation. For example, a small-membership congregation may not be able to recruit volunteers to offer a Sunday school for the children of young couples in the neighborhood who are church shopping. Older, less physically agile members or young and overscheduled members may not have the energy or commitment to take on this role, even though they hold strong convictions that their church ought to have a Sunday school. A congregation that has agreed to pick up trash along a stretch of public road may recruit volunteers who will do this task for months or years but find over time that people no longer find this a worthwhile ministry and stop volunteering.

2. *In the downside of Duty, dedication can be exploited, with the result that dedicated people burn out.* The pool of people in a congregation who respond to an appeal to their sense of duty may not be large. Hence, the same people are called upon repeatedly to carry out the less exciting or less rewarding tasks within a congregation. Most likely, there will always be more tasks to be done than there are dutiful people to do them. But there is little joy for people whose sense of duty is exploited. In such situations, the congregation needs to say to its members, "Until God sends us the people we need to carry out this task, we won't try to do it."

To continually ask the few people who respond out of a sense of duty to take on more tasks will lead to their burnout. They may become exhausted, cynical, and disillusioned. Burned-out volunteers do not make the best witnesses for their congregation. They can become so disillusioned that after they complete a strenuous term of office, they leave the church. Some congregations lose their best people through the back door simply because they were not the best stewards of their members' volunteer energies. Some members take their burnt-out bodies and souls to another congregation, perhaps one that is much larger, where they can hide and avoid getting involved in the tasks that keep the church moving. Others simply drop out and don't even look for another church to join. This may happen especially in the case of committee chairs or project managers who try to do a job themselves because no one volunteers to help them. When congregations sense that they are losing some of their workers after these members have been overinvolved, leaders need to reassess whether they are supportive enough of faithful workers or people in tough roles.

3. *In the downside of Duty, a congregation can get stuck in antiquated roles.* A good number of congregations continue to try to fill all the volunteer roles that were filled in the past. Little thought is given to the possibility that some of those roles no longer meet members' and nonmembers' needs. At one time most congregations had separate committees for finance, stewardship, evangelism, social ministry, Christian education, youth ministry, and property. When members no longer volunteer to serve on those committees, a congregation has an opportunity to re-examine the way it structures itself. As long as dutiful members continue to fill the roles, this re-examination may not take place.

At the same time, when people are responding out of a sense of duty, their real gifts may not be valued. Members may not even be asked what they would really like to do to help the congregation accomplish its mission. As a result, members don't think along those lines. They assume that the clergy and other congregational leaders know what needs doing and that their role is to respond to these leaders.

Some congregations hold to the norm that it is not OK to say no to a request from a church leader. As a result, people say yes to some pretty boring and mundane jobs. They may also say yes to jobs that lie well beyond their abilities or come into conflict with their values. Because of this norm, it doesn't occur to members to question whether such tasks should be given priority by the congregation. As a result, old structures continue even when they are outdated or no longer serve a congregational need.

4. *In the downside of Duty, an overemphasis on duty may foster self-righteousness among some volunteers.* These people may begin to feel superior to those they believe do not help out enough in the congregation. As other people begin to sense this attitude, they may come to resent their second-class status within the church.

5. *In the downside of Duty, opportunities are missed when members are not challenged to identify their call.* When clergy welcome new members, they may not think to explore what the newcomers would be highly motivated to offer the church. Instead, they think of the roles that are now going unfilled that this new member might assume. A congregation that has no process for helping members identify their sense of God's call to service has missed an opportunity to help members grow spiritually.

Responding to the concept that God calls all of us to certain tasks and roles requires spiritual maturity. People of prayer are more likely to discern a call. We generally pray about the things that trouble us, and out of such prayer may come a call to address one of those concerns. We might say that it is God who brought us to the point of being troubled. God may open the eyes of the troubled person and allow her to see that she could do something positive to address a distressing situation. The more we become involved in the pain of others, unjust situations, or crying needs, the more we will learn and the more we will turn to God for strength, courage, and resources.

Managing the Polarity Poorly: Early Warnings

The following warning signs may indicate that your congregation is overemphasizing one pole of the *Call AND Duty* polarity. Congregation members might choose other warning signs for either malaise.

Early Warnings for Call

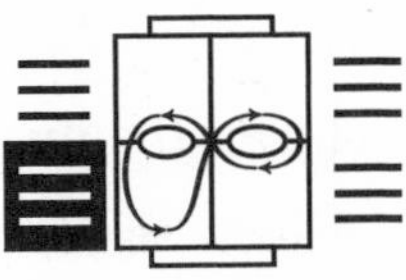

Early Warnings Left

1. Committee chairs increasingly complain that members won't serve on a committee because it doesn't fit their call.

2. Congregational leaders frequently comment that fewer and fewer people in the congregation are willing to do the menial jobs.
3. The congregation has difficulty getting members to stay with certain roles that require an extended commitment, as members often feel called to new roles and simply abandon their old ones.
4. Members' loved ones are increasingly concerned that a member's pursuit of his call has led to the neglect of other duties, such as spending time with family members or taking better care of himself.
5. Some members begin to distinguish between "*we,* who are called," and "*they,* who do the routine tasks around here." Those who feel called may think that their ministry makes them more pleasing in the sight of God.

Early Warnings for Duty

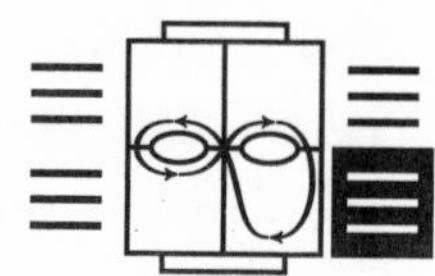

Early Warnings Right

1. Certain hardworking members begin complaining about other church members who "rarely lift a finger" to help out with the menial work.
2. People increasingly commiserate with each other about how hard they are working and how underappreciated they are.
3. Eventually, members rarely feel called to do anything for the congregation. They labor hard and long in various activities or roles, but nothing appears to bring the congregation to greater health and vitality.
4. The congregation begins to notice that some members leave the church after completing a tough project or a strenuous term of office.
5. The congregation knows that some members will say yes to anything church leaders ask of them; it is noticed that members who respond to an appeal to duty tend to be overused.

Managing the Polarity Well: Action Steps

Given the importance that we all function out of both a sense of call and a sense of duty, we now turn to those Action Steps that ensure our remaining in the two upper quadrants of this polarity.

Action Steps for Call

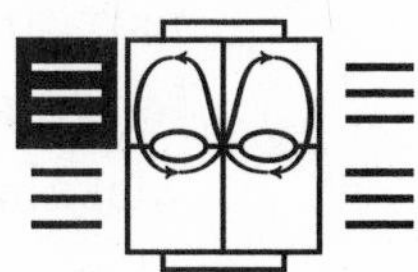
Action Steps Left

1. Develop a strategy for asking members what they would really like to do to help the congregation attain its mission.
2. Form a study group or Sunday adult forum to explore Bible stories about the many ways God has called people into service.
3. Hold a Sunday church forum where members, in small groups, talk about the people over whom they weep, whether in the congregation or other parts of the world. That very process can inspire the congregation to develop a ministry to those who are so identified, as we generally feel called to address the pain of those for whom we weep.
4. Ask congregational nominating committees to read Marlene Wilson's book *How to Mobilize Church Volunteers*, and to begin thinking about what motivates members to take on a specific responsibility. Make nominations from that frame of reference.
5. Invite members to give a five-minute talk during Sunday worship on their call to a specific vocation or ministry opportunity.

Action Steps for Duty

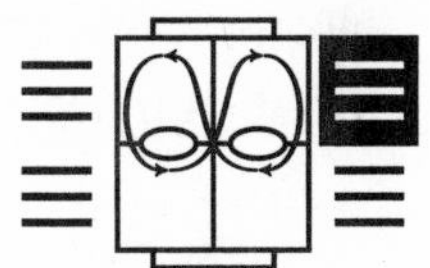
Action Steps Right

1. When there are menial tasks to be done in the congregation, take care to ensure that participants have fun and are appropriately thanked.
2. Throw a surprise party for an outstanding volunteer, perhaps one who is retiring from a position in the congregation.
3. When volunteers are canvassing a neighborhood to invite children to the congregation's vacation Bible school, plan for them to meet at the church first for encouragement and prayer and then return to the church for refreshments and to talk about their experience.
4. When it becomes clear that there is more work to do than can be handled by willing volunteers, raise the money to hire a staff person to do the work. For example, a small-membership congregation that

used volunteers to do its janitorial work might raise funds to hire a part-time custodian when it becomes clear that the work has become too much of a burden on church members.

5. Make sure that church leaders and staff regularly show their appreciation to those who have completed a task or fulfilled a role. Thought should go into showing appreciation in new and creative ways each year.

Summary

The motivated energy of laypeople is one of the greatest resources of a congregation or service agency. Yes, money is important in keeping a church going, but it is the many ministries that laypeople take on that make a church great. People look for a community of faith that shows enthusiasm about what is happening within the congregation. They want to see people joyfully putting their faith into action by assuming responsibility within the church, whether out of a sense of call or a sense of duty. When a congregation is filled with members who are enthusiastic about their church and their role in making it great, newcomers want to join. Longtime members and new members alike volunteer for activities simply because they enjoy spending time with people who are excited about their congregation.

As map 9.2 on pages 210–211 illustrates, when this polarity is well managed, huge amounts of energy are funneled into the church. Congregations that manage this polarity well are good at helping members identify their calling and at supporting their efforts to develop the capacity to fulfill that call. These congregations also know that there are some essential jobs that nobody will feel called to do. Members of the congregation accept the responsibility individually and collectively to fulfill their duty to get these jobs done. Neither the "call" work nor the "duty" work is limited to a few. It is shared broadly so that the individuals and the congregation benefit from attending to both in a way that is sustainable.

This kind of congregation also communicates to visitors and newcomers that members are expected to become actively engaged in making the congregation better. There is great latitude in the roles newcomers will assume, and assistance is offered to help them find their call or their next "growing edge," but if they want to be part of the fun, they will need to find a ministry that suits who they are and what they believe their call to be.

When a congregation is not managing this polarity well, it usually experiences financial woes. A congregation's biggest financial contributors are normally those people most engaged in congregational life. When a congregation is in financial straits, one of its long-term stewardship goals should be to work at managing this polarity better. When a congregation begins to manage this polarity more effectively, many more people will become engaged in the life of the congregation. As a byproduct of this involvement, financial contributions will increase.

A Final Word

In our opening chapter we indicated that polarities are interdependent pairs of truths that are a natural and integral part of our daily lives. Like all other natural phenomena, they are gifts from God. There is a grace that prevails when we deal with polarities. We have stated that polarities are unavoidable, unsolvable and indestructible—that is, even if you manage them poorly, you have an ongoing opportunity to learn from mistakes and try to manage them better in the future. A congregation may be destroyed and go out of existence from the mismanagement of key polarities, but the polarities will remain in any existing congregation, new or old. In that sense, polarities are like grace. They cannot be destroyed and are always there to be tapped.

If you have a GPS system in your car, you know how helpful it can be as you try to reach a destination. It never scolds you. Whenever you make a wrong turn, it doesn't berate you for being stupid or stubborn. It simply says, "Recalculating," and then begins to offer an alternate route. Polarities function a bit like a GPS system.

This is especially true of the Greater Purpose Statement (GPS) at the top of each map. The GPS for your congregation may be something different from "Thriving Congregation." Like the rest of the content we have suggested, the content of your GPS is up to you. Whenever we work on a polarity that we experience within a congregation, the insights produced can be enormously helpful. Seeing a polarity represented on a polarity map, we are given an opportunity to manage it well by taking congregational life in a

Polarity Management®

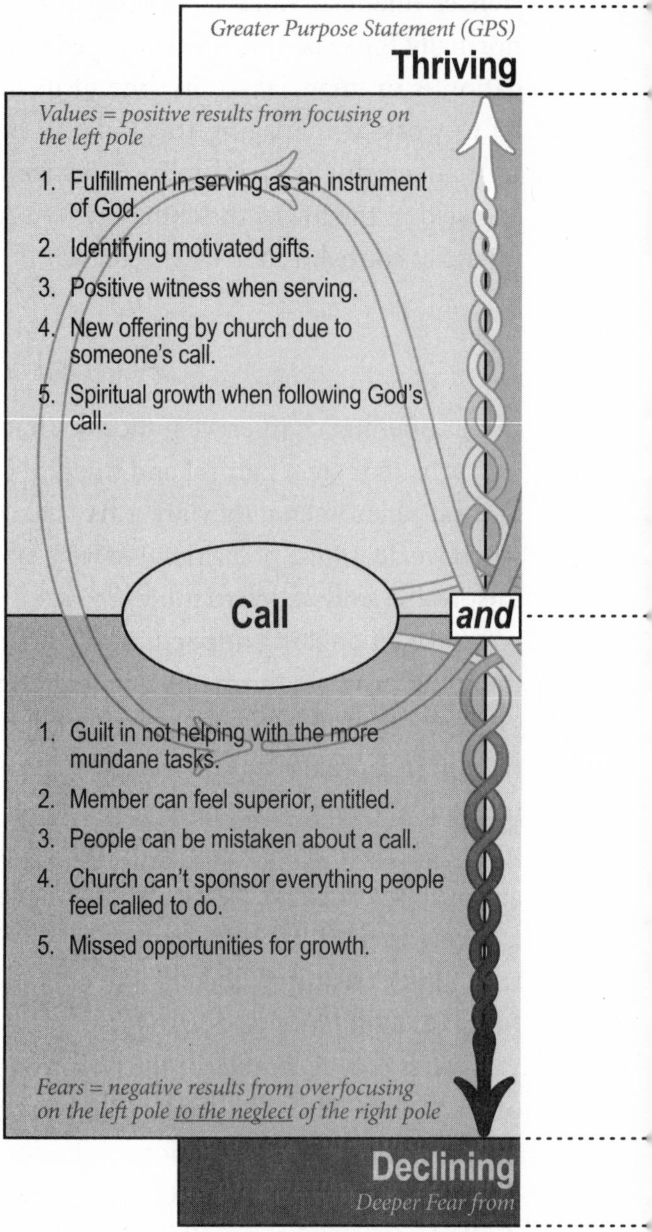

Action Steps

How will we gain or maintain the positive results from focusing on this left pole? What? Who? By when? Measures?

1. Members are asked what they would do to help the congregation attain its mission.
2. Bible stories about the many ways God has called people to service.
3. Do people feel called to minister to those for whom they weep?
4. Nominating committee considers what motivates people to serve.
5. Five-minute talks in worship from people who feel called to a specific vocation or ministry.

Early Warnings

Measurable indicators (things you can count) that will let you know that you are getting into the downside of this left pole.

1. Complaints that members won't serve because it doesn't fit their call.
2. Few people willing to take on menial jobs.
3. When a new call comes, people abandon old roles—hurting the congregation.
4. When pursuing a call people can neglect other duties.
5. When feeling called, people may think they are more pleasing in the sight of God.

Greater Purpose Statement (GPS)

Thriving

Values = positive results from focusing on the left pole

1. Fulfillment in serving as an instrument of God.
2. Identifying motivated gifts.
3. Positive witness when serving.
4. New offering by church due to someone's call.
5. Spiritual growth when following God's call.

Call

and

1. Guilt in not helping with the more mundane tasks.
2. Member can feel superior, entitled.
3. People can be mistaken about a call.
4. Church can't sponsor everything people feel called to do.
5. Missed opportunities for growth.

Fears = negative results from overfocusing on the left pole to the neglect of the right pole

Declining

Deeper Fear from

Map

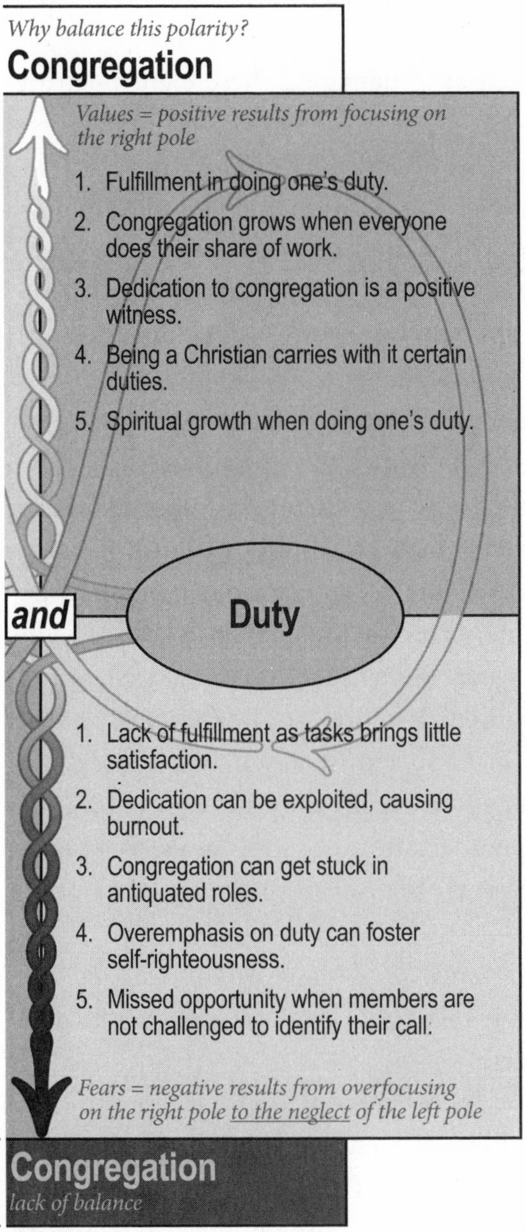

Why balance this polarity?

Congregation

Values = positive results from focusing on the right pole

1. Fulfillment in doing one's duty.
2. Congregation grows when everyone does their share of work.
3. Dedication to congregation is a positive witness.
4. Being a Christian carries with it certain duties.
5. Spiritual growth when doing one's duty.

and **Duty**

1. Lack of fulfillment as tasks brings little satisfaction.
2. Dedication can be exploited, causing burnout.
3. Congregation can get stuck in antiquated roles.
4. Overemphasis on duty can foster self-righteousness.
5. Missed opportunity when members are not challenged to identify their call.

Fears = negative results from overfocusing on the right pole to the neglect of the left pole

Congregation

lack of balance

Action Steps

How will we gain or maintain the positive results from focusing on this right pole? What? Who? By when? Measures?

1. Find ways to make menial tasks fun.
2. Hold a surprise party for outstanding volunteers.
3. When doing tough tasks, build in fellowship time.
4. When tasks become too much, hire a part-time person.
5. Find creative ways to thank the congregation's hard-working volunteers.

Early Warnings

Measurable indicators (things you can count) that will let you know that you are getting into the downside of this right pole.

1. Complaints: "People rarely lift a finger around here."
2. People feel they are working hard and are underappreciated.
3. People experience discouragement when their efforts don't increase the congregation's health and vitality.
4. People burn out and leave the church.
5. Certain members are exploited because of their keen sense of duty.

Map 9.2

direction that maximizes the two upsides and minimizes the two downsides. As we continue to manage the polarity, we will learn new things about it. We can continue to expand the polarity map to describe more completely how it can be managed better. Again, polarities are like grace, because the polarity map always offers another chance.

Let us cite four reasons for seeing and managing these eight polarities and others in your congregation:

1. *To reduce vicious circles.* When we treat a polarity as a problem and regard one pole as the solution, we are in trouble from that point forward. That approach leads to vicious circles, chronic problems, unnecessary conflicts, increased resistance, and unsustainable "solutions." If you want to guarantee that a congregational change effort will not be sustainable, tie it to one pole of a polarity.
2. *To create virtuous circles.* The point is not only to reduce what we regard as problems. We also want to tap the great potential within any polarity. If we can't see the polarities, we're less able to tap them. If we can identify and tap them, each polarity is a powerful energy field that can enhance the life of the congregation. These eight polarities and others can become virtuous circles that lead to thriving congregations. Since polarities are indestructible, tying a change effort to a few key polarities will enhance the sustainability of change. Even when we make some inevitable mistakes in the process, the polarity remains available for us to tap in the future. It is an indestructible gift from God, a manifestation of God's grace. A polarity within a congregation will cease to exist only if the congregation itself ceases to exist.
3. *To improve our effectiveness as clergy, laity, congregations, and denominations.* The result of the first two benefits is to increase overall effectiveness and the ability to thrive.
4. *To enlarge our capacity to love.* Increasing our ability to identify and tap polarities helps us see others, our congregations, and ourselves more completely. Seeing is loving. Each of us and each of our congregations are doing the best we can in the moment, given our history. When we can see values, fears, and behavior in the context of our history, we can "love the sinner" (showing mercy) AND "challenge the

sin" (seeking justice.) Our inability to love ourselves, our neighbor, or our congregation is a reflection of our inability to see. One of our primary tasks is to see each of these more completely. The polarity perspective can help.

We hope you have enjoyed exploring these eight congregational polarities with us. We know that every thriving congregation is managing most of these eight well. We encourage you to review these eight polarities regularly and assess how your congregation is managing them. Such a review is another way of assessing a congregation's well-being. We encourage you to visit our websites from time to time and to use our congregational assessment tool, which provides specific and measurable ways to increase your congregation's vitality.

Here's hoping we will meet again soon.

Blessings,

Roy AND Barry

APPENDIX A

Polarities in Small Groups

In the body of this book, we examined eight key polarities which, when managed well, can contribute to a thriving congregation. In this section, we discuss four polarities that can make a difference in small-group ministries. All the principles you have learned about polarities apply to these four and to any other polarities you might identify in your congregation. Reviewing these polarities may also assist you in training small-group leaders as well as in introducing polarity theory to a congregation.

There are the four polarities that stand out for us with small-group ministries:

Content AND Process
Challenge AND Support
Effective Leaders AND Effective Participants
Long-Term Groups AND Short-Term Groups

The Content AND Process Polarity

The *content* of a small group is the subject matter to be addressed when the small group gathers. Sometimes the content or subject matter is the stated purpose of the small group—to see how the Gospel of John relates to our daily living, to pray for concerns brought by the congregation, or to discern how the congregation can best minister to homeless people in the community.

The *process* of a group is the way group members interact as they go about the group's task. *Process* issues may be the subject of group reflection. A group might reflect on how members worked together in the meeting—for example, what they liked about the way they accomplished their task, what concerned them about the group's functioning, and how the group

Polarity Management® Map

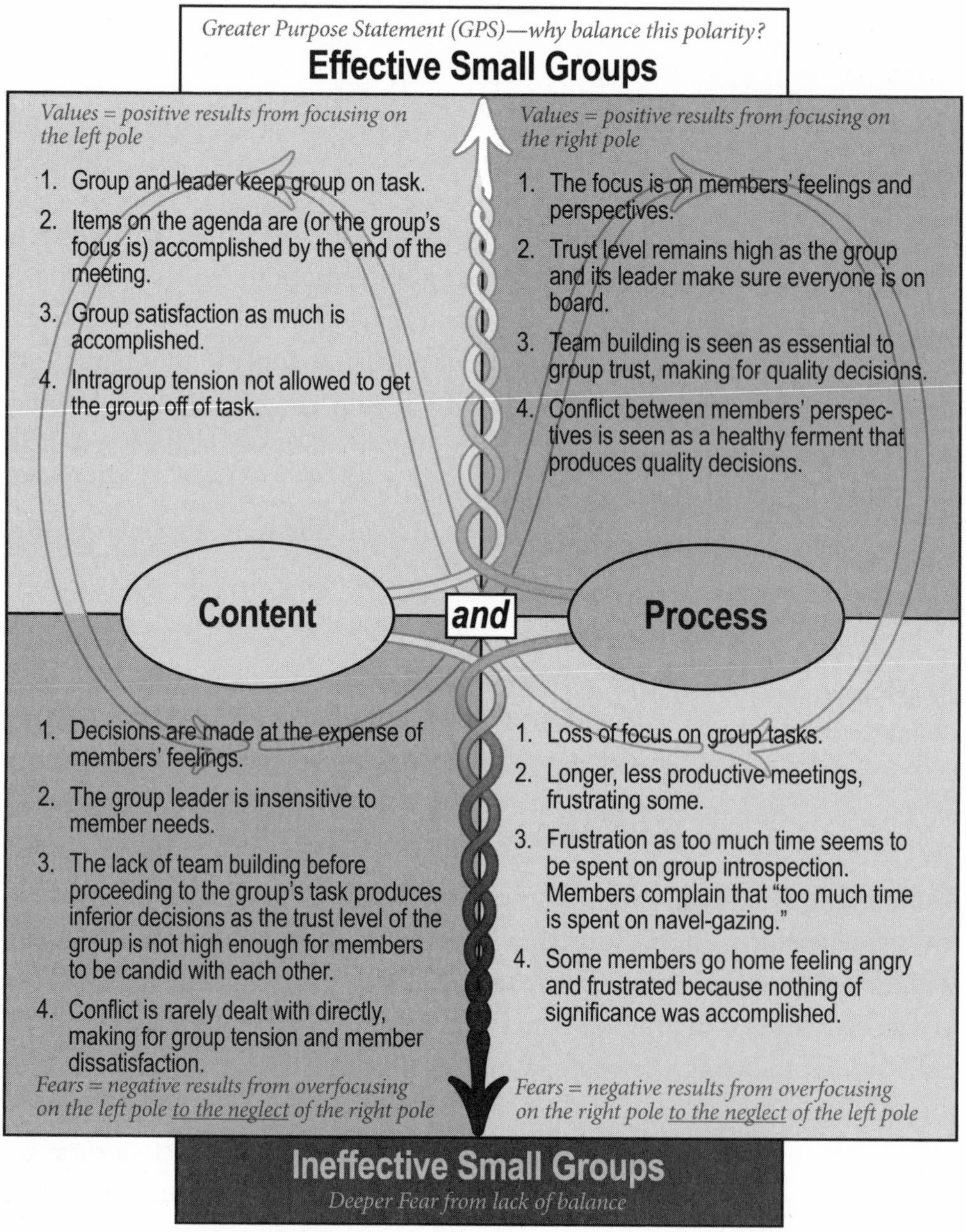

Greater Purpose Statement (GPS)—why balance this polarity?

Effective Small Groups

Values = positive results from focusing on the left pole

1. Group and leader keep group on task.
2. Items on the agenda are (or the group's focus is) accomplished by the end of the meeting.
3. Group satisfaction as much is accomplished.
4. Intragroup tension not allowed to get the group off of task.

Values = positive results from focusing on the right pole

1. The focus is on members' feelings and perspectives.
2. Trust level remains high as the group and its leader make sure everyone is on board.
3. Team building is seen as essential to group trust, making for quality decisions.
4. Conflict between members' perspectives is seen as a healthy ferment that produces quality decisions.

Content **and** **Process**

1. Decisions are made at the expense of members' feelings.
2. The group leader is insensitive to member needs.
3. The lack of team building before proceeding to the group's task produces inferior decisions as the trust level of the group is not high enough for members to be candid with each other.
4. Conflict is rarely dealt with directly, making for group tension and member dissatisfaction.

Fears = negative results from overfocusing on the left pole to the neglect of the right pole

1. Loss of focus on group tasks.
2. Longer, less productive meetings, frustrating some.
3. Frustration as too much time seems to be spent on group introspection. Members complain that "too much time is spent on navel-gazing."
4. Some members go home feeling angry and frustrated because nothing of significance was accomplished.

Fears = negative results from overfocusing on the right pole to the neglect of the left pole

Ineffective Small Groups

Deeper Fear from lack of balance

Map A.1

could have been more effective. The effectiveness of any group depends on its capacity to give equal attention to process and content.

Map A.1 on page 216 summarizes this polarity.

The Upside of Content

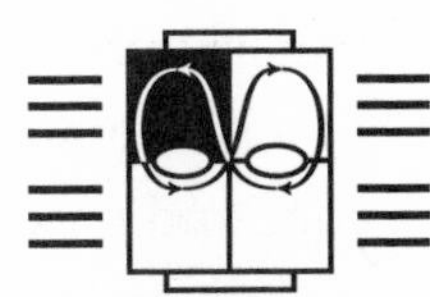

Upside Left

1. *In the upside of Content, the group and the leader keep the group on task.* For group members to feel a sense of satisfaction at the end of a meeting, both the leader and the group need to attend to this effort. A leader's efforts can be sabotaged by group members. At such times, other group members need to come to the aid of the designated leader.

2. *In the upside of Content, the group focuses on its agenda and accomplishes its goals.* Groups that work well are able to accomplish at each meeting what they set out to do. Every thriving congregation needs groups that function well. Leadership groups make wise decisions that are owned by the members. A spiritual-growth group states a focus and explores it to the satisfaction of its participants.

3. *In the upside of Content, group life is satisfying when much is accomplished.* All of us like to belong to groups that complete significant tasks. When a group's decisions have a visible impact on the congregation, its members deserve a pat on the back. In a study or prayer group, tangible results may not be expected, but members should feel that their time was well spent, because they came away with an altered perspective or were enriched by the ideas, feelings, or experiences shared.

4. *In the upside of Content, conflict between members' perspectives is seen as healthy and necessary to produce wise decisions.* Group members expect differences of opinion and do not allow these to derail group progress.

The Upside of Process

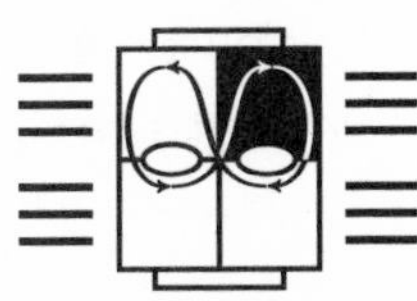

Upside Right

1. *In the upside of Process, the group focuses on members' feelings and makes sure all members are heard.* An effective group takes time to listen to its members' feelings and perspectives, and allows these to influence the decisions

made. Group members will not necessarily agree with a member's opinion on a topic or issue, but members leave the meeting knowing that they were heard.

2. *In the upside of Process, team building creates group trust, making for shrewd decisions.* Research has documented that groups that engage in effective team building develop trust, take more risks, and make better decisions. In a spiritual-growth group, members often want to identify their growing edge and need to face their vulnerabilities and fears. When the trust level in growth groups is high, people are more likely to take such risks and to experience personal transformation.

3. *In the upside of Process, the trust level remains high as group and leader make sure everyone is on board.* Once group members are engaged with each other, the leader and the group make sure they stay engaged so that they continue to participate in the meeting. Not everyone needs the same amount of "airtime," but the group leader or another group member ensures that everyone feels welcome to participate.

4. *In the upside of Process, conflict between members is seen as healthy ferment.* When the trust level of a group is high, conflict is not seen as negative. Members should fight hard for their ideas and not take it personally when their ideas are not accepted. Without this healthy ferment, the quality of group decision making will likely be inferior. When members do not feel free to express their way-out ideas, little creativity will develop. Some groups come up with creative solutions to problems simply because one member was unafraid to share a wacky idea.

The Downside of Content

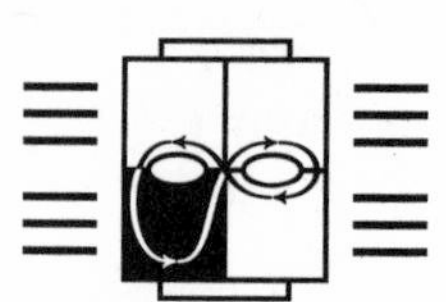
Downside Left

1. *In the downside of Content, decisions may be made at the expense of members' feelings.* Each of us is probably aware of people who have left a congregation or have simply become furious about the way a decision was made. A controversial decision may be made in an autocratic way by the pastor or board chair, without involving members in discussion. Group members get the sense that their perspective is not valued by a leader.

2. *In the downside of Content, group leaders may be insensitive to members' needs.* Some leaders are simply not adroit at recognizing the feelings of others. In the new science of emotional intelligence, we would say that these leaders lack the capacity for empathy. They can't be or choose not to be in touch with what is in the minds and hearts of group members. Inevitably this inattention leads to poor decision making and to group members' feeling a low level of satisfaction.

3. *In the downside of Content, the lack of team building produces inferior decisions.* Trust is necessary if a group is to function well. Without trust, the quality of decision making in a task group suffers. In a spiritual-growth group, the lack of trust usually leads people to withhold their deeper fears and vulnerabilities, so personal growth and transformation are much less likely. Groups that do not take time for team building have difficulty developing trust and are less likely to function well.

4. *In the downside of Content, failure to deal directly with conflict creates group tension and member dissatisfaction.* When conflict is not addressed directly, little of significance will take place. Some members simply withdraw. Others resort to blaming or complaining. The unresolved tension festers, and meetings are rarely satisfying. This can happen when group facilitators press the agenda of the meeting without stopping to acknowledge the conflict and to explore ways of dealing with it.

The Downside of Process

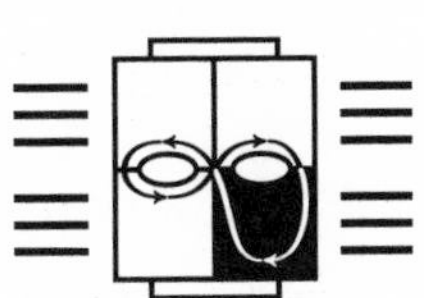

Downside Right

1. *In the downside of Process, the group may fail to focus on its task.* A group can get so caught up in personal sharing that it loses focus on why members gathered. We are speaking here mainly of congregational decision-making groups. Within a spiritual-growth group, the subject matter for the gathering may continually lose focus as members continue to reflect on how the group is functioning. This habit becomes a problem since people joined the group to focus on an aspect of spiritual enrichment. When the group rarely focuses on this subject matter, participants feel betrayed by those who structured the growth experience.

2. *In the downside of Process, longer, less productive meetings frustrate group members.* Attention to process can result in shorter and more productive meetings when members continually bring the group discussion back on focus. Members can go overboard with process, however, sometimes inflaming a disagreement and certainly lengthening the meeting.

3. *In the downside of Process, members feel frustrated when they think too much time is spent on group introspection.* Some people are invested in the content of the group and see process comments as distractions. They think attending to process makes meetings "touchy-feely" when they would prefer to focus on content.

4. *In the downside of Process, narcissism may be encouraged when members use process time to overfocus on how the process affected them personally.* Some hard-driving, goal-oriented folk think that any time spent on team building or process is wasted, leaving less time to accomplish the tasks they see as important. People may leave meetings angry and frustrated, or may quit the group because they think it does nothing but waste time.

Managing the Polarity Poorly: Early Warnings for Content

Early Warnings Left

1. *Group members don't check in with one another in the opening moments of a meeting and thus fail to generate trust for the meeting.* Without setting aside time for group members to get caught up with each other's lives, the group chair launches right into business items.

2. *Members' comments about process are ignored.* Some group members may speak up when they don't like what seems to be happening in the group, but these comments are simply ignored, and members dive right back into content issues.

3. *When a group's agenda is completed, members simply leave, missing the opportunity to reflect on accomplishments and challenges.* If a group doesn't take a few minutes to reflect on the meeting, it is difficult for the chair or facilitator to learn how the group could go about its tasks more efficiently or to raise the satisfaction level of group members.

4. *Members are allowed to bully others into voting a certain way.* In some groups, a few people dominate discussion and "persuade" others to vote their way. Other group members will feel dissatisfied with the group and lower their commitment to following through on decisions.

Managing the Polarity Poorly: Early Warnings for Process

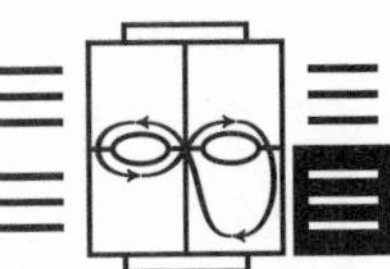
Early Warnings Right

1. *The group usually goes overboard when engaged in personal checking in.* Some groups are so happy just to be connecting with fellow members that they rarely get down to business.

2. *Excessive time is spent on the melodrama of certain members' lives.* Some groups have members who are emotionally needy, and the group may allow itself to get sucked into dealing with these people's issues. This caretaking can eat up a sizable portion of group time, so the group rarely accomplishes its work.

3. *Members are often absent because people rarely feel that anything of significance is accomplished at meetings.* When group process and members' issues dominate a group's life, some members stop attending, out of dissatisfaction that the group accomplishes little.

4. *The group goes overboard making sure that everyone feels good about the meeting.* In some groups, the quality of work accomplished is less important than the goal that everyone should come out of the meeting feeling good about everyone else. These conflict-avoiding groups are rarely creative since members are reluctant to share ideas, fearing they might upset others in the group.

Managing the Polarity Well: Action Steps for Content

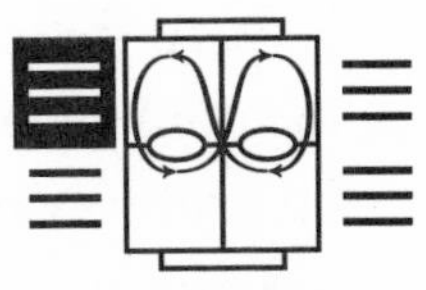
Action Steps Left

1. *Groups have a clear focus for every meeting.* The facilitator articulates the purpose of the meeting, either by preparing an agenda or by stating the focus at the begin-

ning of the gathering. Members of the group feel free to share their concerns about the focus or to express their investment in it.

2. *As a meeting begins, the agenda is agreed upon by those participating.* Even when an agenda has been mailed out ahead of time, effective facilitators ask whether group members want to add to the agenda or express concern about agenda items. Group members are able to express those concerns without engaging the group in an immediate discussion of them. This discussion gets group members to buy into the agenda for the session.

3. *Time limits are set for each agenda item or each phase of a group's meeting.* Members of task groups or governing boards often complain about the length of meetings. To address this issue, the facilitator asks the group, before it tackles the first item on the agenda, to determine how long members want to spend on each item. Someone is then designated as timekeeper. When time has been called for an item, the facilitator asks whether the group wants to extend the discussion, and if so, for how long.

4. *Leaders are selected for their ability to get things done at a task meeting or to keep a growth group moving toward greater depth.* Not only does the congregation choose leaders who have skills in decision-making processes or in facilitating a growth or support group; it also holds training seminars to further develop effective leaders. Members who are already effective leaders lead those training seminars.

Managing the Polarity Well: Action Steps for Process

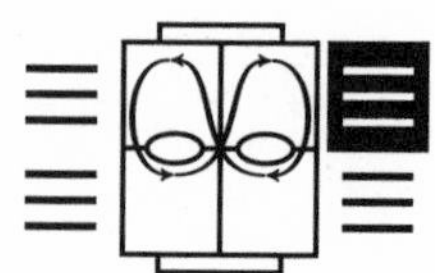

Action Steps Right

1. *Each meeting begins with team building.* At the beginning of each meeting, each person shares briefly, perhaps responding to a question, letting other group members know what frame of mind he or she is bringing to the meeting.

2. *At specific intervals, time is set aside for reflections on process.* Deciding the point at which a group will stop dealing with content and begin to reflect on process can be especially helpful if a group is trying to change the way it functions. For example, a group can decide to get its work done in a shorter time. Checking with the group periodically to see how members feel about

the more rapid pace is often a good move. Regularly reflecting on process tends over the long term to help a group develop new norms for the way members work together.

3. *Every meeting concludes with reflection on how the group went about its task.* When the group adopts a norm that no meeting or other gathering will end without group reflection on how the meeting went, it tends to have shorter and more productive meetings. Such a norm also helps group facilitators develop their skills. At times they are affirmed for the way they managed the group, and at other times they hear how the group would prefer to use its time.

4. *Leaders are selected for their understanding of process.* Process work requires specific skills and sensitivities that are not picked up easily and that come more naturally for some people. A congregation would do well to ensure that every group has at least one member who has these skills—a person who is self-aware, is able to observe what is going on in a group and how members are participating, and is aware of watching the process.

As with all polarities, the question is "How do we maximize both upsides and minimize both downsides?" Gifted leaders are competent in both content and process. They know how to lead a fruitful discussion while keeping an eye on how the group is functioning. Being aware of the importance of process may motivate congregations to hold training seminars on how to lead a small group in a way that values both content and process. Modeling is another way of helping people acquire skills in group facilitation. A person who manages this polarity well when leading a group can work with an understudy who learns though observation how the leader oscillates between content and process to facilitate effective meetings.

Challenge AND Support

This second small-group polarity is central to the growth and development of group members. At times group members feel bad about themselves, beaten up and abused, or simply vulnerable. At such times, what they need most is tender loving care. They need to be surrounded by people who will support and protect them. A small group that has developed trust is often one to which members will bring their brokenness, knowing that they will be cared for.

Polarity Management® Map

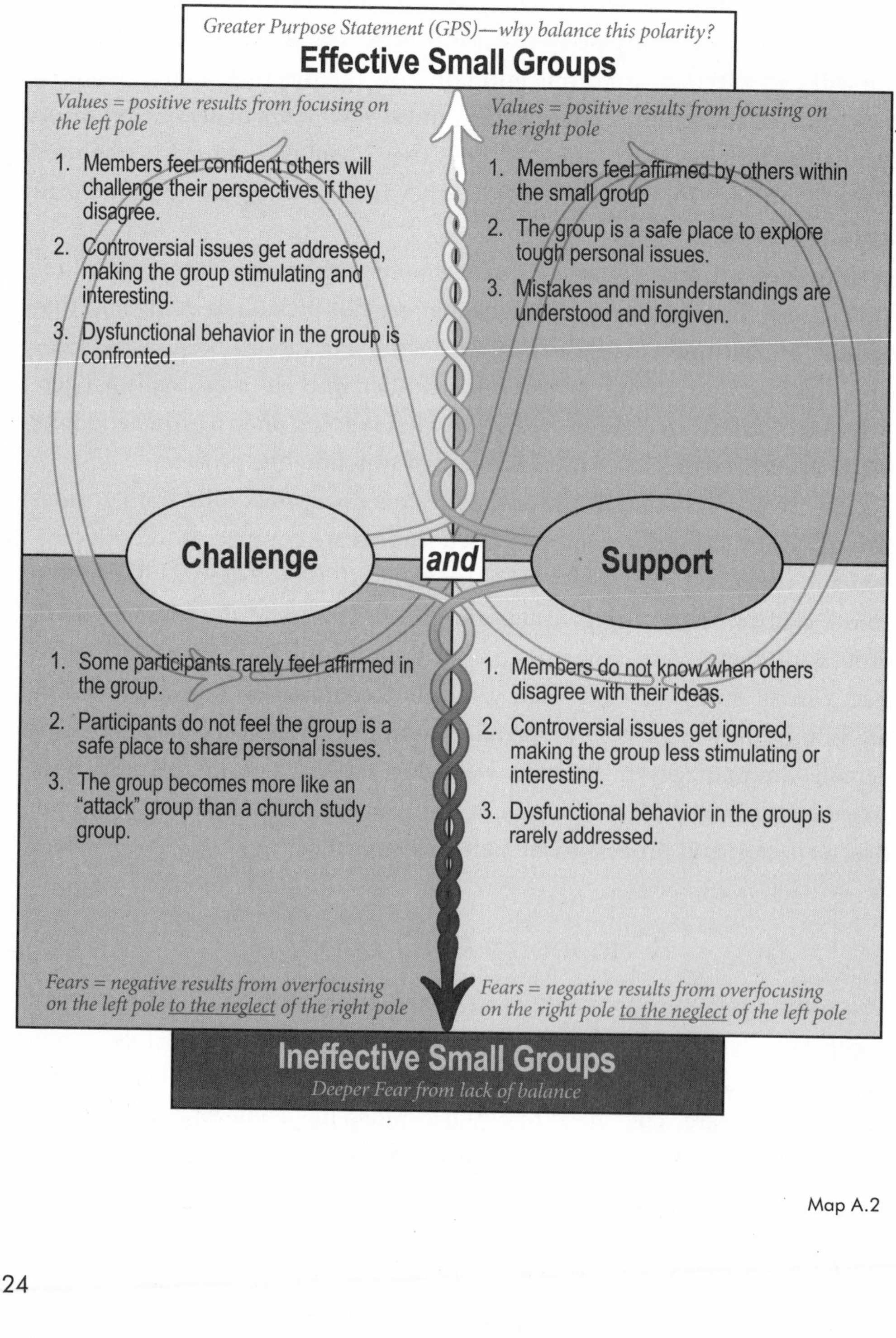

Greater Purpose Statement (GPS)—why balance this polarity?

Effective Small Groups

Values = positive results from focusing on the left pole

1. Members feel confident others will challenge their perspectives if they disagree.
2. Controversial issues get addressed, making the group stimulating and interesting.
3. Dysfunctional behavior in the group is confronted.

Values = positive results from focusing on the right pole

1. Members feel affirmed by others within the small group
2. The group is a safe place to explore tough personal issues.
3. Mistakes and misunderstandings are understood and forgiven.

Challenge *and* **Support**

1. Some participants rarely feel affirmed in the group.
2. Participants do not feel the group is a safe place to share personal issues.
3. The group becomes more like an "attack" group than a church study group.

Fears = negative results from overfocusing on the left pole to the neglect of the right pole

1. Members do not know when others disagree with their ideas.
2. Controversial issues get ignored, making the group less stimulating or interesting.
3. Dysfunctional behavior in the group is rarely addressed.

Fears = negative results from overfocusing on the right pole to the neglect of the left pole

Ineffective Small Groups

Deeper Fear from lack of balance

Map A.2

At other times, members need someone in the group who will level with them, perhaps letting them know they are functioning immaturely and need to grow up. This critical feedback can relate to how they are functioning as group members, or it can relate to their opinions about the subject matter. In short, critical feedback can relate to both content and process. For example, someone may be told that she interrupts others, dominates a meeting by commenting on anything offered by other group members, or fails to follow through on her commitments to the group. Other members may receive critical feedback about a stance on issues that leads others to conclude that they are not concerned about homeless, hungry, or marginalized people. Similar criticism may be given to a person who talks constantly about how poorly women, minorities, and handicapped people are treated. There are parallels between this small-group polarity and the *Nurture AND Transformation* polarity. We will not go into explaining each point in each quadrant, as the meaning of each should be self-evident without discussing Action Steps or Early Warning Signs. (See map A.2 on page 224.)

Effective Leaders AND Effective Participants

This polarity may seem to be a continuum rather than a polarity. In fact, social scientists Robert Tannenbaum and Warren Schmidt placed these two aspects of leadership on a continuum—autocratic leadership and laissez-faire leadership—and tried to discern which style is better. They could not document that one style was more effective than another. Rather, they discovered that the most effective leadership style in any community is the leadership that meets the expectations of those who are led. In other words, if people were used to autocratic leadership, they responded best to that leadership style. If they were used to laissez-faire leadership, they responded best to a leader who allowed group participation.

To place the leadership issue in a polarity map, we might think about the two poles as *Effective Leaders AND Effective Participants*. Let's take a look at how this polarity would look on a polarity map. (See map A.3 on page 226.)

This polarity is similar to the *Strong Clergy Leadership AND Strong Lay Leadership* polarity discussed in chapter 5. The leader of a small group needs constantly to pay attention to what is going on in the group and to respond

Polarity Management® Map

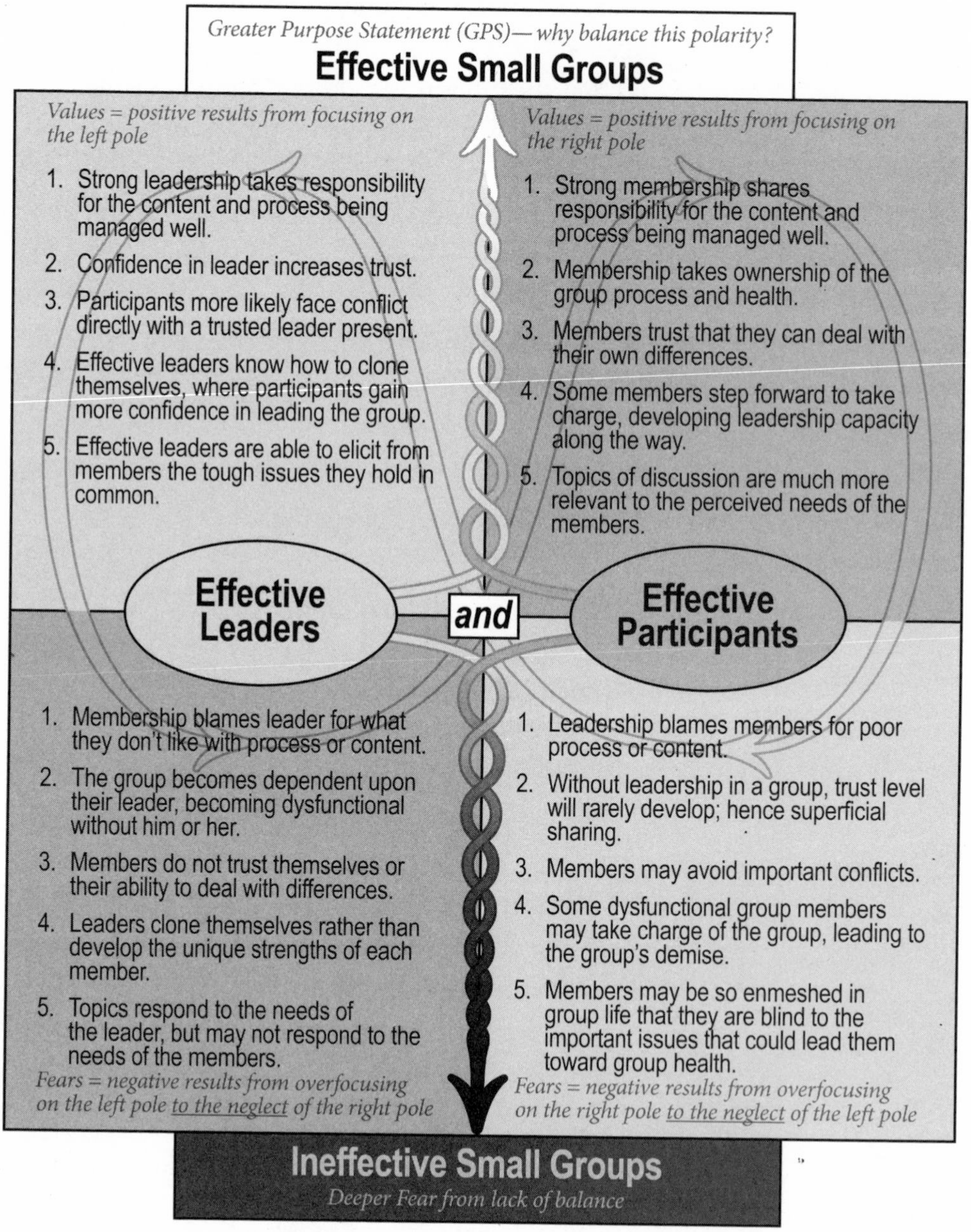

Greater Purpose Statement (GPS)— why balance this polarity?

Effective Small Groups

Values = positive results from focusing on the left pole

1. Strong leadership takes responsibility for the content and process being managed well.
2. Confidence in leader increases trust.
3. Participants more likely face conflict directly with a trusted leader present.
4. Effective leaders know how to clone themselves, where participants gain more confidence in leading the group.
5. Effective leaders are able to elicit from members the tough issues they hold in common.

Values = positive results from focusing on the right pole

1. Strong membership shares responsibility for the content and process being managed well.
2. Membership takes ownership of the group process and health.
3. Members trust that they can deal with their own differences.
4. Some members step forward to take charge, developing leadership capacity along the way.
5. Topics of discussion are much more relevant to the perceived needs of the members.

Effective Leaders ***and*** **Effective Participants**

1. Membership blames leader for what they don't like with process or content.
2. The group becomes dependent upon their leader, becoming dysfunctional without him or her.
3. Members do not trust themselves or their ability to deal with differences.
4. Leaders clone themselves rather than develop the unique strengths of each member.
5. Topics respond to the needs of the leader, but may not respond to the needs of the members.

Fears = negative results from overfocusing on the left pole to the neglect of the right pole

1. Leadership blames members for poor process or content.
2. Without leadership in a group, trust level will rarely develop; hence superficial sharing.
3. Members may avoid important conflicts.
4. Some dysfunctional group members may take charge of the group, leading to the group's demise.
5. Members may be so enmeshed in group life that they are blind to the important issues that could lead them toward group health.

Fears = negative results from overfocusing on the right pole to the neglect of the left pole

Ineffective Small Groups

Deeper Fear from lack of balance

Map A.3

accordingly. Sometimes that means taking firm control of the group and advocating a way to proceed that will be most helpful to the group in the long run. At other times, it is important to allow the group's agenda to unfold without any direction. In this way, members will feel free to explore and share in a way that lends depth and breadth to a group as they gain important insights into themselves and their spiritual path. Finding effective facilitators to enable meaningful small-group experiences can be a challenge. For this reason we recommend that congregations identify people who have the potential to become effective facilitators and ask them to work as understudies to skilled facilitators.

Long-Term Groups AND Short-Term Groups

As Roy travels around the country consulting with congregations, he occasionally comes upon a congregation whose small groups have been together for many years. In one Disciples of Christ congregation in the Midwest, each adult Sunday school class had had its own room, its own format, and pretty much the same participants for a span of time ranging from ten to fifty years. For example, the Victory Class, made up of people from the GI generation, had been meeting regularly since the end of World War II. Other classes had been together for shorter periods and reflected a variety of age groups and agendas. Yet the norm of the congregation was that members would stick with one Sunday school class more or less permanently. In another church consultation, Roy discovered four small groups that had been together for years. This congregation had a tendency to chew up its clergy. As the consultation continued, it became clear that decisions in the congregation were not made by the elected governing board. They were being made within these long-term groups, which could easily sabotage any decision made by either the pastor or the governing board. Yet when it was suggested that these groups break up to form new groups, the resistance was overwhelming.

As we might guess, there is both an upside and a downside to that kind of small-group stability. Some congregations discourage small-group continuity and encourage small groups to continually divide like cells and receive new members. There is an upside and a downside to this approach as well.

Polarity Management® Map

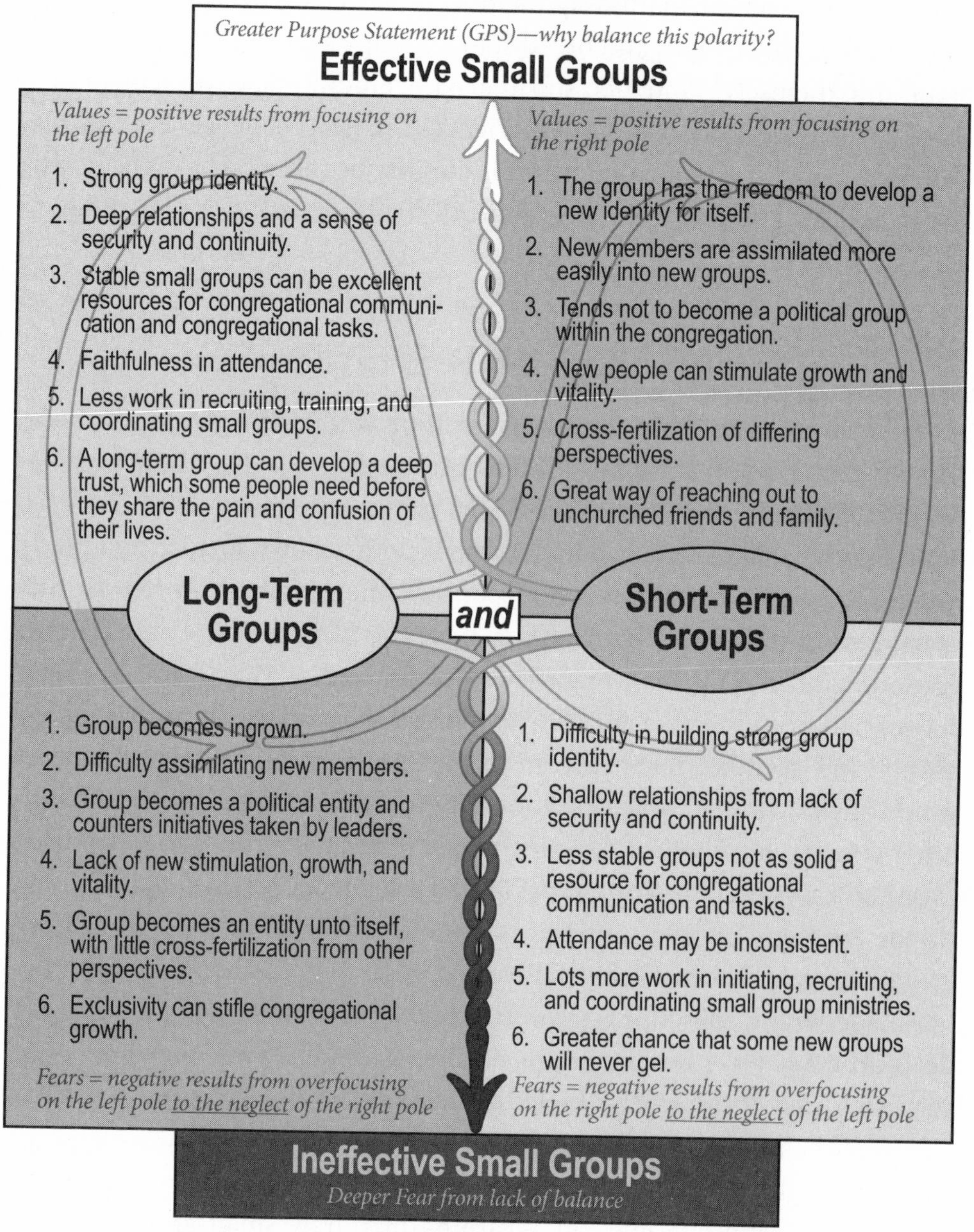

Greater Purpose Statement (GPS)—why balance this polarity?

Effective Small Groups

Values = positive results from focusing on the left pole

1. Strong group identity.
2. Deep relationships and a sense of security and continuity.
3. Stable small groups can be excellent resources for congregational communication and congregational tasks.
4. Faithfulness in attendance.
5. Less work in recruiting, training, and coordinating small groups.
6. A long-term group can develop a deep trust, which some people need before they share the pain and confusion of their lives.

Values = positive results from focusing on the right pole

1. The group has the freedom to develop a new identity for itself.
2. New members are assimilated more easily into new groups.
3. Tends not to become a political group within the congregation.
4. New people can stimulate growth and vitality.
5. Cross-fertilization of differing perspectives.
6. Great way of reaching out to unchurched friends and family.

Long-Term Groups *and* **Short-Term Groups**

1. Group becomes ingrown.
2. Difficulty assimilating new members.
3. Group becomes a political entity and counters initiatives taken by leaders.
4. Lack of new stimulation, growth, and vitality.
5. Group becomes an entity unto itself, with little cross-fertilization from other perspectives.
6. Exclusivity can stifle congregational growth.

Fears = negative results from overfocusing on the left pole to the neglect of the right pole

1. Difficulty in building strong group identity.
2. Shallow relationships from lack of security and continuity.
3. Less stable groups not as solid a resource for congregational communication and tasks.
4. Attendance may be inconsistent.
5. Lots more work in initiating, recruiting, and coordinating small group ministries.
6. Greater chance that some new groups will never gel.

Fears = negative results from overfocusing on the right pole to the neglect of the left pole

Ineffective Small Groups

Deeper Fear from lack of balance

Map A.4

The truths held in each approach are interdependent and thus form a polarity. Let look at how this polarity might look on a map. (See map A.4 on page 228.)

As we observe the truth of this polarity, we recommend that every church group be able to meet as a unit, possibly for three to six months, before being open to new members. It is difficult to develop trust within a small group when the membership changes every Sunday. Ideally, members covenant that they will attempt to attend regularly for a certain period, whether that be during the six weeks of Lent or for the nine months from mid-September to mid-June.

Facilitating a long-term group is much easier than facilitating a group that is starting up or has just taken on new members. At times a long-term group does not even need facilitation, because over time the group has developed rituals and norms that carry the group. The norms the group has developed, consciously or unconsciously, determine members' behavior whenever the group is in session. When starting a new group, the group facilitator must quickly find ways of determining what every group member expects from the experience and where individual agendas may be in conflict. Because trust is central to effective small-group ministries, the facilitator needs to design ways group members can build trust and share important information about themselves so that the group can then settle into the agenda the members have chosen.

Determining when a new group is ready to take on new members is not simple. The decision depends in part on who the new members are, in particular whether group members already know the newcomers and how familiar the newcomers are with the congregation. It may be up to the group's facilitator to judge whether the group has bonded sufficiently to be able to welcome a new individual or couple and whether group members should be encouraged to think about a few people they would like to see in their group, be they friends, neighbors, or other members of the congregation.

While groups need time to gel, those that meet for more than a year can begin to manifest the downside of an exclusive group. They can become a clique within the congregation, perhaps one that resists decisions made by committees or the board. In addition, the spiritual growth of members within a group may begin to slow when new members are not invited in to contribute new perspectives. A congregation that wrestles with this polarity strives to affirm both stable and ever-changing groups.

Conclusion

The ability of a congregation to manage these four polarities, central to small-group functioning, will determine the type and quality of the small group in the congregation. When small groups are initiated but fail to grow into stable, productive groups, the governing board of a congregation or other leadership group may want to revisit these four polarities and consider why small groups are not satisfying to the membership and fail to develop.

APPENDIX B

Methods for Working with Polarities in Groups

When members of a group—whether three people or an auditorium full—strongly disagree about a matter, a wise leader first helps the group determine whether it is dealing with a problem to solve or a polarity to manage.

Asking two key questions will help:

1. Is the issue ongoing? That is, "Is it likely that we will still be dealing with this issue five years from now? Ten years from now?" Because polarities are unavoidable and unsolvable, they will be with the congregation throughout its life—just as inhaling and exhaling are with each of us throughout our lives.
2. Are the two alternatives interdependent? That is: Can you focus on one for only so long before you are *required* to focus on the other to be successful over time? You can be active for only so long before you are required to rest. You can focus on inreach for only so long before you are required to pay attention also to outreach if you are to succeed over time.

If the answer to these two questions is yes, you probably have a polarity to manage. That you can identify two positions, each with an upside and a downside, does not make it a polarity to manage. You can argue over where to go for lunch, debating the upsides and downsides of the two restaurants you have in mind, but that does not make the question a polarity to manage. When you choose one of the restaurants, nothing in the relationship between the two options will require you to choose the other restaurant next time—or ever! The two restaurants represent independent options rather than interdependent options.

If you build a polarity map around alternatives that you think may constitute a polarity, ask two other questions after the map has been filled out:

1. Is it necessary over time to have both upsides?
2. Will focusing on one upside to the neglect of the other eventually undermine our efforts to move toward our Greater Purpose?

If the answer to these two questions is yes, you probably have a polarity to manage. If the answer to all four questions above is no, you probably have a problem to solve.

When you have a problem to solve—for example, deciding whether to build new classrooms connected to the sanctuary—important polarities may need to be considered. For instance, "How might the new structure be a response to our desire for both inreach and outreach?

Likewise, when you have a polarity to manage, you will also be solving problems to ensure that you manage it well. For example: What is the content of the map? What are some effective Action Steps we can take to empower both upsides? Our point is that you do not give up problem solving when you are managing polarities, and you don't necessarily give up managing polarities when you are solving problems.

Once a group, or at least the group facilitator, has determined that it is dealing with a polarity, the nature of the issues will become clearer to everyone if a polarity map is created. Members of a community will find a polarity map most useful and will experience the wisdom of the polarity when they agree on the content of the map. It is an advantage, particularly in dealing with a contentious polarity, to use a polarity map completed by the people who are at odds. People are most likely to agree on the content of a map and to own it if they see their own ideas expressed in it. For this reason, we often involve groups in developing the contents of each quadrant. This can be done in several ways.

Method One

One way to develop a polarity map in a group is to work with large sheets of newsprint, an overhead projector, or an editable blank map in PowerPoint with an LCD projector. A group member or staff assistant can write the suggestions offered by the group. (The overhead or LCD projector is especially useful when the leader is working with a large meeting.) First, simply state the two neutral poles of the polarity.

Both poles should have neutral names—first, so that they have the same relative value for the stakeholders involved. Second, a neutral name is often easier to identify as having an upside and a downside. If you cannot think of a neutral name for each pole, pick positive attributes for each pole and let those be the pole names. It does not work for one pole name to sound positive, reflecting the values and language of the stakeholders, and for the other to sound negative. The group would automatically overfocus on the pole with the positive name.

For example, it would not work to name the poles "Take Care of Our Members AND Neglect Our Members." One is positive and the other is negative. In such a situation you can convert to more neutral names like *"Inreach AND Outreach."* If you cannot think of neutral names, use positive names like "Take Care of Our Members AND Take Care of the Community."

Once you have neutral or positive names for both poles, you can begin filling out the rest of the map. Sometimes groups start with the Greater Purpose Statement at the top and the Deeper Fear at the bottom. When these two elements are clear, it sometimes becomes easier to fill out the rest of the map. If the Greater Purpose is not yet clear, you can fill out the upsides and downsides of the four quadrants first. As the map becomes richer in content, it may become easier to identify the Greater Purpose.

When you start to fill out the map, we recommend that in most cases you start with the two upper quadrants. Those quadrants represent values that may be held strongly by different people. As the upside content is created, both those valuing the upside of the left pole and those valuing the upside of the right pole are provided with a "place to stand." The values they hold dear are being affirmed.

Once you have recognized *my* value as a "good thing" by putting its positive results in the upside of a pole, I am more willing to recognize that it's possible to have "too much of a good thing." This element is represented by the downside of my pole. This awareness is balanced by the recognition that the other pole has its own downside.

Which upside should you fill in first? We suggest filling in the upside of the pole favored by those who feel most vulnerable in the process. Because of their vulnerability, they are the ones least likely to be able to participate fully and to hear the other group's point of view. If they feel heard and respected for the upside they value, they are more likely to be able to hear and recognize a second upside.

We suggest that in generating content for each quadrant of the map, you begin with simple brainstorming without judgment of the content. Be open to possibilities and produce an unqualified list. Once you have the list, look back through it and see whether the values represented in the content will work for everyone in the group. Do all participants think they know what is meant by each word in the quadrant? Do they agree that each word fits in this particular quadrant? If not, this is an ideal time to clarify what people mean by certain words and the values they associate with those words.

The goal is to put words in each quadrant that work for those present and, to the extent we can imagine, for other stakeholders. When filling out a map, it is a good idea to see it as a draft that can be changed as others look at it and need to add or change words to make it work for them. This is why we have repeatedly suggested that you feel free to modify the maps in this book so that they work for you.

Then ask, "What are the positive results from focusing on this pole?" Work to complete that upside first, keeping in mind that you can go back later and add items to this and each of the other quadrants—and you will, as people in the room come up with fresh points for each quadrant. We have also had the experience of naming two neutral poles but, as work progressed, finding that words in the quadrants suggested alternative names for the poles. A group might decide to shift to the new names and then continue to develop its lists for each quadrant.

Let's use as an example the polarity of *Leader Empowerment AND Participant Empowerment.* Begin with the upside of Leader Empowerment. Write down all positive results. When a contribution does not seem to fit the quadrant you are working on, briefly discuss where it belongs. Then ask the group for thoughts about the upside of Participant Empowerment. When participants have finished offering suggestions for both upper quadrants, ask, "All right, now what are the negative results you get when you overfocus on Leader Empowerment to the neglect of Participant Empowerment?" Everyone should feel free to contribute. Brainstorm, and then review. Do the same for the opposite pole. When an item is suggested for the list by one participant and someone else in the group does not think it belongs in the quadrant, a brief discussion will help everyone agree on each item that goes on the list. Sometimes the leader or another participant suggests that an item might better fit in another quadrant. When this happens, it is important to assume that both participants have a legitimate point of view. The group then has an opportunity to clarify values and language between the two points of view. After the group has worked through all four quadrants, the map should contain content that most people in the group will agree on. They can then go on to discuss such issues as, "What would it take for this congregation or group to live most of its life in the two upper quadrants of this polarity?"

As participants work on the map, people who don't believe that movement toward the opposite pole is wise will come up with more reasons for the group to embrace only their preferred pole, usually by pointing to the downside of the opposite pole. The facilitator simply thanks objectors for their observations and adds their reasons to the list on the downside of the pole they oppose. The facilitator also thanks the speakers for contributing to a fuller understanding of the whole polarity.

Method Two

An even more engaging way to develop a polarity map in a group begins with using masking tape to mark a map on the floor of your meeting room. Simply take two long strips of masking tape and make a big cross on the floor. In the middle of each upper quadrant, make a big plus sign, and put a minus sign in the middle of each lower quadrant. Then divide the group into four subgroups. At least two people will be standing in each of the four quadrants. On the wall in front of them, post a polarity map with only the two neutral poles filled in at the end of the central axis. As participants look at the map on the wall and then at the quadrant in which they are standing, they will see what part of the polarity they are to address. Each subgroup will need a scribe to record its statements.

Give the subgroups three minutes to brainstorm the statements that they think describe the quadrant in which they are standing. After three minutes, call time, and ask the scribe of each subgroup to place the sheet with its statements face down in the quadrant. Then have each subgroup rotate to the next quadrant in the normal flow of the infinity loop (lower left to upper right to lower right to upper left). All four subgroups are now standing in a new quadrant, and they brainstorm the statements they think belong in that quadrant. After three minutes, call time, and have the scribes place their subgroup's page of statements face down on top of the first page of notes in the quadrant. Ask the subgroups to move to new quadrants, brainstorm for three minutes, and add their notes (face down) to the pile in the quadrant and then repeat the process for the final quadrant.

Now instruct each subgroup to pick up the four brainstorming lists in the quadrant where its members are standing. Give the subgroups ten minutes to collate the items from all four lists into one list on a sheet of newsprint. Then tape all four sheets of newsprint to the wall, using the pattern of the polarity map. Once everyone is seated facing the polarity map on the wall, have a spokesperson from each subgroup walk the full group through the list that his or her subgroup collated. Start with the upside of one of the poles, usually the pole that is most popular in the church. Ask the full group to reflect on whether all items listed on that newsprint sheet belong in that quadrant of the polarity map. Move next to the downside of that pole. Again, ask the whole group to reflect on the accuracy of the items. It may come as a shock to some participants that the downside of their favorite pole can be so ugly or have such devastating implications. Then do the same thing with the upside and downside of the opposite pole.

The results are often stunning. More than likely, the four quadrants of the polarity will contain much fuller lists than they would have if the group had brainstormed as a whole the contents of each quadrant. What's more, everyone in the room, with the exception of the leader, had some input into each of the four quadrants; the group therefore can take ownership of the map.

Once the group has had a chance to talk about what group members learned by creating this polarity map, ask what it would take for the group or the congregation to manage this polarity better—to stay in the two upper quadrants of the polarity. If the group develops a conviction that it is important to oscillate between the two upper quadrants, move on to Action Steps and Early Warning statements. Again divide the group into four subgroups—one for each Action Step list and one for each Early Warning list. Ask each subgroup to discuss its assignment and write its statements on newsprint. Allow the subgroups twenty minutes to develop their lists. When they have finished, ask them to tape the results in the appropriate place next to the polarity map on the wall.

Dealing with Opposition

Proponents of opposite sides of a polarity often focus on the downside of the opposition's point of view. The wind is taken out of their sails when a leader can point to a polarity map, particularly one the group itself has created, and say, "Yes, there are some downsides to that approach. We have just listed them here." When participants see that you are willing to acknowledge downsides to the position they oppose, they usually feel heard and acknowledged. When an issue has not been included on the downside of the relevant pole, a group leader can add it to the list.

Groups soon realize that there are two "right" answers to the dilemma. In fact, members can acknowledge the downside of their preferred pole while maintaining that the presence of these negatives does not mean that moving toward that pole is unwise. In addition, when advocates for either pole see that their opponents are willing to acknowledge the downside of their preferred pole, they may be more ready to embrace the upside of their opponents' case.

Conclusion

At times, when a group argument does not have two neutral poles, a decision is made, the problem is addressed, and the group agrees on a solution. If the argument persists, however, you may find, using the four criteria at the beginning of this appendix, that a polarity lies beneath the argument and needs to be addressed first. It may be one of the eight polarities we are surfacing in this book.

Dealing with a named polarity by using a polarity map will do much to minimize church arguments. Without the polarity map in front of them, contestants will continue to call attention to the downside of the pole they resist. When their opposition returns fire by pointing to the downside of the opposite pole, no one feels heard. When their objections are acknowledged and presented in a polarity map, however, people will calm down, because they believe their perspective is being take seriously. Laying out a polarity conflict this way makes it much more manageable.

APPENDIX C

Polarity Principles

Polarity principles summarize key ideas about how polarities function. Below are listed the fifteen principles that have been presented in this book.

Chapter 1

1. Polarities are interdependent pairs of truths that are a natural and integral part of our daily lives. Like all other natural phenomena, they are a gift from God.

2. We are constantly managing polarities, because they are embedded in congregational life. The polarity map and principles are intended to build on the intuitive and tacit wisdom about polarities that we have acquired by dealing with them more or less well our whole life. The map and principles provide a common model, language, and understanding of this phenomenon. This understanding will allow us to be more collaborative and intentional about tapping this phenomenon to create or maintain a thriving congregation.

3. Either/or thinking, though essential in some situations, does not enable us to manage polarities effectively. To manage polarities well, we must supplement our either/or thinking with both/and thinking.

4. If we treat a polarity to manage as if it were a problem to solve, we will find that we are dealing with unnecessary, often painful and draining power struggles in which the congregation loses twice. It loses the first time because energy is wasted and relationships are damaged during the struggle. It loses again when one side "wins," and the congregation has to deal with the downside of the winners' preferred pole.

5. The normal flow of energy in all polarities is an infinity loop, which reflects the ongoing self-correction of the polarity from the downside of one

pole to the upside of the other. Over time, the upside of one pole will reach its limits, especially if it is focused upon to the neglect of the other pole, and we will begin to experience the downside of the pole. As we anticipate or experience the downside of a pole, we are naturally driven in a self-regulating way to the upside of the opposite pole.

6. A polarity map contains two pole names with an *"AND"* box between them; an upside and downside for each pole; a Greater Purpose Statement (GPS) and a Deeper Fear; positively reinforcing Synergy Arrows leading in a virtuous circle toward the GPS; and negatively reinforcing Synergy Arrows leading in a vicious circle toward the Deeper Fear.

7. A polarity can be managed well. First, it must be recognized as a polarity to be managed rather than a problem to be solved. To manage it well, we have to create Action Steps to get to the upside of each pole and identify Early Warnings to let us know when we are moving to a downside.

Chapter 2

8. All polarity maps contain two "points of view." The point of view is composed of the upside of one pole, which is valued, and the downside of the opposite pole, which is feared.

Chapter 3

9. If you are building a map with a group of people that includes two subgroups, each of which feels strongly about one pole, it is best to deal with both upsides first. A wise facilitator will start with the upside supported by the group most anxious about being heard. Once that group's upside has been affirmed, its members are more likely to be able to hear that there is a second upside as well.

10. When your Early Warnings indicate that you are getting into the downside of a pole, revisit your Action Steps for the upside of the opposite pole. If you are doing the planned Action Steps and are still getting the Early Warnings, you may need to identify additional Action Steps for a course correction and to minimize the downside of the pole.

Chapter 4

11. A polarity can exist within one or both poles of a larger polarity. For example, to support both *Spiritual Health AND Institutional Health*, a congregation needs both *Management AND Leadership*.

12. Sometimes when thinking of Action Steps to get to the upside of one pole, a group realizes that the Action Steps for one pole could also support the upside of the other pole. We call these High-leverage Action Steps and list them for both upsides.

Chapter 5

13. The overfocus on one pole will eventually lead to the downside of both poles.

Chapter 7

14. The more individuals or groups value the upside of one pole and fear the downside of the other pole, the more difficult it will be for them to gain access to the upside of the other pole.

15. When a power struggle erupts between advocates of the two poles of a polarity, the smaller a group or the less powerful its advocates, the more it needs to be listened to.

APPENDIX D

References on the Importance of Polarities

Numerous books indicate that leaders and organizations that manage paradox, dilemmas, or polarities well outperform those that do not. Below is an annotated list of key books that address this skill.

Collins, Jim, and Jerry I. Porras. *Built to Last: Successful Habits of Visionary Companies.* New York: HarperCollins, 1994.

Authors identify the "Genius of the 'AND'" as a central variable that distinguishes "Gold" companies from "Silver" companies. The book is based on managing the polarity of "Preserve the Core AND Stimulate Progress." This polarity could also be seen as Stability AND Change.

Collins, Jim. *Good to Great: Why Some Companies Make the Leap . . . and Others Don't.* New York: HarperCollins, 2001.

The "Genius of the 'And'" continues to appear as an important variable in this book; it is identified as a key characteristic of leaders who move companies "from Good to Great." Ten polarities are identified as central to becoming a "Level 5" leader.

Dodd, Dominic, and Ken Favaro. *The Three Tensions: Winning the Struggle to Perform Without Compromise.* San Francisco: Jossey-Bass, 2007.

Authors interview executives from two hundred companies and identify three important tensions (polarities) central to their organization's effectiveness: "Profitability & Growth," "Today & Tomorrow," and "The Whole & Its Parts."

De Wit, Bob, and Ron Meyer. *Strategy Synthesis: Resolving Strategy Paradoxes to Create Competitive Advantage.* London: Thomson, 1999.

De Wit and Meyer identify ten paradoxes (polarities) that are at the heart of strategic management.

Elsner, Richard, and Bridget Farrands. *Lost in Transition: How Business Leaders Can Successfully Take Charge in New Roles.* London: Marshall Cavendish Limited, 2006.

The authors identify eight tensions (polarities) that, when managed well, contribute significantly to success in new jobs.

Fletcher, Jerry, and Kelle Olwyler. *Paradoxical Thinking: How to Profit from Your Contradictions.* San Francisco: Berrett-Koehler, 1997.

"After more than fifteen years of studying thousands of detailed examples of people performing at their best, Fletcher and Olwyler have found that individuals are always paradoxical when performing optimally and that each person has a particular combination of contradictory and paradoxical [polarity] qualities that work together to produce that person's best work."

Hammett, Pete. *Unbalanced Influence: Recognizing and Resolving the Impact of Myth and Paradox in Executive Performance.* Mountain View, Calif.: Davies-Black Publishing, 2007.

Ten years of research indicate the importance of paradox in executive performance.

Hampden-Turner, Charles. *Charting the Corporate Mind: Graphic Solutions to Business Conflicts.* New York: Free Press, 1990.

Hampden-Turner has written several books on the advantage of managing dilemmas. His research shows that companies that manage key dilemmas well outperform those that don't.

Hampden-Turner, Charles, and Alfons Trompenaars. *The Seven Cultures of Capitalism: Value Systems for Creating Wealth in the United States, Japan, Germany, France, Britain, Sweden, and The Netherlands.* New York: Doubleday, 1993.

———. *Building Cross-Cultural Competence: How to Create Wealth from Conflicting Values.* Chichester, U.K.: John Wiley & Sons, 2000.

Hampden-Turner and Trompenaars identify six dilemmas (polarities) that must be managed to support cross-cultural competence.

Handy, Charles. *The Age of Paradox.* Boston: Harvard Business School Press, 1994.

Handy builds on his earlier work, *The Age of Unreason,* to assert that the balancing of paradoxes (polarities) is at the heart not just of effective personal and organizational life but also of our survival as a world community.

Hickman, Craig R. *Mind of a Manager, Soul of a Leader.* Hoboken, N.J.: John Wiley & Sons, 1990.

Support for the benefits of paradoxical thinking shows up also in Hickman's book, whose title is a fundamental polarity in leadership.

Hofstede, Geert. *Culture's Consequences: Comparing Values, Behaviors, Institutions, and Organizations across Nations.* London: Sage Publications, Ltd., 2001.

Hofstede identifies five dimensions (polarities) of national culture to help us tap national differences as a resource.

Johnson, Barry. *Polarity Management: Identifying and Managing Unsolvable Problems.* Amherst, Mass.: HRD Press, 1994.

Johnson shares a number of case examples in which the shift from seeing an issue as a problem to solve to seeing it as a polarity to be managed added value for leaders and organizations.

Johnston, Charles M. *Necessary Wisdom: Meeting the Challenge of a New Cultural Maturity.* Seattle: ICD Press, 1991.

Johnston identifies five key polarity domains within culture and asserts the importance of understanding and bridging polarities. Managing polarities is at the heart of wisdom and cultural maturity and the way we "must learn to think and act if our future is to be a healthy one."

Pascale, Richard Tanner. *Managing on the Edge: How the Smartest Companies Use Conflict to Stay Ahead.* New York: Simon & Schuster, 1991.

Pascale identifies "managing contention better" as the key variable that separated the fourteen companies that kept their "excellent" rating from the twenty-nine that did not in a comparison of the forty-three companies identified in Thomas J. Peters and Robert H. Waterman's book *In Search of Excellence* (New York: HarperCollins, 2004). What Pascale means by "managing contention" is managing polarities/dilemmas/paradoxes, and he identifies seven, giving examples of each.

Quinn, Robert E. *Beyond Rational Management: Mastering the Paradoxes and Competing Demands of High Performance.* San Francisco: Jossey-Bass, 1988.

Quinn asserts that mastering paradox (polarity) is central to high performance.

———. *Building the Bridge as You Walk on It: A Guide for Leading Change.* San Francisco: Jossey-Bass, 2004.

Quinn identifies eight polarities as "the fundamental state of leadership."

Seidler, Margaret. *Power Surge: A Conduit for Enlightened Leadership.* Amherst, Mass.: HRD Press, 2008.

Leaders and organizations that manage polarities well outperform those that don't. Seidler translates the principles of Polarity Management to both personal and work relationships.

Sisodia, Raj, Jag Sheth, and David B. Wolfe. *Firms of Endearment: How World Class Companies Profit from Passion and Purpose.* Philadelphia: Wharton School Publishing, 2007.

According to the authors, the key indicator of whether a company is a great investment is the degree to which it manages the polarity of taking care of stockholders and stakeholders—in other words, attending to company interests and the interests of the larger community in which the company operates.

NOTES

Chapter 1

1. Barry Johnson, *Polarity Management: Identifying and Managing Unsolvable Problems* (Amherst, Mass.: HRD Press, 1992).

Chapter 2

1. Jim Collins and Jerry I. Porras, *Built to Last: Successful Habits of Visionary Companies* (New York: HarperCollins, 1994).

2. Loren Mead, *The Once and Future Church: Reinventing the Congregation for a New Mission Frontier* (Bethesda, Md.: Alban Institute, 1995).

3. For a discussion of the Holmes and Rahe Life Changes Rating Scale, see Roy M. Oswald, *Clergy Self-Care: Finding a Balance for Effective Ministry* (Bethesda, Md.: Alban Institute, 1991).

4. A discussion of the Strain Response Inventory is also found in Oswald, *Clergy Self-Care.*

5. Martin F. Saarinen, *The Life Cycle of a Congregation* (Bethesda, Md.: Alban Institute, 1984).

6. Marcus Borg, *Meeting Jesus Again for the First Time: The Historical Jesus and the Heart of Contemporary Faith* (New York: HarperCollins, 1994) and Marcus Borg, *Reading the Bible Again for the First Time: Taking the Bible Seriously but Not Literally* (New York: HarperCollins, 2001).

Chapter 3

1. *Disciple: Becoming Disciples through Bible Study* (Nashville: Abingdon, n.d.); order from Cokesbury, (800) 672-1789.

2. Loren Mead, *More Than Numbers: The Ways Churches Grow* (Bethesda, Md.: Alban Institute, 1993).

3. Credence Cassettes, Credence Communications, 6134 Brookside Plaza, Kansas City, MO 61114; (816) 333-0800.

4. Taize songs, written by Jacques Berthier and others at the ecumenical Taize community in France, are available in books and on CDs from GIA Publications, Inc., (800) 442-1358. Most newer denominational hymnals contain a few easy-to-sing Taize songs.

5. Alpha, *www.alphausa.org.*

6. Cursillo, *www.national-cursillo.org.*

Chapter 4

1. Craig R. Hickman, *Mind of a Manager, Soul of a Leader* (Hoboken, N.J.: John Wiley & Sons, 1990).

2. John P. Kotter, *Leading Change* (Boston: Harvard Business School Press, 1996), 35, 51, 67, 85.

Chapter 5

1. The Center for Emotional Intelligence and Human Relations Skills, at *eq-hrctr@myactv.net,* (301) 432-8933; 5930 Moser Rd., Boonsboro, MD 21713, offers weeklong training workshops in emotional intelligence and human resources at seminaries across the country. Ordained clergy and other church professionals are also invited to these workshops held near a seminary.

2. Daniel Goleman, *Emotional Intelligence: Why It Can Matter More Than IQ* (New York: Bantam Books, 1995), 186.

3. John D. Mayer, Peter R. Caruso, and Peter Salovey, "Selecting a Measure of Emotional Intelligence: The Case for Ability Scales," in Reuven Bar-On and James D. A. Parker, eds., *The Handbook of Emotional Intelligence: Theory, Development, Assessment, and Application at Home, School, and in the Workplace* (San Francisco: Jossey-Bass, 2000), 187.

4. Speed B. Leas, "The Involuntary Termination of Clergy" (unpublished research for the Alban Institute).

5. Personal communication between Mahan Siler and Roy Oswald.

Chapter 6

1. Brian D. McLaren, *Everything Must Change: Jesus, Global Crises, and a Revolution of Hope* (Nashville: Thomas Nelson, 2007).

2. M. Scott Peck, *The Road Less Traveled: A New Psychology of Love, Traditional Values, and Spiritual Growth* (New York: Simon & Schuster/Touchstone Books, 1975).

3. Percept can be reached at (800) 524-1445; Visions/Decisions at (800) 524-1445.

Chapter 7

1. Alcoholics Anonymous, *The Big Book Online*, 4th ed. (New York: Alcoholics Anonymous World Services, Inc., 2001), 59.

2. John Harris, *Stress, Power, and Ministry* (Washington, D.C.: Alban Institute, 1976), 113.

3. Cursillo, *www.national-cursillo.org;* Walk to Emmaus, *www.lighthouse-trails.com/walktoemmaus.htm;* Via de Cristo, *www.viadecristo.org;* Alpha, *www.alphausa.org.*

4. Living the Questions, *www.livingthequestions.com.*

5. For a sample of such a CD, contact Rev. Tom Williamson, Gloria Dei Lutheran Church, 461 College Parkway, Arnold, MD 21012-1818, *gloriadei@juno.com*, (410) 544-3799. Another CD, "Centering in Grace," by Roy Oswald, is available from Life Structure Resources, (800) 723-0625, *www.LifeStructure.org*, 5930 Moser Rd., Boonsboro, MD 21713.

Chapter 9

1. Marlene Wilson, *How to Mobilize Church Volunteers* (Minneapolis: Augsburg, 1983).

2. For an overview of the Myers-Briggs concepts, see Otto Kroeger and Janet M. Thuesen, *Type Talk: The 16 Personality Types That Determine How We Live, Love, and Work* (New York: Doubleday/Dell, 1988).

ABOUT THE AUTHORS

Roy M. Oswald

Roy M. Oswald is an Evangelical Lutheran Church in America pastor and author of numerous books published by The Alban Institute, including *Discerning Your Congregation's Future: A Strategic and Spiritual Approach* (1996), *Clergy Self-Care: Finding a Balance for Effective Ministry* (1991), and *Personality Type and Religious Leadership* (with Otto Kroeger), 1988, as well as the video *Why You Should Give Your Pastor a Sabbatical* (2001).

Roy M. Oswald
Executive Director, Center for EQ-HR Skills
5930 Moser Road
Boonsboro, MD 21713
(301) 432-2616
roymoswald@aol.com
http://lifestructure.org

Barry Johnson

Barry Johnson is the originator of Polarity Management® and author of *Polarity Management®: Identifying and Managing Unsolvable Problems* (HRD Press, 1992 and 1996).

Barry Johnson
Founder and President, Polarity Management Associates
1496 Manitou Lane
Middleville, Michigan 49333
(269) 205-4263
bjohnson@polaritymanagement.com
www.polaritymanagement.com